Giraffes, Black Dragons, and Other Pianos

GIRAFFES, BLACK DRAGONS,
AND OTHER Pianos

A Technological History from Cristofori to the Modern

Concert Grand   EDWIN M. GOOD

STANFORD UNIVERSITY PRESS

STANFORD, CALIFORNIA

1982

Stanford University Press
Stanford, California
© 1982 by the Board of Trustees of the
Leland Stanford Junior University
Printed in the United States of America
ISBN 0-8047-1120-8
LC 81-50787

To WALTER G. VINCENTI
Friend, Colleague, and Patient Mentor

Preface

---◄─◆─►---

If the zoological motif in the title suggests to any reader that this book will put forth an evolutionary history of the piano's progress, I must immediately register a correction. Evolutionary perhaps— the metaphor here signifies only a history of change, and the piano has undergone technological alteration over the years.

But change is not synonymous with improvement or with prog- ress. One of the reasons I decided to write this book was that too many of my predecessors seemed to take it as axiomatic that the piano has advanced, that the Steinways, Bechsteins, and Kawais of our day are without question better than the Steins, Broad- woods, and Könnickes of earlier days. Affectionate as I am toward any good piano that I find under my fingers, whether made in 1790 or 1970, I think that Mozart was not mistaken in his enthusiasm for Johann Andreas Stein's pianos in 1777, nor was Ignaz Mos- cheles making the best of a bad job when in 1831 he exclaimed with pleasure over his new Erard, "A very violoncello!" That the piano has been improved in certain objective ways I do not doubt: it stays better in tune, it holds greater tension, it has strings of higher quality, it puts forth more volume. But I am unwilling to conclude that for certain musical purposes—such as playing music by Mo- zart, Beethoven, Schubert, Schumann, Chopin, perhaps even Brahms—the modern piano is in all respects better than older ones. It is different from them. To that series of differences I have sought to draw attention.

The primary sources for this history are the pianos themselves, and I have organized the book, except the first and last chapters, around specific existing pianos (and the last chapter takes up specific contemporary types of pianos). In examining an instrument or in reading the detailed description of one, I often realized that an innovation made some years earlier was not embodied in it. This forced me to ponder the fact that a delay always occurred between the entrance of something new on the scene and its adoption by any maker other than the originator, let alone by most other makers. The difference between invention and acceptance is a major leitmotif running through the book.

Consider only one example, important in the design of the modern piano. In 1828, Henri Pape in Paris introduced "cross-stringing" for very small uprights, where the long bass strings run above and across the plane of the short higher strings, in order to use the longest strings possible in a small case. During the 1830's, some American and English makers tried it temporarily in square pianos. A few cross-strung instruments were exhibited at the Great Exhibition in London in 1851, and in the early 1850's other American patents were granted. But the earliest cross-strung piano examined in this book was made in 1853. Only in 1859, 31 years after Pape's innovation, did Steinway successfully cross-string grands. Johannes Brahms, who died in 1897, never owned a cross-strung piano. Erard, the largest maker in Paris, made its first cross-strung grand in 1901, 73 years after the invention, holding out, to be sure, against an arrangement that most makers had adopted by then. Holdout or not, it is at least as important in understanding the pianos of the nineteenth century to realize that most makers did *not* use cross-stringing until far into the second half of the century as it is to know that Pape invented it in 1828. If the date of innovation were the only important fact, we could check off cross-stringing as available after 1828—and totally misconstrue the actual pianos that people played and built.

This lag between innovation and acceptance is a commonplace among historians of technology, but it has seldom been noticed in histories of the piano. I believe, then, that in this and other respects, I tell a more accurate story than my predecessors have told. At the same time, many of them have been enormously valuable to me. Three books stand out among all the rest: Rosamond E. M. Harding's *The Piano-Forte* (1933; 2d ed., 1978), Arthur Loesser's *Men, Women, and Pianos* (1954), and Cyril Ehrlich's *The Piano: A History* (1976). That Rosamond Harding took her story only to

1851 is reason enough to go beyond her. She gathered together an incredible amount of information, little of which I have found mistaken, and proved herself to be the finest drafter of action diagrams in the literature. But her book is confusingly organized and difficult to read, and it is disappointing that the second edition, exhibiting all the virtues of the first, eliminates none of its vices. Arthur Loesser, on the other hand, superbly wrote a superbly ordered story. I know few books on any subject that are so constantly engaging and interesting. Focusing on the piano as a social artifact, Loesser commented on technology now and again, but these comments were sporadic enough and often enough somewhat off the mark that I think of my book as a complement to and partial correction of his.

Cyril Ehrlich, an economic historian who has studied the piano industry after 1851—and who distinctly knows the difference between invention and adoption in technology—has paid special attention to manufacturing technology. I have shamelessly filched many facts from his extremely fine book, but at the same time I propose a picture of European piano technology in the later nineteenth century rather different from his, not in the facts of the matter but in their interpretation. The success of the modern piano on Steinway's model and the failure of the conservative makers like Erard, who stood pat on the older technology, is the point of Ehrlich's story, and there I depart from him. I admire what Steinway did, but I am not ready to suppose that where others did something else, they were misguided or out of touch with reality.

Some readers may think that one subject ought to be more prominent here than it is. I have done little to correlate the pianos described and discussed with the music written on and for them. To do so properly would fatten the book out of all decent proportion. But I have not resisted the temptation here and there to discuss the implications of the instrument at particular times for the music that was played on it. And though I did not go out of my way to find as examples pianos that belonged to or were associated with famous musicians, except for Beethoven (Chapter Three), I have more or less serendipitously used a few in Chapters Six, Seven, and Eight.

The book would not have been conceived were I not a participant in the Program in Values, Technology, and Society at Stanford University, where in constant learning from colleagues in several disciplines, the lines of connection between technology and other aspects of human life began to come clear for me. That I have dedicated the book to one of those colleagues in appreciation for unusual stimulation I trust the others will take as reflecting likewise toward them. Students enrolled in a course in the program on the subject of the book have helped me to sharpen my understanding and expression of the material. I am also grateful to Stanford's Department of Music for allowing me to play two recitals on the Broadwood grand discussed in Chapter Three. Intimate acquaintance with one instrument eased the way to real friendship with others.

One hears of editors who improve books, but I have never before come across one. Barbara Mnookin tried to keep me from getting away with anything and succeeded in repairing more unclear and infelicitous statements than I care to admit. Where any remain, it is because I was more stubborn than I should have been.

A Tenured Faculty Development Grant from Stanford University partially funded a sabbatical leave during which most of the research was done.

Stanford, California   E.M.G.

Acknowledgments

---◆---

A book like this cannot be completed without the help of many people in providing information, material, and encouragement. I am happy to acknowledge the aid of the following:

Professor Malcolm Bilson, Cornell University, Ithaca, N.Y.; Q. David Bowers, Wolfeburg, N.H.; Susan T. Brombaugh, Yale University Collection of Musical Instruments, New Haven, Conn.; Bruce Carlson, The Schubert Club, Saint Paul, Minn.; Professor Albert Cohen, Stanford University; Bjarne B. Dahl, Sunnyvale, Calif.; Dr. Rudolf Distelberger, Kunsthistorisches Museum, Vienna; Dr. and Mrs. G. Norman Eddy, Cambridge, Mass.; LaRoy Edwards, Yamaha International, Buena Park, Calif.; Edmund Michael Fredericks, Walhonding, Ohio; William E. Garlick, Boston; Joe Green, Yamaha International, Buena Park, Calif.; Alberto Hashimoto, Nippon Gakki Company, Ltd., Hamamatsu, Japan; Dr. Hubert Henkel, Musikinstrumenten-Museum, Karl-Marx-Universität, Leipzig; Professor William E. Hettrick, Hofstra University, Hempstead, L.I., N.Y.; Thomas Higgins, Saint Louis, Mo.; Sally Hoffmann, Helen Foresman Spencer Museum of Art, University of Kansas, Lawrence; Helen Rice Hollis, Smithsonian Institution, Washington, D.C.; Cynthia Adams Hoover, Smithsonian Institution, Washington, D.C.; Professor Eric Hutchinson, Stanford University; John H. Jervis, Sohmer & Company, New York; Barbara Lambert, Museum of Fine Arts, Boston; Dr. Laurence Libin, Metropolitan Museum of Art, New York; Tom O'Donnell, CBS Musical Instruments, Fullerton, Calif.; Dr. Jerry Persons, Music Library, Stanford University; Stewart Pollens, Metropolitan

Museum of Art, New York; Professor Ronald V. Ratcliffe, California Polytechnic University, San Luis Obispo; Dr. Richard Rephann, Yale University Collection of Musical Instruments, New Haven, Conn.; Harvey Roehl, The Vestal Press, Vestal, N.Y.; Dr. Konrad Sasse, Händel-Haus, Halle, GDR; Eugene Schachter, Long Beach, Calif.; Dr. Howard Schott, Tenafly, N.J.; Sally J. Silberman, Kimball Piano and Organ Company, Jasper, Ind.; Willard Sims, Baldwin Piano and Organ Company, Cincinnati, Ohio; Robert Smith, Somerville, Mass.; Harvey J. Sohmer, Sohmer & Company, New York; Gretchen Steffy-Bond, Palo Alto, Calif.; John H. Steinway, Steinway & Sons, New York; Dr. John Henry van der Meer, Germanisches Nationalmuseum, Nuremberg; Anne Voglewede, The Schubert Club, Saint Paul, Minn.; Dr. Kurt Wegerer, Kunsthistorisches Museum, Vienna; Roger Weisensteiner, Kimball Piano and Organ Company, French Lick, Ind.; Professor Robert Winter, University of California, Los Angeles.

Contents

———◆▶————

Illustrations

————◄◆►————

(1) The ranges of pianos and references to specific pitches are notated on the following scheme:

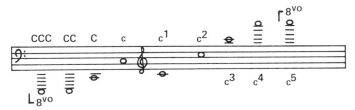

Pitches in the octave above any C are noted like that C; the d above c^1 is d^1, that above CC is DD, and so on.

(2) In Chapters Two through Ten, the photograph of each piano discussed is captioned in the following format:

Type of piano, maker, location, date. Serial number, if any, or model number and designation. Inscription, if of interest. Action type, dampers; hammer-covering material. Stops: number, types, and functions, left to right. Range. Stringing: patterns of single-, double-, triple-strung notes; wound and plain strings; mode of stringing (straight, cross, etc.); speaking lengths of bottom string, c^2, top string. Placement of tuning pins, if significant. Other aspects of vibrators if significant. Framing. Case: material, dimensions. Location of piano. Catalog or other collection number, if any. Comments on the instrument, if any.

Giraffes, Black Dragons, and Other Pianos

1

Technology and the Piano

In 1774, the Marquise du Deffand asked the French wit and philosopher Voltaire to contribute some verses for her Christmas entertainment. They were to be sung to the accompaniment of a new instrument called the fortepiano. Voltaire sent some verses he pronounced not very good, "but," he continued, "they are good enough for the fortepiano, which is a tinker's kettle" (*instrument de chaudronnier*). That Madame du Deffand's aristocratic *salon* would harbor a fortepiano and not a harpsichord in 1774 is unexpected; some decades would pass in France before the former would fully supplant the latter. But it is of not merely passing interest that in the year before Voltaire wrote his poor verses, a seventeen-year-old virtuoso from Salzburg named Wolfgang Amadeus Mozart wrote the first of the piano concertos (in D major, K. 175) with which he would set in train a musical revolution.

Voltaire's sarcasm reflects the estimate in which he held the tinker's plebeian technology. A *chaudronnier* made and repaired metal objects for household use—the relation of the word to the English "cauldron," a large kettle, is clear enough. Voltaire, to be sure, actually said "a tinker's instrument," but any instrument that a tinker made was more likely a kettle than anything else (hence my somewhat free translation of the phrase). The point is that, the kettle being a product of technology, Voltaire dismissed the piano's worth in technological terms. The piano has come a long distance since 1774, but like the tinker's kettle, it is a product of technology, whether low or high. That fact is the subject of this book. The piano's history has been written in terms of several different approaches: the social history of the instrument, its economic history, the piano as the vehicle for music, and the history of pianists and piano-playing, which must refer to the instruments.[1] My purpose is to write a technological history of the piano.

The piano is a machine. That may not be the first word that comes to mind to define the instrument, but it is perhaps the most inclusive, and it is the necessary presupposition of our subject. A machine accomplishes work, that is, it applies energy to some end. The piano's energy produces musical sound vibrations.

All sound is vibration in the air. What differentiates music from other kinds of sound is the regularity of the vibrations. There is a great deal more to the physics of musical sound than this superficial statement, but for our purposes at the moment it is enough.[2] The regularity of vibration implies *pitch*, the "height" or "depth" of the tone, measured by the rapidity of vibration; *timbre*, or *tone quality*, a function of the number and relative strengths of subsidiary vibrations, overtones, within the fundamental one; and *volume*, or *loudness*, a function of the amount of vibrational energy being applied.

The piano differs from other musical instruments in the way it produces sound. In its simplest essentials, the pressure of the player's finger on the key activates a set of levers that flings a hammer to strike strings. The strings, being stretched tight, respond to the hammer's blow by vibrating. The energy of vibrating strings needs amplification in order to be heard. One end of each string passes across a hardwood bridge, which is glued to a large, thin plate of wood beneath it, the soundboard. The vibrations are transmitted from the string through the bridge to the soundboard, which sympathetically reproduces the vibrations over its own wide surface, setting the air in contact with it into vibration.

The piano has, therefore, three essential parts: a *vibrator*, which produces the sound vibrations, and which in the piano is the string; an *activator*, which causes the vibrator to vibrate, and which in the piano is the hammer and the rest of the mechanism attached to the key (technically the *action*); and a *resonator*, which amplifies the relatively weak vibrations of the vibrator, and which in the piano is the soundboard.

Every musical instrument must have a vibrator and an activator, though not every one needs a resonator. The present standard system of classifying musical instruments, based on the kinds of vibrators used, recognizes four classes of instruments.[3] One is the idiophones (from Greek *idios*, the thing itself, plus *phōnē*, sound), in which the vibrator is the instrument itself, e.g., cymbals, rattles, and xylophones. A second class, the membranophones, has as the vibrator a stretched skin or other material that, when struck or otherwise disturbed, gives out a musical tone, e.g., drums. In a third class, the aerophones, the vibrator is a column of air enclosed within walls (usually a tube), which vibrates in response to the player's blowing into or across the tube. The aerophones are the wind instruments: clarinets, flutes, tubas, pipe organs, and others.

The fourth class of instruments has as the vibrator stretched strings. These are the chordophones (Greek *chordé*, string). There are three effective ways, and one ineffective way, to start a string vibrating. The ineffective way is to pass air across it, as in the so-called Aeolian harp. The effective ways are by plucking (guitars, banjos, harpsichords), by friction on the string, usually with a bow (violins and their relatives), and by striking (dulcimers, clavichords, pianos). And there we have placed the piano among musical instruments: it is a struck chordophone.*

———————◆▶———————

This book investigates technology in the history of the piano. Before beginning on the history, I shall look in some detail at the machinery of the modern piano. This chapter is intended to exhibit the technological problems of the instrument, to establish the nomenclature of its parts, and to show how the parts are related to each other. The rest of the book will follow those technological problems from the piano's beginnings back to the present.

There are two ways of laying out the strings, the piano's essential vibrators: horizontally and vertically. Theoretically one could hang them at any angle between the two, but no experiments in doing so have lasted. The horizontal configuration is represented

---

*Some students of musical instruments propose a fifth class of instruments, namely "electrophones" or "electronophones," on the ground that electric or electronic impulses are the vibrating element. Others argue that those impulses are the activators, becoming *sound* vibrations only on being transformed by a loudspeaker. On this view, which I accept, the loudspeaker is the vibrator, and it is to be classed as a membranophone.

in the modern day by the grand piano (pictured from directly above in Fig. 1.1), the word grand originally meaning simply big. The vertical (Fig. 1.2) is generically called the upright piano.

Apart from accommodating the string layout, which carries implications for the design of the action, the case of the piano is merely the box that contains the machine. It has no function with respect to the instrument's work, does not affect the tone or otherwise have musical value. There is one exception: the opened lid

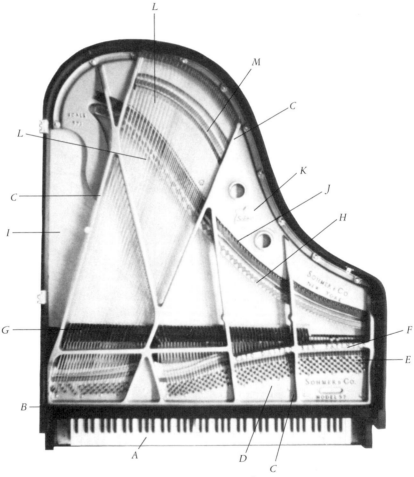

FIG. 1.1. *Plan view of a grand piano.* A, keyboard; B, case; C, frame; D, pin block (under the frame); E, tuning pins; F, capo tasto bar; G, dampers; H, bridge; I, soundboard; J, hitch-pins; K, string plate; L, cross-strung strings; M, bass bridge.

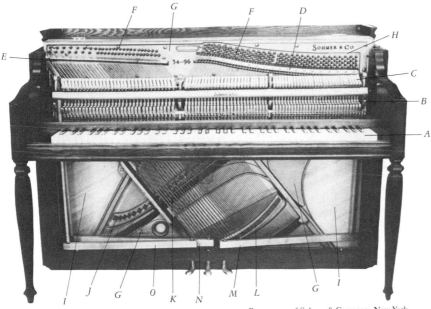

FIG. 1.2. *Plan view of an upright piano.*   *A*, keyboard; *B*, action; *C*, hammers; *D*, pressure bar; *E*, nut bridge; *F*, tuning pins; *G*, frame; *H*, pin block (under the frame); *I*, soundboard; *J*, bridge; *K*, cross-strung strings; *L*, bass bridge; *M*, damper pedal lever; *N*, bass damper pedal lever; *O*, "soft" pedal lever (moves hammer rail forward).

of the grand piano serves as a reflector, directing sound into the room. When it is closed, the instrument may sound somewhat softer or slightly muffled. But the sound of the grand does not come only from the top; as much comes out the bottom, which is not closed in modern grands (in early ones it was). The raised lid does not modify or enhance the *tone*, but has to do only with available loudness. One can raise the lid of an upright too, with a similar but lesser effect.

The machine itself may be divided into three distinct but interrelated mechanisms, corresponding to the three acoustic functions discussed above: the vibrator mechanism, the activator mechanism, and the resonator mechanism.

The *vibrator* is the set of strings and what keeps them in place. In most modern pianos, the lowest eight or so notes have one string to each note (what will hereafter be called single-strung), a quite thick piece of wire composed of an inner core of steel around which a smaller copper wire is closely wound. About the next 18 notes also have wound wire, and each note has two strings (double-strung). The rest of the strings are unwrapped steel, and each note has three strings (triple-strung). Triple-stringing over most of the range is now nearly universal, and the determination of where to begin the double-stringing and single-stringing and where to use wound wire is an element of design. Thus there may be minor variations from one make and model to another. The strings, as can be observed in Figures 1.1 and 1.2, are shorter as they are higher in pitch, and they are also thinner. Again, the lengths of the strings and the gauges of wire used for various pitches are decided by the designer.

Pitch is determined by the string's rate of vibration. The more vibration cycles in a given time, the higher the pitch. To produce vibrations at rates that the human ear can hear, the string must be stretched relatively tightly. Stretched too tightly, it will break, but too loosely stretched, it will not vibrate fast enough to produce an audible sound. The pitch of any string is determined by the combination of its length, the tension with which it is stretched, and its mass or thickness. The shorter the string, the higher its pitch; the more the tension on the string, the higher its pitch; the smaller the string's mass, the higher its pitch. Any change of length, mass, or tension will change the pitch.

If two strings are under precisely the same tension and of exactly the same thickness, and one is exactly half as long as the other, the shorter string will vibrate exactly twice as fast as the longer and will sound a pitch exactly an octave higher. The octave has a proportion of two to one in *frequency*, or the rate of vibration. If the longer string vibrates at 100 vibration cycles per second (or 100 Hz),* and the shorter one is an octave higher, its frequency is 200 Hz.

We run here into a problem of design. Suppose that the A above middle C (a¹ in the chart of pitches on p. xix), which has a frequency of 440 Hz, has a vibrating length (technically, *speaking*

---

*Short for Hertz, after the German physicist Heinrich Rudolf Hertz, who first measured electromagnetic waves. One Hz is one complete vibration cycle, where the vibrating body ends the cycle in the same position in which it started.

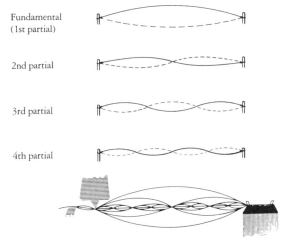

Fundamental
(1st partial)

2nd partial

3rd partial

4th partial

Fɪɢ. 1.3. *Partials in a vibrating string*.   The lowest figure in the diagram shows the simultaneous vibration patterns of the first, second, fourth, and eighth partials. Diagram by John Ellingsen from Arthur Reblitz, *Piano Servicing, Tuning, & Rebuilding* (Vestal, N.Y., 1976).

length) of 15 inches. If the A an octave below (a) is of the same gauge wire and at the same tension, it must be 30 inches long, the next one down (A), 60 inches, the next (AA), 120 inches. Still another is the lowest note on the standard modern piano (AAA), and under these conditions it would have a speaking length of 240 inches, or 20 feet! It will not do. Here the other factors in the pitch of a string come into play, which explains why the lower strings are not only longer but also thicker than the higher ones. In order to avoid too long a string, you must have a heavier one. The strings become longer as the pitches go lower, but not in the proportions that would be needed if they did not also become thicker.

The lowest strings are wound in order to be as heavy as necessary without excessive stiffness. The amount of stiffness in a piano wire is important, because on it depend the overtones in the sound and therefore the tone quality. A string vibrates not only with a motion over its entire length, but also with subsidiary motions along parts of the string. The portions of the string, being shorter than the whole, produce higher but fainter pitches. The diagram in Figure 1.3 shows schematically some of the simultaneous vibrations that go on in this complex pattern. The subsidiary vibrations are called *overtones*, or, more precisely for the piano, *partial tones* or *partials*.

The relative strengths of the fundamental tone and of each of the partials determine the quality of sound. Stiffness in a wire is an impediment to the vibration of partials. Indeed, the very top strings are so short and under so much tension that the wire is extremely stiff and produces few partials. To be sure, the frequencies of those upper partials of the high strings begin very quickly to be too high for the human ear. But the lower strings, which are both longer and under relatively less tension than the upper ones, freely produce partials.

Certain of those weaker but still audible tones vibrate at frequencies that make the string sound harsh and out of tune. There is reason, then, to do away with the harsher higher partials. One wants the mixture of fundamental and partials to produce a full, mellow, round tone with a certain amount of brilliance in it. Brilliance, which can be described as a somewhat hard-edged, sharp sound, is produced by relatively strong higher partials. If there are few higher partials, the tone is somewhat thick and fuzzy, perhaps even a bit hollow. If the relative strength of the higher partials is too great, the sound is strident, very hard, and what has come to be called tinny.

The quality of the wires is a very important factor in timbre. Evenness and regularity of vibration are possible only if the string has the same mass throughout its length, is perfectly round (any tendency toward an oval shape destroys regularity of vibration), and is completely free of twisting. Impurities in the steel itself, of course, will also hinder proper vibration. Given wires of sufficiently high quality, the timbre depends on the relations among the string's length, mass, tension, and stiffness. The ideal string, the string that acoustic theory assumes, has no stiffness, but there is no such object as an ideal string. Every string is more or less stiff, and the more tension is on the string, the more the stiffness comes into play. Thus a relatively long string in the high treble must have very high tension, whereas a relatively short string in the bass must have less-than-normal tension. A necessary compromise is involved. Up to a certain point of tension, the string's elasticity is improved, and it produces a tone increasingly rich in partials. Beyond that point, however, the increasing tension brings out stiffness, which damps out partials, and the tone goes dead. By careful increase of the gauge (mass) from top notes to bottom, one may end up in the bass with rather thick but not too stiff wires that are both long enough to give a good sound and short enough to fit inside a case of reasonable proportions. In a very small case, the lowest strings must be relatively short, therefore both quite thick—and correspondingly stiff—and under low tension with a correspondingly low elasticity. The resulting tone is considerably poorer than the optimum. For that reason, a "baby" grand may have a less desirable sound than a large upright. The trade-off in design and materials in pianos produces not perfection but a more or less acceptable, sometimes splendidly successful, compromise.

Timbre also depends on other factors. The material of the activator has an effect on tone quality; the harder it is and the faster the blow, the more upper partials are generated in the sound. The point on the string at which the hammer strikes also affects the tone quality. The diagram of partials (Fig. 1.3) shows that, as the string vibrates, certain points along it are relatively at rest because they mark the points corresponding to the partials. These points of relative but not absolute rest are called *nodes*. One node occurs at the midpoint of the string, because the second partial divides the string into two equal segments. Another set of nodes is one-third and two-thirds of the way along the string, because the third partial divides the string into three. The partials begin to sound a bit out of tune at about the seventh partial, which sounds a slightly flat minor seventh in the third octave above the fundamental. A hammer blow at one of the nodes tends to damp out partials corresponding to that node.[4] The reason is that a node is a relative point of rest in the string, but the hammer blow moves the string to its widest amplitude of vibration, thus canceling out a point of rest there. If the hammer should strike the string exactly in the middle, all of the even-numbered partials will be damped out, because all of them have a node in the middle of the string. Such a tone would be dull and hollow. Attempts to match piano tone with the striking point of the hammers have resulted in the conclusion that the best striking point is between one-seventh and one-ninth of the length of the string. This striking point tends to damp the seventh, eighth, and ninth partials, though recent tone analysis shows that these partials are not completely damped out.[5]

The strings are wound around metal pins at one end, in a grand at the front of the instrument, in an upright at the top. These are the *tuning pins* (in England, wrest pins), and turning them with a wrench made for the purpose—a tuning hammer—lessens or increases the tension, thus changing the pitch. The tuning pins are driven into the *pin block* (in England, the wrest plank), in the modern piano usually laminated of hardwood, in earlier pianos a solid block of maple or beech. The pin block is glued to the sides of the case. The other end of the string is led around a smaller pin, the *hitch-pin*, which is driven or sometimes cast into the metal frame. The upper strings in most modern pianos go around the hitch-pin and run back to the adjacent tuning pin, whereas the lowest, wound strings are looped singly on the hitch-pins.* By the tuning pin at one end and the hitch-pin at the other, the string is kept in the right tension and therefore in tune.

Most of the tension, however, is taken by the *frame*, a single piece of cast iron with holes over the pin block through which the tuning pins protrude. This metal frame is bolted to the pin block on one side and to the wooden underframing at the other, and in a modern concert grand may hold a total tension of 30 tons. Though the tension is less in smaller grands and uprights, it is still quite enough—as much as 15–18 tons in an upright. The development of the frame to resist so much force was a considerable issue in the history of the piano, and we will discuss it a good deal. The frame is now ordinarily made of what is called gray cast iron, though a few makers have experimented with cast steel and with aluminum alloys. Cast iron is cheap, not too heavy, and resistant to the compressive forces that the frame undergoes.

We must finally come back to the strings. The tuning pins and hitch-pins do not determine the speaking lengths of the strings. At the tuning-pin end, the top strings pass under a somewhat blunt metal bar, part of the cast frame, the rest of the strings through holes in small brass studs screwed into the frame (see Fig. 1.4).

*In a few modern makes of grands, all of the strings are looped singly on the hitch-pins, as was the pattern in all early grands. To use one piece of wire for two adjacent strings saves material and money, though the strings do not stay in tune as well as with single looping.

FIG. 1.4. *Capo tasto bar and agraffes in a grand piano.* ("Capo d'astro" is a trade name.) The strings bear upward against the capo tasto and the agraffes. The agraffes are the small studs with holes in them, two of which are just visible at the extreme left of the picture.

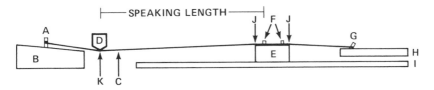

FIG. 1.5. *Speaking length of the string.* *A*, tuning pin; *B*, pin block; *C*, string; *D*, capo tasto; *E*, bridge; *F*, bridge pins; *G*, hitch-pin; *H*, frame; *I*, soundboard; *J*, downward bearing of string on bridge; *K*, upward bearing of string on capo tasto. Drawing by Bayard H. Colyear III.

The bar is called the *capo tasto* bar (Italian, "cap of the key"—some makers call it *capo d'astro*, which sounds nice but means nothing). The studs with holes in them are called *agraffes*. The capo tasto and the agraffes hold the strings down so that the strings' tension bears upward on them (shown in Fig. 1.5). This is most important on grands, where the blow of the hammer comes from below. On early pianos, before the agraffe and the capo tasto were invented, a really hard blow from the hammer could dislodge the string from

By courtesy of Sohmer & Company, New York

FIG. 1.6. *Bridge and hitch-pins in a grand piano.* The strings are led across the bridge at an angle by the two sets of bridge pins and are looped around the hitch-pins.

its bearing on a bridge near the tuning pins, thus instantly putting it out of tune. With these downward-bearing pieces, such a displacement of the string is impossible.* The agraffe and the capo tasto also determine one end of the speaking length of the strings and, by determining the upward bearing of the strings at one end, exactly fix the angle of down-bearing on the bridge, an angle that has an important effect on string tone. Each string passes across the bridge, led by two small pins at angles (see Fig. 1.6). At this end, the string bears downward on the bridge, and the angling of its passage aids in keeping it from being dislodged.

The lowest strings are strung at an angle across the body of the piano, crossing over some of the shorter strings, as Figures 1.1 and 1.2 show. Cross-stringing, or over-stringing as it is sometimes

---

*This interpretation of the reason behind agraffes and capo tasto has been challenged to me by Malcolm Bilson on the ground that in some years of tuning and playing fortepianos, and using hard hammer blows to do it, he has never seen strings knocked off the bridge. My interpretation comes, I admit, at second hand, from Samuel Wolfenden (*A Treatise*, p. 106), Rosamond Harding (*Piano-Forte*, p. 187), and Helen Rice Hollis (*The Piano*, p. 62)—and anecdotally from more than one technician. Some other writers do not mention the problem of dislodging strings from the bridge. It is worth noting that Wolfenden (pp. 108–9) explains the capo tasto (or pressure) bar as also relieving strain from the pin block.

called, permits the longest strings commensurate with the size of the case. The relative flexibility of longer strings allows a richer mix of partials in the tone, and the development of cross-stringing was a signal point in the evolution of the modern piano.

————————◀◆▶————————

We may conveniently begin discussing the *resonator* where we finished with the vibrator, namely with the *bridge*. Besides its function of determining one end of the string's speaking length, the bridge has to do with resonating the tone. Much of the string's vibrating energy is transmitted into the bridge, and that piece of laminated maple conducts the vibrations to the soundboard. Thus the bridge is the necessary connector between the vibrating string, which needs amplification, and the soundboard, which amplifies.

The bridge is glued to the *soundboard*, an expanse of planks glued edge to edge to form a single plate and held at the sides by the frame. Spruce has been the material for soundboards since there have been makers of stringed keyboard instruments, and nothing better has yet been found. One wants to use spruce with straight, close graining (several modern makers specify wood with no fewer than eight annual growth rings per inch, and more growth rings are desirable), which allows the vibrations to run freely through the wood so that the entire soundboard vibrates quickly in sympathy with the strings. Experiments with other materials, such as laminated boards with woods other than spruce in them, or even metal ones, have been reported not to affect the tone adversely.

The soundboard is thickest where the bridge is, measuring about ³⁄₈ inch toward the center and tapering to about ³⁄₁₆ inch at the sides. The taper is intended to overcome the board's stiffness at the edges, since stiffness in a board, as in strings, detracts from its quick response. Some makers make the soundboard thicker at the treble than at the bass. Sound waves travel along the grain of the board at a speed of about 15,000 feet per second and across the grain at about 3,800 feet per second.[6] Ribs of the same wood as the board are glued to the back of the soundboard, running across the grain (see Fig 1.7). These ribs, according to traditional wisdom, increase the cross-grain speed, though it is not certain whether they actually do so. Their most important function is to help to maintain the shape of the soundboard. In the modern piano, the

FIG. 1.7. *Back of the soundboard in an upright piano.* The ribs run across the grain of the soundboard. The lines of round buttons are the fastenings of the bridge through the soundboard.

soundboard has about ³⁄₁₆ inch of convexity (*crown*) toward the bridge. It is sometimes alleged that the crown assures the board's elasticity and quick vibrational response. The important thing is that the soundboard be in the closest possible contact with the bridge, for otherwise the vibrations will not be transmitted to the board. The downward bearing of the strings on the bridge puts nearly a ton of pressure on the soundboard. Thus the crown in the board resists the downward pressure, and that resistance may increase the board's elasticity.

We probably know less about the acoustics of soundboards than about any other parts of the piano. For example, some treatises on piano construction say that the grain of the soundboard must run parallel to the bridge, whereas others say that it ought to be at 90 degrees to the line of the bridge.[7] Some writers think the ribs should be attached across the grain, others think they ought to run in both directions to make squares, and still others argue for a fan-shaped arrangement.[8]

What is certain is that the soundboard is an efficient amplifier of vibration. A vibrating string presents very little surface to the air around it, and thus it displaces very little air. That is one reason why the sound of an unresonated string is so feeble. When those same vibrations are transmitted to a large plate that vibrates in sympathy with the string, the vibrating surface of the plate affects all of the air in contact with both sides of it, and the air transmits the vibrations very efficiently to the listening ear.

———————◄•►————————

Neither vibrator nor resonator is of any use unless something starts the strings vibrating. In the piano, the *activator* is the *action*.

Consider the following fictional design order:

Design a mechanical means to activate by pressure of the human finger a set of stretched strings at specific pitches. The mechanism shall have the following characteristics:

(1) The strings shall begin to sound as nearly simultaneously with the finger pressure as possible, with no noticeable lag.

(2) The mechanism shall be noiseless and shall remain noiseless through repeated hard usage.

(3) The loudness of the sound produced by the vibrating strings, properly resonated, shall be directly proportional to the weight of the finger pressure and shall remain so no matter how rapidly or frequently the finger pressure is applied; the loudness shall be equally proportional throughout the entire pitch range; and the range of possible loudness shall be from the barely audible to the extremely loud.

(4) The mechanism shall be consistently easy enough to activate that it can be used continuously for many hours without causing undue muscular fatigue and must be strong enough to withstand heavy use over long periods of time by muscular players.

(5) The cessation of finger pressure shall cause the strings immediately to stop vibrating and the sound to cease.

(6) A means shall be devised whereby strings can be allowed to continue to vibrate if the player wishes, even though finger pressure has stopped, and the strings can then be stopped at the player's will.

That somewhat pedantic piece of fiction describes fairly accurately the problem of the piano action. Its job is both to set the strings vibrating and to stop or damp them. It must do so consistently, accurately, instantaneously, noiselessly, and for long times, whether played by small or big people. The loudness of sound must always correspond precisely to the pressure of the player's finger on the key. That is no mean piece of machinery. The action is the machine par excellence within the larger machine that is the piano. Indeed, the Germans call the action *die Mechanik*, the French, *le mécanisme*.

Figure 1.8, with some simplification, shows the three stages of the motion of the action in a grand piano. In the first stage, the hammer is at rest. When the player's finger pushes down the key lever, *A*, at one end, the other end rises. The capstan, *B*, mounted on the key, pushes up against the wippen, *C*, to one end of which is pivoted the jack, *D*. The upper end of the jack rests against the knuckle, *E*, a leather-covered roller mounted on the lower side of the hammer shank, *F*, which is hinged on the.hammer rail, *G*. When the key lever moves up, two things happen simultaneously. The extreme end of the key pushes up the damper lever, *H*, to which the damper wire, *I*, is pivoted, which raises the damper, *J*, from the string. At the same time, the jack, *D*, pushes against the knuckle, *E*, and propels the hammer, *K*, up against the string. At this point we are at the second stage, where the hammer momentarily (for about $1/250$th of a second) strikes the string. The tail of the jack, *D*, has met the regulating button, *L*, which pivots the jack behind the knuckle (to the right in the side view in the diagram). At the same time, the rising of the wippen, *C*, causes the repetition lever, *M*, to rise, its top end coming to rest just under the flange of the hammer. In the third stage, as the hammer, *K*, falls back from the string, the knuckle, *E*, pushes the repetition lever, *M*, down. The jack, *D*, whose end protrudes through a slot in the repetition lever, remains offset from the knuckle. The hammer butt, *N*, catches on the check, *O*, which rose with the key. As long as the key is held down, the action remains in this position. But the slightest release of the key causes the check, *O*, to release the hammer. The repetition lever, *M*, which is sprung to rise, pushes the hammer shank upward so that the jack, *D*, under pressure of the jack spring, *P*, resumes its position under the knuckle, *E*. Even without allowing the key to return all the way to its rest position, a new blow of the hammer can be struck.

The diagrams in Figure 1.9 are of one type of upright action. Three problems must be overcome here. First, the vertical motion of the end of the key must be transformed into the hammer's hori-

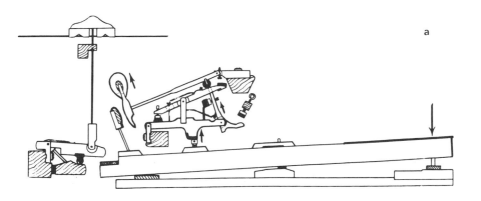

a

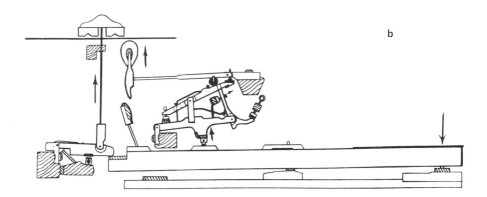

b

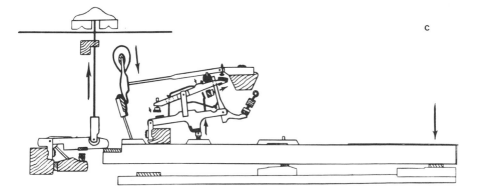

c

FIG. 1.8. *Grand piano action in three positions:* (a) hammer at rest; (b) hammer at the string; (c) hammer in check position. Diagram by John Ellingsen from Arthur Reblitz, *Piano Servicing, Tuning & Rebuilding* (Vestal, N.Y., 1976).

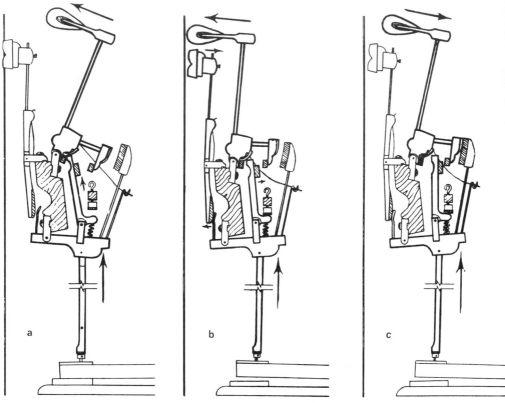

By permission of The Vestal Press, Vestal, N.Y.

FIG. 1.9. *Upright piano action in three positions:* (a) hammer at rest; (b) hammer at the string; (c) hammer in check position. Diagram by John Ellingsen from Arthur Reblitz, *Piano Servicing, Tuning & Rebuilding* (Vestal, N.Y., 1976).

zontal motion. Second, where the hammer in the action of the grand falls from the string mostly by gravity, in the upright action it must bounce back from the string and be prevented from rebounding forward. Third, the damper also moves horizontally, but in the opposite direction from the hammer. As the hammer comes to the string, the damper goes away from it, and when the hammer has moved away from the string, the damper returns to it, both motions by mechanical means rather than by gravity. Because of the mechanical complexity of the upright action, it has never been as satisfactory in operation as the action of the grand. It tends to be sluggish and to feel a bit mushy, and is much less precise, subtle, and consistent.

In any action, the hammer must leave the string immediately on striking it. Should the hammer stay in contact with the string, it will act as a damper on vibration, and the result will be not a ringing tone, but a mere thud (technically called *blocking*). The part of the action that propels the hammer upward or forward must give it enough play that it can return to its resting-place. This problem was solved by an *escapement*. In the action of the grand, the jack, having pushed against the knuckle on the bottom of the hammer shank and flung the hammer upward, is pivoted backward by encountering the regulating button, and this "escape" permits the hammer to fall back. With the upright action, the jack, pushing against the butt of the hammer, hits the offset button and is pivoted backward, escaping from the notch in the hammer butt. Without the escapement, the hammer might be blocked against the string, or it might bounce back and forth, giving two or three tones where the player wishes only one.

In the grand, the combined action of the escapement and the *check* allows the hammer to fall back only part of the way to its resting-point as long as the key is held down. With this arrangement, notes can be repeated very quickly, for an agile finger can strike the key again before the hammer has fallen to its original position, and the hammer has less distance to go to the string. The principle was first conceived by Sébastian Erard in Paris and patented in 1821.* He proudly called it a "repetition" action, and from his basic design was developed the action of the modern grand.

The *hammer* is the business end of the action. Hammers for the lower strings are larger and heavier than those for the upper ones, because the thicker bass string needs a weightier blow to make it vibrate. The bottom hammer is usually almost exactly twice as heavy as the top one.[9] The designer of the action must balance its leverage so that the pianist can obtain the same loudness with almost the same strength of blow for the heavier bass hammers as for the lighter treble ones. The hammer is a piece of wood around which usually a hard inner and a softer outer layer of felt are attached. Sometimes there is no separate inner layer.

The search for the perfect material for hammers went on for many decades, and, it may be argued, it is still under way. If the material is too soft, the tone will be thick and fuzzy from an ab-

---

*Rather than clutter up the text with the dates of birth and death of persons who have a part in the story, I have put those dates in the Index.

sence of upper partials, without the clear definition that piano tone is expected to have. If the material is too hard, upper partials will be too prominent, and the tone will be harsh and hard. The perfect hammer-covering material is hard enough for solidity and definition of tone and soft enough for mellowness and richness; never compacts in the slightest; and is absolutely resistant to the cutting properties of metal wire. Whatever that perfect material may be, we have not yet found it.

Felt is far from perfect, but it is the material now universally used. Long usage tends to harden felt hammer heads and to flatten them as repeated blows compress the material at the tip. Moreover, since the strings always meet the hammer at the same places on its surface, they cut grooves in the felt. Then the tuner must "voice" the hammers by sanding off felt around the grooves, pricking the top of the hammer to loosen and soften the felt, and reshaping the striking surface. Voicing must be done every so often, depending on how much and how hard usage the instrument has had. Time comes when the voicing has removed so much felt that the remaining layer is too thin and hard to make a full sound. One must then either buy a new piano or pay a sizable sum for a new set of hammers.

The *damper* mechanism is very important. The action is so arranged, as we have seen, that when the key is depressed the damper leaves the string, allowing it to vibrate freely. When the key is released, the damper returns to its place against the string, and its felt surface stops the vibrations—or is supposed to stop them. One sometimes hears an annoying snarl from the strings if the damper does not seat firmly and instantly on the string. The material must be soft, so that touching the strings makes no noisy thump. But the damper must be heavy enough to stop the vibrations instantly, even with a heavy string, yet light enough not to add too much weight to the action. The highest notes on modern pianos do not have dampers. The strings are so short and stiff that the vibration diminishes very quickly, and no damper is needed.

The action contains a pedal to lift all of the dampers at once and hold them away from the string as long as the player wishes. In the wrong hands (or feet), this can produce a horrendous noise, but with good players it is a very important expressive device. Figure

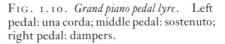

FIG. 1.10. *Grand piano pedal lyre.*   Left pedal: una corda; middle pedal: sostenuto; right pedal: dampers.

By courtesy of Sohmer & Company, New York

1.10 shows the lyre of a grand piano with the standard three pedals. The right pedal on all modern pianos works the dampers. On a grand, a vertical rod leads from the back of the pedal to a horizontal rod attached to all the damper lifters. On an upright, the pedal is attached inside the case to a horizontal wooden bar that operates a vertical rod (shown in Fig. 1.2). As long as the pedal is held down, the dampers stay off the strings. This pedal is sometimes wrongly called the "loud" pedal. It does not actually make the sound louder, though non-pianists who batter the keys while holding down the damper pedal make the noise seem terribly loud.

The left pedal is the so-called soft pedal. On an upright, it works a rod that moves all the hammers forward so that they have a shorter distance than usual to travel to the string, resulting on the whole in a softer sound for the same finger pressure. On a grand, the left pedal is imprecisely called the *una corda* pedal ("one string" in Italian). It moves the entire keyboard and action to the right (in a few makes, to the left) about ⅛ inch, so that the hammer strikes two of the triple-strung strings and one of the double-strung ones. The name una corda is a holdover from pianos of the late eighteenth and early nineteeth centuries, in which the pedal moved the action so that the hammer struck only one string. The effect on those fortepianos is a markedly different tone quality. On the modern piano, the timbre is subtly different, but many people cannot hear it. In that respect, at least, the modern piano does not give the player the flexibility of changing tone quality that early ones did.*

If an upright has a third pedal, between the other two, it may have one of several functions. On some, the middle pedal lowers a rod to move a strip of wool or felt between the hammers and the strings. The hammer strikes through the intervening cloth, producing a muted sound. On others, the middle pedal is a way to keep the "soft" pedal down without holding it down, the pedal sliding into a groove that keeps it down. On still others the middle pedal operates only the bass dampers. On a very few, it serves the same function as the middle pedal on a grand and is called a *sostenuto*, or sustaining, pedal. If one plays a chord and, while holding down the keys, puts down the sostenuto pedal, that chord will continue to sound, but no other dampers are affected. The mechanism, patented by Theodore Steinway in 1875, achieves this effect by eccentric buttons activated by the pedal, which catch and hold up only dampers that are already up. Most American and Japanese grands and many grands made elsewhere for export to the United States have the sostenuto pedal. Europeans have not liked it as Americans have, though it has recently become more common.

————————◆————————

We have examined the various parts of the machine, their functions, and their operation. It is important to bear in mind that, like any machine that is a conglomeration of several acting parts, the piano is a system, the interrelations of whose parts spell the difference between a good instrument and a poor one.

That interrelationship is a technological matter. To trace technology in the history of the piano, which is the task of this book, is to notice how the years have brought changes in the relations of

*The modern upright cannot have an una corda pedal because the strings run at such an oblique angle to the hammers that if the action were moved sideways, the hammer might strike one string of the wrong note.

the parts with one another. For this reason, the history in the chapters to follow is organized around descriptions and discussions of specific instruments. The pianos themselves are the primary sources for such a history, and their similarities to and differences from one another are the stuff of the story.

Had there been no differences, there would be no history of the piano, and the description just passed would be all we need. But the instrument changed over the years, as typical ideals of sound and of music changed. The piano sounds that audiences wished and expected to hear in Mozart's time were quite different from those that they wished and expected to hear in Liszt's time, which in their turn were different from what we expect today. To explain such changes in musical taste is beyond our scope. The subject will come up from time to time along the way, but no definitive treatment of it will be attempted. This book proposes, by describing and explaining the technological systems of a number of different instruments, discussed roughly in chronological order, to show what pianos were throughout the history of the instrument.

I shall not attempt an air-tight definition of technology. For our purposes, the word can be used more or less loosely to signify the means, physical and intellectual, of producing the machine that is the piano. Included in those means are three distinguishable but interrelated kinds of technology.

One is the *technology of design*. I have spoken of the piano as a system with necessarily interacting parts. Design is the beginning of the interrelationship in which the functioning of the parts is envisioned, thought through, and perhaps sketched out in a plan. I call this design rather than invention. To be sure, invention may in specific instances be an element of design. When Alpheus Babcock made the first one-piece metal frame for a piano in 1825, he invented something. But the invention was only one aspect of the total design of the instrument he wished to improve. Even Bartolomeo Cristofori, the inventor of the piano itself, did not conceive an entirely new machine. He invented a new kind of keyboard activator for stretched strings, but nothing else about the instrument would have distinguished it from a harpsichord. The pianoforte action was only part—perhaps in Cristofori's mind the most important part—of a total design. He was even willing to call the instrument by the same name he used for the harpsichords he was employed to make and repair in Florence. As far as Cristofori was concerned, this box contained a new kind of harpsichord.

I do not mean that invention is unimportant. Many inventions will be discussed in the pages that follow. But all of them were conceived as parts of wholes, elements of design in a machine that transcended the specific invention. The technology of design, then, has to do with the conception of the instrument, however and in whatever degree that conception may differ from earlier or contemporary conceptions.

A second kind of technology is the *technology of materials*. This technology is closely related to that of design, for specific material to be used in a particular part may affect the design and vice versa. If, for example, the framing that holds the string tension is of wood—and for well over a century after the piano's invention nothing else was conceivable—the material, length, and mass of the strings must be designed accordingly. As we will see, stronger and heavier strings, ultimately of steel, came to be used, and the increasing force of the strings required framing stronger than wood. To be sure, some aspects of the technology of materials have not changed very much: soundboards are still made from spruce, as they were in the earliest pianos and in the harpsichords and clavichords that preceded them. But the glues that hold the spruce boards together today are very different from those used in the eighteenth and nineteenth centuries.

Sometimes it is difficult to know why a particular material is used for a part—why, for example, one manual specifies pear wood for damper heads and holly or sycamore for various action parts, but maple or mahogany for hammer moldings.[10] Perhaps those materials were prescribed because they had always been used, and long trial had shown them to be best. Such lore is an element of technology. Some materials have little or no effect on the instrument's sound; such a technique as veneering obviously affects only the appearance. But with the materials of strings, frames, hammer coverings, and dampers, the musical ramifications may be very wide indeed.

The third kind of technology is the *technology of manufacture*. The piano, like almost any artifact made in both the eighteenth and nineteenth centuries, was first made by hand in a craftsman's shop and later at least partly by machine in a factory. In the earlier days, every part of the instrument was made by workers in the shop, but later some or all parts were bought ready-made from specialist firms. In craft-shop manufacture, each worker typically put together an entire instrument from the ground up, but in factory work each had only one specific task to do. The craftsman formed and assembled parts with hand tools, whereas in the factory some parts were made and assembled by machine. I make no value judgments for or against machines. Some pianos made entirely by hand are superb, some are junk. Some made with extensive use of machines are offensive to eye and ear alike, and others are splendid vehicles for the most skilled pianist.

Two aspects of the manufacturing technology of the piano bear special mention. Instruments made in small shops are always few in number and may be expensive out of proportion to their quality. Economies of scale allowing a firm to make large numbers of pianos certainly led to lower prices and not always to inferior instruments. Second, as the piano industry grew, some companies came to specialize in making frames or soundboards or actions for sale to firms that assembled the completed instruments. The supply industry fostered designs involving interchangeable parts, another aspect of the economy of scale, which lowered costs to purchasing manufacturers. It also positively affected the subindustry of tuners and technicians. Like all machines, pianos need repair. If the work can be done quickly and inexpensively, so much the more pleasant for the player. To be sure, interchangeable parts may produce a certain homogeneity among instruments, and if that influence tends toward mediocre products, the economies may defeat the aspirations of musicians.

As we will see, the hoary tradition of the small craft and the handworker retained its hold on piano manufacture for a very long time. The persistence of the craft mentality had its effect in turn on the technology of materials. As late as the 1920's, the director of a French firm still stoutly maintained that an iron frame did not necessarily improve the tone. It has always been a conservative industry, and we will have to inquire for reasons as the investigation goes along. Even Steinway & Sons, the company that for over a hundred years has by common consent been in the technological forefront of design and manufacture of pianos, said recently in an advertisement, "The craft [of making pianos] has hardly changed in a hundred years." If the statement is true and not mere sentimental puffery, we shall need to ask why.

————————◄◆►————————

The history of the piano as a machine, then, is our subject. It is tempting in what looks like a narrow focus to try to bring out everything. Even in so confined an area, that would swell the discussion beyond reason and make for confusion. I have stayed pretty much on the main roads of development, only now and then pursuing a by-way for interest's sake.

Throughout these chapters, I have organized the story around descriptions of specific instruments, guided by the perception of the piano as a technological system. Each piano is described and discussed in terms of its own characteristic interrelationships of parts and of the influences on it. The wider story of the instrument is woven together around these "stop-action" shots of pianos.

The Classic Piano

Like most innovations, the piano made its way slowly. Though it had its origin in what historians of music call the Baroque period, about 1700, its ascendancy began only during the Classic period in the late eighteenth century, the time of Mozart, Haydn, and the young Beethoven. The pianos in the last decade of the century represent, for the most part, developed and standardized forms of the earliest experimental instruments.

Those settled forms involved both mechanism and shape. By 1800, two principal types of action were to be found, the "English" and the "Viennese." The British and nearly all of the French pianos had the English type; the German and Austrian ones had the Viennese type. The shapes were mainly two: the grand and the square (which was not square but rectangular), both horizontal types of piano. By 1800, some vertical instruments were being made, resuming experiments that had been carried out in the mid-eighteenth century (I will defer discussing those instruments to Chapter Four). These various types of pianos had undergone a fair amount of development, especially in the actions. The lines of influence from earlier predecessors are relatively clear, but some of the details of the process are lost. We do not know, for example, who first designed square pianos, or when it was done.

Conveniently for the historian, the piano has a definite beginning in time, or at least a last possible date of invention. We shall begin with a piano made by the inventor—but not his original invention, which, as far as anyone knows, no longer exists.

The instrument pictured in Figure 2.1, by Bartolomeo Cristofori, was originally in the collection of the Kraus family in Flor-

FIG. 2.1. *Grand piano, Bartolomeo Cristofori, Florence, 1726. Inscription:* "Bartholomaeus de' Christophoris Patavinus inventor faciebat Florentiae MDCCXXVI." *Action:* Cristofori jack action with escapement; hammers parchment cylinders with leather tips. *Stops:* Hand stop on cheek blocks: una corda. *Range:* C–c³. *Stringing:* Double-strung plain; C 195.4 cm, c² 27.3 cm, c³ 13.9 cm. *Framing:* Wood. *Case:* Double case: outer case decorated, inner case (pictured) undecorated cypress; 250 cm long, 91.5 cm wide. *Location:* Musikinstrumenten-Museum, Karl-Marx-Universität, Leipzig, GDR. Catalog no. 170.

ence, came from them in the late nineteenth century to the collection of Wilhelm Heyer in Cologne, and in 1927, with much of the Heyer Collection, was transferred to the University collection in Leipzig. During the Second World War some of the instruments in the collection were destroyed, but the Cristofori piano survived. The University is now the Karl-Marx-Universität, and the Cristofori is part of a large collection of pianos and other instruments.

Bartolomeo Cristofori was a Paduan harpsichord maker, employed from about 1693 by Prince Ferdinand de' Medici in Florence. He must have had an enviable reputation. Ferdinand was an enthusiastic harpsichordist with both the money and the motivation to hire the best person available to build and care for his harpsichords. Indeed, those who have examined Cristofori's surviving instruments have often remarked on his artistry as a craftsman.

He had to be more than a craftsman to do what he did in inventing the piano. It was a momentous step in a new direction. We who are so accustomed to the piano may wonder why someone did not think of it before. Such a question cannot really be answered, though it is probably adequate to the musical situation to say that no one particularly needed to think of it. At the same time, there is enough evidence that musicians were becoming dissatisfied with the capabilities of the keyboard instruments at their disposal to justify the thought that a new solution would have come sooner or later. Indeed, within a few years of Cristofori's invention in or before 1700, designs for something like it were drawn up independently in both France and Germany.

Cristofori set to work on an alternative to the harpsichord (he may have thought it only an improvement) at the express wish of Prince Ferdinand.[1] A specific shortcoming of the harpsichord was the target of the change. The instrument has for certain purposes a problem that can be overcome only by suggestion and artistic sleight of hand. The harpsichord makes its sound by plucking. A plectrum, which in Cristofori's day was a crow quill and in most modern instruments is made of plastic, is mounted on a jack so that when the key is depressed, the quill rises past the string and plucks it (see Fig. 2.2). When the key is released, the jack falls back to its resting-place by gravity, and a damper attached to it stops the string's vibration.

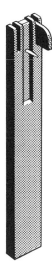

FIG. 2.2. *Harpsichord jack.* Drawing by Bayard H. Colyear III.

The problem of the harpsichord is that the player cannot affect either the timbre or the loudness of the sound. Hitting the key harder makes no difference, except to cause a thump when the key strikes the key-frame below it, because the loudness of the sound depends not on the speed with which the plucking is done, but on the mass of the plectrum that comes into contact with the string. That mass is determined by the way the quill is set into the jack, and it cannot be modified during playing. Thus it is impossible to produce gradations of loudness on the harpsichord. Some harpsichords, to be sure, had two or even three manuals (keyboards) placed one above the other, each with its own set of strings and each producing different timbres and volumes. Most Italian harpsichords had a single manual, but even the two- or three-manual instruments could not produce crescendo, diminuendo or accents, in which one note stands out in loudness or timbre above others being played simultaneously or in series. Audiences may think they hear accents when excellent harpsichordists simulate them by carefully delaying the attack of a note or holding it slightly too long. That suggestion of accent is art, not science. The notes are not louder; the player attracts attention to them, and they seem louder.

In Italy, where by 1700 opera had already become a public and not merely a princely entertainment, and where a long tradition of the world's finest makers of violins and other stringed instruments had been established, the dynamic inflections of vocal and violin music were known and loved. The organist and composer Giovanni Casini emphasized that music should have "the speech of the heart, now with the delicate touch of an angel, now with violent eruptions of passion." And regrettably, "the harpsichord does not fulfill all the expressions of human sentiment."[2] Such considerations must have animated Prince Ferdinand in wishing Cristofori to improve the harpsichord.

The work, begun in 1698, had been completed by 1700, the year of Ferdinand's jubilee.* An inventory of his instruments compiled in that year mentions among others:

An *Arpicembalo* of Bartolomeo Cristofori, of new invention, that produces *piano* [soft] and *forte* [loud], with two principal unison registers, with a soundboard of cypress without a rose, with bands and framing half-circles alike, with veneer of ebony, with jacks (*saltarelli*), with red cloth, that touch the strings, and hammers (*martelli*) that produce the *piano* and *forte*; and the entire instrument well closed and covered with a sheet of cypress veneered with ebony, with a keyboard of boxwood and ebony, without breaks, which begins on C (stretched [= full] octave) and ends on C, with the number of forty-nine keys (both white and black), with two black side blocks, with which one lifts and sets out [the instrument from its box] with two small black knobs above, length 3⅞ *braccie*, width at the front one *braccia* and six *soldi*,† with a desk of cypress and an outer case of white poplar, and a covering of red leather, lined with green taffeta and edged with gold ribbon.[3]

---

*This date was established by Mario Fabbri ("Il primo pianoforte") and is now generally accepted. Earlier histories cited 1709 as the year of Cristofori's invention. In that year, Scipione Maffei saw Cristofori's instruments in Florence. Since Maffei was the first to print anything about the piano, the date of his first view of them was taken as the date of invention. But Fabbri's discovery of an inventory of 1700 has pushed the date back. (I am indebted to Helen Rice Hollis for supplying me with a copy of Fabbri's article.)

†*Braccia* and *soldi* are units of measurement; I have been unable to discover their equivalents.

This is an extraordinarily interesting document. The term ar-picembalo is so rare that even Sibyl Marcuse, in two books crammed full of detailed information, never mentions it.[4] It probably refers to a harpsichord shaped like a harp lying on its side, as opposed to the rectangular virginals or the more irregularly shaped *spinetto*.* The writer of the inventory uses the word saltarelli, which usually meant the jacks (Fig. 2.2), to refer to the damper mechanism. This arpicembalo had precisely the range of the 1726 piano pictured in Figure 2.1, the four octaves from C to c^3.

What is most interesting technologically about the 1726 Cristofori and its predecessors is that it is different in only one respect from the harpsichords that Cristofori was employed by Ferdinand de' Medici to make. The length of the case and its disposition, complete to an outer case that holds a removable inner one, the C–c^3 range, the stringing, the soundboard, the design of bridges—all are quite familiar to anyone acquainted with Italian harpsichords of the late seventeenth century. The instrument, in its inner, undecorated case, could be removed for performance from the larger, highly decorated outer case. Most Italian harpsichords had but one manual, which could engage two sets of jacks, each plucking a different set of strings. Thus each note of the harpsichord had access to two strings of different tone quality. To change from one set of strings to the other, one pulled the manual out toward oneself or pushed it in; to play both at once, the manual was left in the middle position, where both sets of jacks engaged the strings. Thus there were two sets of tuning pins and two of hitch-pins. Since the two sets of strings were usually tuned in unison (one comes occasionally across four-foot registers, tuned an octave higher than the key),[5] only one bridge was needed. And the C–c^3 range, though not uniform in Italian harpsichords, was common enough. The lowest octave was often a "short octave,"

---

*Unless it refers to a harpsichord standing upright like a harp. Such an instrument was called a clavicytherium, and Cristofori is known to have made them (Sibyl Marcuse, *A Survey*, p. 282). I find it very difficult to conceive his using that unsatisfactory instrument as the model of his first pianoforte. The crucial evidence against the idea is that the inventory gives dimensions of length and width, not of height and width. But the use of the very rare word arpicembalo instead of the usual gravecembalo may suggest something more unusual about the instrument than its action. Scipione Maffei wrote that he saw in 1709 "three [instruments] of the ordinary size of other harpsichords" ("Nuova invenzione," p. 145) and also one of another shape, with "simpler structure" (*ibid*, p. 154). Unfortunately, he did not describe the other.

hence the reference in the 1700 inventory to a stretched octave.* The 49 keys referred to in the inventory require that the lowest octave be a full one.

The ingenious, if not genius, Cristofori went far beyond what he may have thought. His activator, demonstrably derived from the harpsichord action, employs a completely different principle. Whether some other instrument suggested this action to the Paduan inventor cannot now be determined. The action pictured in Figure 2.3 is from the Leipzig piano of 1726 in Figure 2.1, not from the arpicembalo of the 1700 inventory or from the instruments that Maffei saw in 1709 (see below and Fig. 2.4). There is already development from the original idea.

Notice first the damper. It is a harpsichord jack without a plectrum, which rises from the string when the key goes down and falls back to it by gravity when the key is released. Every harpsichord jack had a damper that worked exactly so (see Fig. 2.2), and Cristofori simply adapted what he well knew. The new principle is the hammer action, and it is a measure of Cristofori's genius that not only this design, but earlier forms that he is known to have developed, solved in principle most of the problems inherent in the action mechanism of the horizontal piano. The hammer must strike the string with speed proportional to the weight of the player's touch on the key. It is therefore flung at the string, not pushed against it. There must be a space of free flight where the hammer is not in contact with whatever moved it. The hammer must rebound instantly from the string so that it serves as an activator for the vibration, rather than as a damper. Its being flung at the string is one assurance that it will bounce away in free fall. Cristofori has devised an escapement: the jack, having delivered the blow to the hammer shank, slips to the side of the surface it struck, allowing that lever to fall immediately to its original position. When the key is released, a spring of hog's bristle returns the jack to its position under the escapement, ready to be played again.

The hammer, having struck the string and bounced away, must not be allowed to bounce back to the string by the force of its movement. In the 1726 action, Cristofori installed a back check to catch and hold the hammer head when it fell. The material of the

*The short octave looks as if it reaches down only to E. But the E key sounds C, and the F♯ and G♯ keys play D and E, respectively.

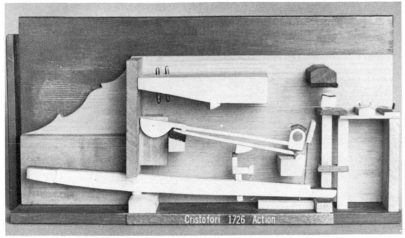

FIG. 2.3. *Cristofori grand action, 1726.* The jack, mounted on the key, strikes the triangular projection on the underside of the intermediate lever, hinged to the rail at right, the left end of which propels the hammer shank upward. Strings are wound on the lower ends of tuning pins driven through the pin block. Model by Ronald V. Ratcliffe.

hammer was a parchment cylinder, rigid enough to give a firm blow but with enough "give" in it not to be excessively hard, to which was glued a piece of soft leather where the hammer met the string. It is interesting that all of the hammers in this instrument, and in the other two existing Cristofori pianos, are the same size.

A number of successful attempts to devise other hammer actions were carried out later, but the action of the modern grand contains only two substantial differences of design and material from Cristofori's action, apart from the increased weight and the leverage to move it. The modern action has a lever that lets the hammer fall back only part of the way from the string while the key is down, allowing quicker repetition of notes, and modern hammers are covered in thick felt. But felt-making was of little significance in 1700, and Cristofori would hardly have thought of that material.

Technologically, the Cristofori piano had a new element of design, an action mechanism on a totally new principle, namely a keyboard activating hammers. Materials for the new hammer design had also to be found. The manufacturing technology was not

at all different from that of the harpsichord. Trial and error may
have persuaded Cristofori to make one other design change,
namely thicker strings than those ordinarily found in harpsichords.[6] These strings may have necessitated a stouter bracing
system inside the case than harpsichords had.

We do not know how many pianos Cristofori made before his
death on January 27, 1732.[7] The 1726 instrument has an "XX"
stamped on the action frame,[8] but this may or may not be a serial
number. So far as anyone knows, only three Cristoforis remain in
existence: the one in Leipzig here described; another of the same
year in the Museo degli Strumenti Musicali in Rome; and a third,
dated 1720, in the Metropolitan Museum of Art in New York. I
have chosen to describe the Leipzig piano because it has most of its
original parts, whereas the New York Cristofori is said to have
later hammers and some other substantial modifications.

Fortunately, Cristofori's influence did not depend on the number of pianos he made. In 1709, a Veronese gentleman, Scipione
Maffei, visited Florence to persuade Prince Ferdinand to give
financial support to a literary journal Maffei proposed to publish.
He must have succeeded, because Volume 5 of the *Giornale de' Letterati d'Italia* (1711) carried the notice, "Under the protection of His
Most Serene Highness, the Prince of Tuscany." In the course of
his visit in 1709, Maffei saw four pianos in Cristofori's workshop.
He published a laudatory article about them in the 1711 edition of
the *Giornale*, the first published reference to the piano (but a
somewhat unfortunate one, since Maffei referred to the inventor
as Cristofali and, in the index to the volume, as Cristofari). In addition to describing the instruments and the principle involved in
them, Maffei gave, from memory he said, a diagram of the action
(Fig. 2.4).

Apart from a somewhat lumpy appearance (which may testify
to Maffei's skill at drawing), this model has two differences from
the one I have described. First, the escapement mechanism here
operates directly on the hammer, rather than on an intermediate
lever as in the 1726 model. Second, the damper in the older model
is positioned under the string, and depressing the key brings it
down from the string. One unexpected aspect of both models is
that Cristofori drove the tuning pins completely through the pin
block and attached the strings to their undersides. He may have
found that if the strings were strung above the pin block, heavy

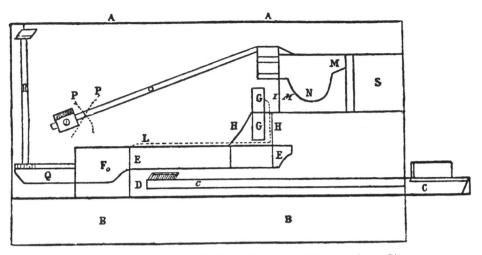

FIG. 2.4. *Scipione Maffei's diagram of Cristofori's action.*   Diagram from *Giornale de' Letterati d'Italia*, 1711.

blows from the hammers could unseat them from the bridge at their keyboard ends. Below the pin block, the hammers strike the strings toward their seating on the nut bridge. But replacing a string was probably somewhat cumbersome.

Maffei's article had little impact in Italy. Indeed, he indicated that Cristofori had encountered some degree of "opposition" to his new instrument, which Maffei called a *gravecembalo col piano e forte*, "harpsichord with soft and loud." Pianos were made in Italy after Cristofori's death, some of them apparently by men trained in his workshop. One of the great singers of the eighteenth century, Farinelli, owned a piano made in 1730 by Giovanni Ferrini, a pupil of Cristofori's. But Italy did not take to the piano—never really adopted the instrument invented within its borders that would soon sweep the European musical world.

It was the Germans who for some time to come fostered the instrument. Maffei's article was translated into German and published in Hamburg in 1725 in *Criticae musicae*. A Dresden organ and clavichord maker named Gottfried Silbermann evidently read the article and attempted to copy the instrument described. According to a contemporary account, Silbermann showed one of his pianos to Johann Sebastian Bach in about 1736, but Bach criticized it for a heavy touch and weak treble tone. Though this rejection badly annoyed Silbermann for some time, he finally took

Bach's criticism to heart and tried again. This time he submitted his work to Frederick the Great of Prussia, who was so impressed that he purchased the whole of Silbermann's inventory, 15 grand pianos.[9]

In 1747, shortly after Frederick had come into possession of the pianos, Bach came to Berlin to visit his son Carl Philipp Emanuel, Frederick's court harpsichordist. Frederick was relatively knowledgeable about music, an enthusiastic flutist, and an admirer of Bach. When the old composer arrived at the Stadtschloss in Potsdam, Frederick dropped everything and welcomed him, showed off his new instruments, and had him try them. He even gave Bach a theme on which, at Silbermann's piano, the composer improvised a fugue, and which he later elaborated into a number of movements and sent to Frederick as "The Musical Offering." The story has it that this time Bach was pleased with Silbermann's work.[10] He was not merely being tactfully polite about an absolute monarch's new toy. Bach is known to have acted as Silbermann's agent for selling pianofortes in Leipzig. A voucher with his signature attests to the sale of a "Piano et Forte" to a Polish count on May 9, 1749, and the scholar who published it even argues that the first movement of "The Musical Offering" coheres with the piano sound, and "performance . . . on the pianoforte seems to be strongly indicated."[11] Though two of Frederick the Great's Silbermann pianos are still in the Sans Souci Palace in Potsdam, the one that Bach played was destroyed with the Stadtschloss in the Second World War.

Silbermann successfully copied Cristofori's design and, by his own work and that of his pupils and apprentices, inaugurated the German manufacture of pianos. There were other, unsuccessful efforts to do what Cristofori had done. Jean Marius of Paris and Christoph Gottlieb Schröter of Saxony independently designed pianofortes in the second decade of the eighteenth century, but neither brought his invention to fruition.[12]

Both Marius and Schröter were influenced by a musical "superstar" of the day. He was a German musician with the unlikely name of Pantaleon Hebenstreit, who designed and who, by backbreaking practice, became a fabulous virtuoso on a huge, nine-foot dulcimer with 186 strings, touring all of nothern Europe with it. Gottfried Silbermann knew Hebenstreit too. In fact, until 1727 Silbermann made Hebenstreit's dulcimers for him.[13] The dulcimer, a trapezoidal frame over a soundboard with strings stretched the long way of the instrument, is played with mallets, somewhat like a stringed marimba or xylophone.* Now the dulcimer was a lower-class instrument, whose common German name was *Hackbrett* ("butcher block"). But Hebenstreit impressed commoners and aristocrats alike, and in 1704 King Louis XIV of France, before whom Hebenstreit performed, suggested that the artist name the instrument for himself, the Pantaleon.

What amazed people about Hebenstreit's performance was that he played a great many notes on a very difficult instrument and played them very expressively. With the mallets he could play both softly and loudly, and the undamped shimmer that he threw over series of arpeggios on his unwieldy monster cast audiences into spasms of ecstasy. Both Marius and Schröter heard Hebenstreit play, and one may surmise that the expressiveness he attained with the hand-held mallets led both to think of attaching hammers to keys. With the Pantaleon, as with all instruments played with hand-held mallets, the stroke was downward against the string and not upward, like the harpsichord's and Cristofori's actions.

Jean Marius submitted four designs of what he called *clavecins à maillets* ("hammer harpsichords") to the French Royal Academy of Sciences in 1716. One looks very much like a clavichord (an instrument we will discuss shortly), and the hammers seem to function in the same way as the tangents of a clavichord. Another is a composite model with one up-striking hammer and two kinds of down-strikers. A third is an upright instrument in which the hammer is a peg, presumably of wood, that strikes the strings from below.† The fourth is a combination harpsichord and piano, in which both jacks and hammers can be activated at once by the same keys, or the hammers can be wedged out of position. It is not

---

*This instrument is not be confused with the "Appalachian dulcimer," an American folk instrument that is not a true dulcimer, but a kind of zither.

†From the diagram (originally published in *Machines et inventions approuvées par l'Académie Royale des Sciences*, 3; Paris, 1735), I cannot imagine that it would work. But we cannot be sure that the drawings accurately represent Marius's design. They were made some 15 years after his death, perhaps from working models (which have of course disappeared), by someone who may or may not have known anything about the subject. Marius, of whom little is known (neither his birthdate nor his birthplace), was apparently a very wide-ranging inventor. He worked on the design of water pumps with Réaumur, the great hydraulic engineer, and invented a folding harpsichord—convenient for traveling but for little else—and the folding umbrella. (I am indebted to my colleague Albert Cohen for this information.)

clear what materials Marius had in mind for his hammers. The Academy approved the designs, which had something of the same effect as granting a patent, but there is no evidence that Marius or anyone else ever built an instrument from them.[14]

Despite the Academy's acceptance of Marius's designs, even the French forgot him. The *Encyclopédie Méthodique*, in its article "Art du faiseur d'instruments de musique et lutherie," published in 1785, attributed the invention of the *"forte-piano ou clavecin à marteau"* to Silbermann in Freiburg, Germany, "about 25 years ago." Not until about 1770 would a piano be made in France, the earliest known being by Jean (or Johann) Kilian Mercken, who was probably either German or Flemish.[15] Pianos were certainly known in France before that. Advertisements for them appear in the late 1750's, and in 1763 Johann Gottfried Eckhardt, who had settled in Paris in 1758, published six sonatas for the harpsichord, which, he said in the preface, could also be played on the *Forte et Piano*.[16]

Christoph Gottlieb Schröter also heard Hebenstreit play the Pantaleon. As a very young harpsichord teacher of aristocratic students (in 1717, when he heard Hebenstreit, he was only eighteen), he was troubled by his students' frustrated wishes to be expressive on the harpsichord. But Schröter was a player and teacher, no mechanic. In 1717, he designed two hammer actions, one up-striking and the other down-striking. A cousin who was a carpenter built a double model incorporating both designs, which Schröter submitted in November 1721 to the Elector of Saxony. Apparently someone at court promised that an instrument would be made—Schröter by his own admission could not have done so under any circumstances. Somehow the model was lost, or Schröter's reputation at the Saxon court was damaged (a vaguely described encounter with a lady-in-waiting led him to leave Dresden abruptly and permanently),[17] and nothing ever happened. To the end of his days, Schröter thought that Silbermann and others had stolen his model and his ideas. In 1738, he advanced his claims to be the rightful inventor in a Leipzig journal.[18] Still later, in 1763, he repeated the claim in another journal,[19] referring to the thief as "a certain gentleman of Dresden," meaning, of course, Silbermann. We will come back to Schröter in due course. He probably deserves some credit he has never been given.

For a long time, Germans and Austrians, Beethoven among them, thought the piano had been invented by a German. It is unlikely that they took Schröter's claims seriously. Like the author in the *Encyclopédie Méthodique*, they probably gave the palm to Silbermann. Beethoven at one point in his life was on a crusade to substitute German musical terms for the conventional Italian ones, and published some of his later works as for the *Hammerklavier* ("hammer keyboard") rather than for the Italian "pianoforte." He though the instrument, being as he believed a German invention, ought to have a good, solid German name.*

Three experiments followed the spread of the piano in Germany and, to a lesser extent, in Italy. One was a long-lasting success, one a long-lasting failure, the other a temporary failure. The success was the development of the so-called square piano, which is not square but rectangular. But square pianos were a long-lasting success only in the sense that they continued to be made until about 1900; they were not a success in the sense of being the best solution to the problems of the instrument. We will examine a rather typical square of the 1760's next.

The long-lasting failure was the attempt to devise a down-striking action, an action in a horizontal piano in which the hammers strike the strings from above. Both Marius and Schröter made down-striking designs, an idea doubtless derived from watching Hebenstreit and other Pantaleonists strike down on the strings with their hand-held mallets. Like others after them, they failed to find a satisfactory design. Getting the hammers to the strings was no problem; indeed, that was the reasonableness of the idea. Getting them away from the strings and preventing their falling back by gravity or rebound was the unsolved and unsolvable difficulty. Attempts to perfect down-striking actions continued until at least 1875; some ingenious people never give up.

The temporary failure was the development of upright pianos.

*Emily Anderson, *Letters of Beethoven*, vol. 2: 267. As late as 1853, one American writer still thought Silbermann was the inventor (P., "The Piano-Forte," *Dwight's Journal of Music*, 2: 2–3; 1852–53), though the Belgian composer and critic François-Joseph Fétis had concluded in 1834 that Marius was first in 1716, Schröter second in 1717, and Cristofori third in 1718 (Fétis, "A Sketch of the History of the Piano-forte and of Pianists" [1834], translated in the same journal, 5: 43; 1854). Fétis did not explain why he dated Cristofori's invention so late. In 1836, the inventor and technician Claude Montal accepted the evidence from Maffei's article that Cristofori (he still called him Cristofali) was the inventor (*L'Art d'accorder*, p. 208).

The first ones were in effect grands set on their heads with the strings running vertically. The shapes were usually but not invariably symmetrical (sometimes called pyramid pianos), and they posed very difficult problems of action design. Two principal makers of eighteenth-century uprights are known. Domenico del Mela da Gagliano in Italy attempted rather crude uprights, one or two of which survive. Del Mela may have been a pupil of Cristofori's, but nothing is known of him or his work except for the pianos, one dated 1739, now in Florence, and an undated one, ascribed to him, in Milan. A pupil of Silbermann's, Christian Ernst Friederici of Gera in Saxony, also produced uprights during the 1740's and 1750's. As far as I can discover, very few if any makers were building these monsters after about 1760, and they were apparently abandoned for the time. We will see in Chapter Four that the experiment, resumed in the last decade of the eighteenth century, issued finally in the smaller uprights that ultimately captured the home market.

———————————◄◆►——————————

The tiny instrument in Figure 2.5 is the earliest existing piano of ordinary construction made in England. A Zumpe of 1766 owned by John Broadwood & Sons, the piano manufacturing company in London, was an experimental model with divided black keys to allow "just" tuning in many keys (see below, p. 75n, on "just" tuning). The maker was a German. Johann Cristoph Zumpe, along with a fair number of others, had been an apprentice in Saxony of Gottfried Silbermann. When the Seven Years War devastated Saxony, beginning in 1756, musical instrument making was drastically affected, and a number of Silbermann's former pupils set out to find their fortunes in England. They seem to have arrived around 1760, and because there were about a dozen of them, they came to be known in the trade later as "the twelve apostles."

These men established the piano industry in England.* No

---

*There are other claimants. The writer of the article "Pianoforte" in Hermann Mendel's *Musikalisches Conversations-Lexicon* (8: 90) claimed that Burkat Schudi brought the hammer action to England in 1732. No evidence supports the contention. There was also a shadowy Father Wood in the early eighteenth century, in whom Edward Rimbault and Rosamond Harding seem to put some credence. I myself think that Father Wood is probably legendary.

FIG. 2.5. *Square piano, Johannes Zumpe, London, 1767.* *Action:* Zumpe single action; leather hammers; dampers originally leather, later red cloth (missing). *Stops:* 2 hand stops inside case: bass dampers, treble dampers. *Range:* GG–f³ (no GG♯). *Stringing:* Double-strung; GG–F♯ brass wound, G–f♯ brass plain, g–f³ iron plain; GG 107 cm, c² 28.8 cm, f³ 10.7 cm. Tuning pins at right. *Framing:* Wood. *Case:* Mahogany with boxwood and holly stringing; 130 cm wide, 47 cm deep. *Location:* Victoria and Albert Museum, London. Inventory no. W.27-1928.

source that I have found has identified all of the twelve apostles, and the identities of some must remain doubtful. By adding those named by some writers to clearly German names in the piano trade in London at an early enough date, I believe that the following men, given in alphabetical order with dates of their activity derived from various London directories by way of Rosamond Harding,[20] are at least most of the group:

Americus Backers, 1767–81
Frederick Beck, 1774–94
Adam Beyer, 1774–?
Gabriel Buntebart, 1769–95
Christopher Ganer, 1774–1807
George Garcka, 1783–92
John Geib, 1786–c. 1800
Meyer, a partner of Zumpe's
    in 1778

Johannes Pohlmann, 1767–93
Schoene, 1784–1820; advertised
    himself as "successor to
    Johannes Zumpe"
Sievers, a partner of Buntebart's
    in 1788 and later
Johannes Zumpe, 1767–84[21]

These craftsmen established themselves first with going instrument makers and later set up independently. Zumpe apparently worked with Burkat Shudi (Tschudi) for a time, and John
Geib was still employed by the firm of Longman and Broderip in
the mid-1780's.

Zumpe doubtless made harpsichords and clavichords as well as
pianos, but he rather quickly found a ready market for his little
squares, which though tiny, as the photograph and dimensions
show, were elegant and quite well made (a number of them survive), and possessed the virtue of novelty. The first public performance on a piano in England took place on May 16, 1767, when
a certain Miss Brickler sang a song from Handel's *Judith* to the accompaniment of Charles Dibdin on, as the advertisement said, "a
new instrument call'd the pianoforte," possibly a Zumpe square
like this one.* It is certain that the first public *solo* performance in
England, by Johann Christian Bach, Johann Sebastian's youngest
son, on June 2, 1768, was played on a Zumpe square, probably
identical to this one, which cost "the London Bach" 50 pounds.
That is a high price for a tiny box. But the piano had begun to
catch on, and Zumpe's instruments were in enough demand that
he could charge what the market would bear, could indeed farm
out his excess orders to others of the "apostles."

We have come here to a new shape. The origin of the convention
of calling these instruments "square" pianos is not known. The
Germans called them *Tafelklavier* ("table piano"), the French,
piano carré ("square piano"), the Italians either *pianoforte da tavola*

---

*Many writers have supposed that this was the first public performance on a piano
anywhere (see, for example, C. F. Colt, *The Early Piano*, p. 12). That has now been dis-
proved by Eva Badura-Skoda's discovery ("Prolegomena," p. 78) of a record of a payment
by the Burgtheater in Vienna to one Johann Baptist Schmid for the performance of a "Concert" (which could mean either concert or concerto) on the "Fortipiano" on March 13, 1763.

or *pianoforte rettangolare* ("table" or "rectangular" piano). The last is, of course, the most nearly accurate. But conventions cannot be readily flouted, and I shall continue to call this type of instrument square.

Like the grand, it is a horizontal piano, but the strings, instead of running down a long case away from the player, run across a wide one. The keyboard is set into the long side, and the strings run diagonally across the case from tuning pins at the right to hitch-pins across the back. The pattern must, of course, reflect the fact that the treble strings are much shorter than the bass ones. One effect of the diagonal direction of the strings in squares was that over time their tension put a twisting torque on the case, which tended to warp diagonally.

Cristofori's type of piano was derived, as we have seen, from the harpsichord, both in its action and in its shape. The square piano's shape was derived from the clavichord. Pictured in Figure 2.6 is a fairly typical eighteenth-century clavichord. Its external disposition is identical to that of Zumpe's piano. The keyboard is set in the long side of a rectangular case; the strings run diagonally across the case from tuning pins at the right. The only differences between this clavichord and the Zumpe square, apart from the clavichord's smaller range, are the actions and the damping mechanism. In the clavichord, the damper is a piece of cloth wound around all the strings at the hitch-pin end, which damps the strings when the key is released.

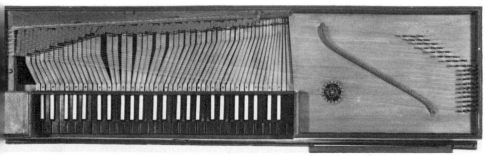

By permission of the Smithsonian Institution, Washington, D.C.

FIG. 2.6. *Eighteenth-century German clavichord.* The maker of this double-strung, fretted clavichord is unknown. Its range is C–f³. Collection of the Smithsonian Institution, Washington, D.C. Catalog no. 60.1394.

The clavichord action is the simplest machine one can imagine. The key is a simple lever with its fulcrum in the middle. At one end is the player's finger and at the other, a small brass strip called a tangent, set vertically into the key with its axis along the length of the key. When the finger pushes down, the tangent rises and strikes the strings (clavichords were ordinarily double-strung). But the tangent is not a hammer. Being rigidly attached to the key, the tangent remains in contact with the strings until the key is released, and being metal, it does not damp the sound. The tangent not only activates the vibration, but also sets one end of the string's speaking length. Indeed, many clavichord makers saved space and costs, and in the opinion of some players, improved the tone, by arranging the keys so that one pair of strings could be struck by two, sometimes even three, adjacent tangents. Since the tangent determines the speaking length of the string, the same pair of strings, struck by the C and then the C♯ tangent, will produce either note. Clavichords so designed (called in English "fretted," in German *gebunden*, "bound together") had their shortcomings. One cannot play the two adjacent notes rapidly in succession, and a trill between the two keys on the same strings is quite impossible.

Clavichords have another feature that some considered a shortcoming. The sound of the clavichord is tiny, scarcely audible 10 feet away. There are at least two reasons for this. The soundboard is confined to one end of the instrument, and it has a relatively small vibrating area, lessened, moreover, by the fact that the pin block takes up some of it. So small a soundboard would need to be considerably thinner than eighteenth-century technology could consistently make it if it was to be an even relatively efficient resonator. The other reason for the clavichord's small volume is the striking point of the tangent. For one thing, the brass dissipates the string's vibrating energy, just as the bridge does. But the bridge transmits the vibrations to the amplifying soundboard, whereas the tangent transmits them only to the key, which is not a resonator. About half of the string's vibrating energy goes where it cannot be resonated—except in the player's soul, one of the pleasures of playing the clavichord being a sense of intimacy with the instrument from feeling the string's vibrations through the key.

Forming one end of the speaking length, the tangent starts the vibration at the end of the fundamental tone's vibrating length, a node of that pitch. We saw in Chapter One that when a string is struck at a node, the striking tends to damp out some of the energy of that particular partial. In this case, the tangent damps energy from the fundamental note of the string, with the result that the energies of the partials are high relative to the energy of the fundamental. Everything about the design of the clavichord conspires to produce a very soft sound.

Whatever its shortcomings, the clavichord had one virtue that the harpsichord did not share. In its fashion it solved the problem that the piano was invented to solve: to vary the intensity of sound according to the amount of pressure on the key. To be sure, the range of possible volume on a clavichord went from the barely audible to the extremely soft. The loudest the clavichord could play without producing an unmusical, albeit very gentle, clunk was so soft that the quietest voice, flute, or violin simply drowned it out. It could not be used in any ensemble, but was strictly a one-person instrument. If a second person in the room breathed too heavily, the third person in the room might lose the music.

We see, then, another reason why something like the piano would probably have been invented sooner or later. The clavichord could not make a large enough sound to be heard in a sizable room. The harpsichord, holding its own in ensemble with voices and other instruments, could not vary its loudness. Something was wanted, as comments from many persons over the years show, that would make at least as much sound as the harpsichord and would be capable of gradations of intensity like the clavichord. As it turned out, that something was the pianoforte, though it might be interesting to speculate on what else it might have been. Surely not Hebenstreit's Pantaleon (interestingly, for some time in the eighteenth century, square pianos with down-striking actions—and there were some—were commonly called pantaleons or pantalons in Germany). The Pantaleon, to begin with, was viciously difficult to play, and its connections with the proletarian *Hackbrett* were clear enough that it would not have made its way in the upper reaches of society, where musical art flourished in the eighteenth century. And surely not the organ, which was available in sizes small enough to fit in a house. The organ at that time had the same problem as the harpsichord, that

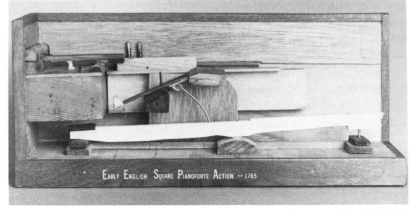

FIG. 2.7. *Zumpe square action.*   The jack is a stiff wire, topped with a leather button ("the old man's head"), which strikes the lighter-colored intermediate lever to propel the hammer to the string. The damper lifter is the light-colored rod under the damper arm at left, lifted by the end of the key. Model by Ronald V. Ratcliffe.

its loudness could be varied only by means of stops, and "chamber organs" had little versatility in this respect. In point of historic fact, it was the pianoforte that was invented and caught on, though acceptance took some time.

Exactly when the first square piano was made can no longer be determined. The earliest existing one is a tiny square in the Neupert Collection in the Germanisches Nationalmuseum in Nuremberg (catalog no. MINe 156), which dates from 1742 and was made by Johann Socher of Sonthofen, in the Allgäu region of Bavaria. That Socher's square was the first is unprovable. The claim that Friederici of Gera invented the square has no evidence to support it.[22]

Zumpe must have made squares in Germany before he came to London in about 1760. He promptly introduced his own action, probably one he had already used in similar instruments. The picture in Figure 2.7 shows how Zumpe radically simplified the Cristofori-type action that he would have learned from Silbermann. The hammer is hinged to a rail, as were Cristofori's hammers. The jack that starts the motion sits on the key. There the close resemblance ends. Zumpe's jack is an iron wire with a little leather button on its top (often jocularly called "the old man's head"), which comes up against a small, wooden intermediate lever hinged to the hammer rail. The intermediate lever pushes the hammer at the rail end of its shank so that it strikes the key and falls back.

There is no escapement, no check to catch the hammer and keep it from bouncing up to the string again. The hammer is a little semicircular piece of wood, scarcely ⅜ inch across, glued to the end of the flat shank and covered with a thin strip of soft leather. In some examples of this kind of piano, the hammers are all of the same size, never mind that some must strike the thicker bass strings. An instrument like this is surely what Voltaire had in mind when in 1774 he called the piano "a tinker's kettle."*

The lowest strings show another derivation from the clavichord, in that they are wound rather than plain. Harpsichords and virginals (rectangular harpsichords shaped like clavichords but larger) did not have wound strings, which would have damaged the quills. The wound string has a core wire of soft iron or brass around which a much thinner wire of copper or brass is wound spirally at fairly wide intervals. Sometimes the winding wire was round, sometimes it was a flat strap. As time went on, the windings became much closer, especially in the later nineteenth century, when winding machines were used. As we saw in Chapter One, the winding increases the mass of the string without seriously increasing its stiffness and thus produces a richer tone. A thicker wire, moreover, has a lower pitch than a thinner one of the same length and tension, and in a case 130 cm wide like the Zumpe's, space for the lowest strings is at a premium. It is not certain that clavichord and square piano makers knew why a wound wire was preferable to an equally thick plain one. They knew only that it was. Grand pianos apparently did not have wound strings until some years into the nineteenth century, but squares had them from the beginning, doubtless because wound wire was common in clavichords.

Zumpe's piano has a different damper system from Cristofori's. Instead of a harpsichord jack lacking a quill, the damper lifter is a stiff wire pushed up by the end of the key. The damper

*The Victoria and Albert Museum's Zumpe has been recorded in works by Johann Christian Bach, Thomas Arne, and Carl Philipp Emanuel Bach, played by Esther Fisher, on Oryx 1811.

sits on the strings on a long wooden arm that is hinged with parchment along the back of the case. A whalebone spring presses the damper down when the key is released. The damper face in the early squares was of cloth or leather, and the damper was more or less ineffective. The immediate cessation of sound on the release of the key is not to be expected from a Zumpe-type square.

In addition to simplifying the action, Zumpe has advanced beyond Cristofori in one other respect: he has incorporated a way to raise all the dampers at once, producing that undamped wash of sound for which Hebenstreit was famous. Zumpe was certainly not the first to do this, for earlier pianos have damper stops, though Cristofori's did not. In this square Zumpe has used two brass hand-stops in the case at the left of the keyboard. Revolving the handle of the closer one upward moves a bar under the arms of the lower dampers, raising them from the strings. Pushing the left handle to the right causes the same to happen with the dampers of the top half of the strings. To use the damper stops, the player either had to go on playing with the right hand alone while moving the stops with the left or had to stop completely and wrestle the handles into place. Or an assistant had to be employed. The hand-stop was nothing new. Harpsichordists and organists had always used it, and organists still do. Its life on the piano was limited, and its function would soon be transferred to the player's legs, either with knee-levers or with pedals.

Though Zumpe's square is a very early English piano, it is like many others built over the next 30 years and more. The range would be extended down to FF in most, in England and on the Continent as well as across the Atlantic, where the first square piano was built by a German named Johann Behrendt in Philadelphia in 1775. Some changes were made. In 1780, John Broadwood first began to put the tuning pins in squares at the back of the case instead of at the right side, and he patented that arrangement in 1783 (English patent no. 1379). The actions were developed toward a bit more complexity, with the reintroduction of an intermediate lever like Cristofori's, an improvement that allowed the pianist better control over the touch. In a piano like Zumpe's, the touch lacks all subtlety, requiring a firm, distinct finger motion but allowing few variations beyond the most obvious difference between loud and soft. As the square developed, the dampers also changed: sometimes they were pushed up directly by the keys instead of being hinged from the case, and sometimes they were placed below the strings.

It is clear that the technological issue par excellence in the entire eighteenth century was the design of the action. Otherwise, except for a necessary strengthening of bracing in response to the increasing use of heavier wires, the technology that had served the harpsichord and clavichord was pressed into the service of the piano. The makers applied their know-how, their ingenuity, and sometimes their guesswork to the problem of the action. The English, being supplied with makers who had been Silbermann's pupils, carried on with Cristofori's principle. Another route was taken in Germany.

The grand by Johann Schmidt in Figure 2.8 epitomizes the classic German and Austrian piano. The FF–f^3 range of notes is typical, though some pianos went up to g^3, a very few to a^3. Schmidt, like his colleagues at this time, used knee-levers for the dampers and a hand-stop for the buff stop, a rail to which tongues of leather are attached, which moves forward when the stop is engaged to place the tongues between the hammers and the strings. The effect of the buff is a somewhat muted tone.* It is also usual to see an Austrian or German piano of this period mostly double-strung; only the top three notes of Schmidt's grand are triple-strung. The sound is small but clear. The lowest strings are not wound, which produces in the bass a relatively thin, sometimes rather nasal clarity of tone without the rich boom one associates with the bass of modern pianos. Several accounts of pianos in the late eighteenth century in Germany show that the sound of the best instruments was often compared to a flute in the treble and to a bassoon in the bass.[23] The bassoon of that period was a much gentler instrument that the modern one, and to hear one is to receive some impression of what was wanted in the lower ranges of the piano.

This is the type of instrument played by Mozart, Haydn, and Beethoven, and probably by Carl Philipp Emanuel Bach after he moved to Hamburg (he had played Silbermann's pianos when he

---

*The buff can be heard at the end of the second movement of Mozart's Sonata in B-flat major, K. 333, recorded by Malcolm Bilson on a Philip Belt copy of a grand made by Anton Walter in about 1780, on Nonesuch N-78004.

was Frederick the Great's court harpsichordist in Berlin). Indeed, Mozart may have known Schmidt's pianos, since his father, Leopold Mozart, had once recommended Schmidt as an organ builder.* Instrument makers in those days did not specialize. Any good craftsman was expected to build equally good harpsichords, clavichords, and pianos, and many built organs as well. Silbermann himself was renowned as both an organ builder and a clavichord maker. In fact, Carl Philipp Emanuel Bach, the greatest exponent in his time of the clavichord, was so attached to his Silbermann clavichord that he wrote a melancholy, affecting "Farewell" to it when he sold it.

I have said that the major technical issue of the classic piano was the action. With the Schmidt, we come to a type of action that was known and used by anyone who played a piano made in Austria or Germany from an unknown early date until early in the twentieth century. Sometimes called the German action, it has come to be known as the Viennese action, geographically too restrictive a term but so conventional that I see no way to avoid it. This was a completely different kind of mechanism from that devised by Cristofori and developed by Silbermann.

The action shown in Figure 2.9 is like the Schmidt's. Notice two things about it. First, the hammers point in the opposite direction from that in the Cristofori and Zumpe actions. They are pivoted in a fork (called a *Kapsel* in German) attached to the key, and a tail of the hammer butt rests in a notch in the rail at the rear of the key. Second, the diagram shows that a spring on the rail, ordinarily of whalebone, keeps it forward. That rail, which the Germans call a *Prelleiste* (*Prell*, "bounce" + *Leiste*, "rail"), gives the action its German name, *Prellmechanik*. When the key is pressed down, the tail of the hammer butt strikes the upper surface of the notch, and the hammer is pivoted upward to the string. With the key raised, the butt of the descending hammer comes down against the front of the rail and pushes the rail backward. As long as the key is held down, the hammer butt rests against the upper

*Helen Rice Hollis, *The Piano*, p. 73. A grand attributed to Schmidt, dated c. 1790–95, in the Metropolitan Museum of Art, New York, may be heard in Mozart's violin sonatas in F major (K. 376), E minor (K. 304), and E-flat major (K. 380) on Pleiades Records P 104. The pianist is Malcolm Bilson, and the violinist, Sonya Monosoff, plays a Stradivarius violin of 1692 from the same collection, restored to Baroque specifications. The same piano is played by James Bonn in works of C. P. E. Bach on Pleiades Records P 105.

FIG. 2.8. *Grand piano, Johann Schmidt, Salzburg, c. 1788. Action:* Viennese action without back checks; leather hammers. *Stops:* 2 knee-levers: all dampers, treble dampers; 1 hand stop in center of nameboard: buff stop. *Range:* FF–f³. *Stringing:* FF–G double-strung brass plain, G♯–d³ double-strung iron, d♯³–f³ triple-strung iron; FF 185.4 cm, c² 27.9 cm, f³ 11.7 cm. *Framing:* Wood. *Case:* Walnut veneered; 213.4 cm long, 96.8 cm wide. *Location:* Smithsonian Institution, Washington, D.C. Catalog no. 303,536.

front surface of the rail. When the key is released, the butt slips back into the notch, the spring on the rail pushes it forward, and we are ready to resume business. The Prelleiste, then, is an escapement rail.

One subsequent improvement perfected the Viennese action and kept it unchanged, except for added weight, until it was abandoned. (In 1909, Bösendorfer, the leading manufacturer in Vienna, stopped offering the Viennese action as an option in grands, and that was the effective end of it.)[24] The improvement was a back check (see Fig. 2.10). We do not know who first introduced the check to this type of action, though all instruments by Anton

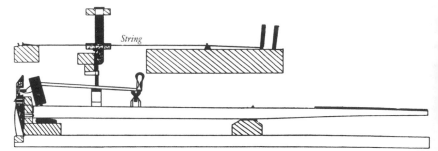

By permission of Gresham Books Ltd., The Gresham Press, Old Woking, England

FIG. 2.9. *Viennese action without back check.*   Diagram from Rosamond E. M. Harding, *The Piano-Forte: Its History Traced to the Great Exhibition of 1851*, 2d ed. (Old Woking, Eng., 1978).

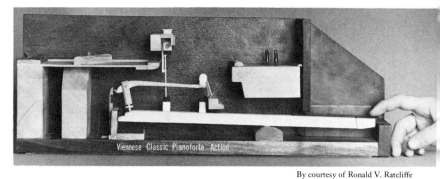

By courtesy of Ronald V. Ratcliffe

FIG. 2.10. *Viennese action with back check.*   Model by Ronald V. Ratcliffe.

Walter and most other pianos made in Vienna have it. Without it, playing too loudly often caused the hammer to bounce back to the strings a second time. With the check, that difficulty was overcome. The escapement rail caught the hammer butt at one end, and the check caught the hammer head at the other, preventing further movement until the release of the key.

No one knows who invented the Viennese mechanism or carried through its first improvements. Both Gottfried Silbermann and his nephew Johann Andreas Silbermann have been nominated for the honor, but there is not sufficient evidence to award it to either of them. The action has two differences from the Cristofori-Silbermann action. First, in the Cristofori-Silbermann action, the hammer is mounted on a stationary rail, whereas in the

Viennese action, the hammer is mounted in its fork on the key itself, suggesting that this design may have an ancestor in the
clavichord action.[25] Second, in the Cristofori-Silbermann action,
the jack on the key pushes against the hammer shank to send the
hammer to the string, whereas in the Viennese action, the hammer butt itself moves against the stationary object, which is the
escapement rail.

The Viennese action has a better leverage ratio than the Cristofori-Silbermann mechanism. The fork is mounted farther back
from the fulcrum than the jack in the English-type actions, so that
the finger pressure on the key moves the fork farther, making the
key a more efficient lever. Moreover, where the jack in the Cristofori-Silbermann action pushes against the hammer shank just
next to the fulcrum at the hammer rail, the motive point on the
hammer in the Viennese action is at the very end of the shank, on
the opposite side of the pivot from the hammer head. The compound leverage (both the finger's leverage on the fork and the
leverage of the escapement rail on the hammer butt) is much more
efficient than that of the English action, an efficiency that accounts
for the Viennese action's characteristic lightness of touch, responsiveness, and shallow "dip" (the distance the key descends under
the finger), as compared with the English type.

We have looked at a developed stage of the Viennese action.
Two of its predecessors deserve mention. In one we have a kind of
reversal of the Cristofori-Silberman action, with the hammers

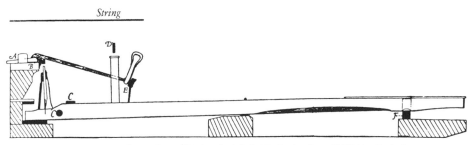

FIG. 2.11. *"Anglo-German" action.* The jack at the end of the key pushes up the
hammer, as in the English action, and the hammer faces the player, as in the
German action. The little piece marked *E*, which looks like a check, does not
function as one, and the maker of the action probably did not know what it was
for. Diagram from Rosamond E. M. Harding, *The Piano-Forte: Its History Traced
to the Great Exhibition of 1851*, 2d ed. (Old Woking, Eng., 1978).

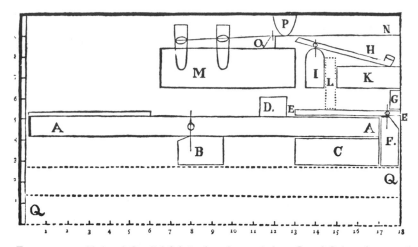

F IG . 2.12. *Christoph Gottlieb Schröter's action.* *A*, key; *B* and *C*, key-frame rails (on rail *C* are guide pins to keep *A*, *E*, and *L* from moving sideways); *D*, key-stop; *E*, "driver" lever; *F*, "driver" lever rail; *G*, "driver" stop rail; *H*, hammer; *I* (*J*), hammer rail; *K*, hammer rest rail; *L*, jack (Schröter's word is Springer); *M*, pin block; *N*, string; *O*, nut bridge; *P*, iron down-bearing bar (a capo tasto); *Q*, key-bed. Schröter's diagram in Friedrich Wilhelm Marpurg, ed., *Kritische Briefe über die Tonkunst*, vol. 3, part 1 (Berlin, 1763–64).

hinged to a rail over the very back of the keys, their heads pointed forward toward the player. As Figure 2.11 shows, they are oper-ated by key-mounted jacks. Rosamond Harding called this the Anglo-German action,[26] because it combines features of both types of action, with the hammers on a rail as in the English action but pointed toward the player as in the Viennese.

The other predecessor (it is not possible to reconstruct the his-torical order of these two types) was a primitive Prellmechanik. Here the "bounce" rail was a real rail, a single, stationary bar of wood all across the back of the key-frame. It was not sprung, nor could it move backward. The hammer, pivoted in its fork on the key—the crucial point in identifying the German-Viennese type of action—came up against the notch in the rail and was flung to the string as in Figure 2.9. But there was neither escapement nor check. The action was very light, simple, and for the most part, without subtlety.

I said above that we do not know who invented the Viennese action. But we can at least credit the person who discovered its underlying principle. That principle, that the key moves the hammer butt against a rail that pivots the hammer to strike the strings, can in fact be traced to none other than Christoph Gottlieb Schröter, that bitterly disappointed inventor from Saxony. In his long self-defense in 1763, Schröter included a diagram of the up-striking action he invented, which is reproduced in Figure 2.12. When the key is depressed, its back end, moving upward, pivots lever *E-E* upward against the rail, *G*, driving the jack, *L*, against the hammer. That lever *E-E* is most interesting, because it embodies the principle of the later Viennese action. An action diagram of a small German square, reproduced in Figure 2.13, shows the hammer attached to the front end of Schröter's lever, omitting his clumsy jack between lever and hammer shank. The action of a square made by Ignace Joseph Senft of Augsburg sometime in the last 30 years of the eighteenth century, modifies Schrö-

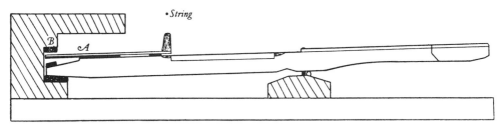

By permission of Gresham Books Ltd., The Gresham Press, Old Woking, England

FIG. 2.13. *Early German action (Prellmechanik).* The hammer lever, *A*, is attached to the hammer by a leather hinge. When the back of the lever strikes the "bounce rail" (Prelleiste), *B*, the lever pivots upward, and the hammer strikes the string. Diagram from Rosamond E. M. Harding, *The Piano-Forte: Its History Traced to the Great Exhibition of 1851*, 2d ed. (Old Woking, Eng., 1978).

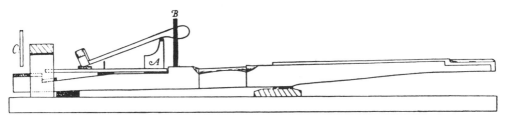

By permission of Gresham Books Ltd., The Gresham Press, Old Woking, England

FIG. 2.14. *Late-eighteenth-century square action.* The jack, *A*, rests on a lever that bumps against the bounce rail at the back, thus causing the hammer to pivot in its key-mounted brass fork, *B*. Diagram from Rosamond E. M. Harding, *The Piano-Forte: Its History Traced to the Great Exhibition of 1851*, 2d ed. (Old Woking, Eng., 1978).

ter's design by retaining the jack and pivoting the hammer in a brass fork mounted on the key (Fig. 2.14). In both of these relatively crude actions is found Schröter's principle of a lever that is pivoted upward by bumping against a rail.

This is precisely the principle of the Viennese action, which is a simplification from Schröter's complicated series of parts. Accordingly, we may fairly suppose, I think, that Schröter was not merely fantasizing when he claimed that people had stolen his idea. Because Schröter himself apparently identified Silbermann as the principle thief, whereas Silbermann's action was clearly derived from Cristofori's, historians have concluded that Schröter was just a grumpy old malcontent. I cannot show all of the steps in the development, nor can I name the artisans who took them. Nevertheless, the evidence in Schröter's diagram allows us to give him his due in the development of the Viennese action.

The person who turned the primitive German-type mechanism into the developed Viennese action, with all its potentiality for responsive subtlety in the hands of a Mozart or a Beethoven, was Johann Andreas Stein of Augsburg, who had learned piano making from Johann Andreas Silbermann of Strasbourg, the nephew of Gottfried Silbermann. Stein contrived the escapement that we have seen by slicing the solid "bounce" rail in the back into sections, one section corresponding to each key. On each section he mounted a spring so that it could both lean backward under the pressure of the returning hammer butt and return forward when the key was released. It was a very economical, elegant solution to a difficult problem.

With that solution, Stein took his place in the general acknowledgment of pianists as a leader among his peers. Mozart visited his shop in Augsburg in 1777 and wrote his father a letter full of praise for Stein, his pianos, and his methods of manufacture. It is worth quoting at some length:

This time I shall begin at once with Stein's pianofortes. Before I had seen any of his make, Späth's claviers had always been my favorites.[27] But now I much prefer Stein's, for they damp ever so much better than the Regensburg instruments. When I strike hard, I can keep my fingers on the note or raise them, but the sound ceases the moment I have produced it. In whatever way I touch the keys, the tone is always even. It never jars [*schebern*],* it is never stronger or weaker or entirely absent; in a word, it is always even. It is true that he does not sell a pianoforte of this kind for less than three hundred gulden, but the trouble and labor which Stein puts into the making of it cannot be paid for. His instruments have this special advantage over others that they are made with escape action. Only one maker in a hundred bothers about this. But without an escapement it is impossible to avoid jangling [blocking] and vibration after the note is struck. When you touch the keys, the hammers fall back again the moment after they have struck the strings, whether you hold down the keys or release them. He himself told me that when he was finished making one of these claviers, he sits down to it and tries all kinds of passages, runs and jumps, and he polishes and works away at it until it can do anything. For he labors solely in the interest of music and not for his own profit; otherwise he would soon finish his work. He often says: "If I were not myself such a passionate lover of music and had not myself some slight skill on the clavier, I should certainly long ago have lost patience with my work. But I do like an instrument which never lets the player down and which is durable." And his claviers certainly do last. He guarantees that the sounding-board will neither break nor split. When he has finished making one for a clavier, he places it in the open air, exposing it to rain, snow, the heat of the sun and all the devils in order that it may crack. Then he inserts wedges and glues them in to make the instrument very strong and firm. He is delighted when it cracks, for then he can be sure that nothing more can happen to it. Indeed, he often cuts into it himself and then glues it together again and strengthens it in this way. He has finished making three pianofortes of this kind. Today I played on one again. . . . Here and at Munich I have played all my six sonatas [K. 279–84] by heart several times. I played the fifth, in G, at that grand concert in the Stube. The last one, in D [the *Dürnitz* Sonata, composed in 1775], sounds exquisite on Stein's pianoforte. The device too, which you work with your knee [the knee-lever for the dampers], is better on his than on other instruments. I have only to touch it and it works; and when you shift your knee the slightest bit, you do not hear the least reverberation.[28]

Mozart shows himself extremely well acquainted with the mechanics of the instrument. To be sure, in those days the player had to be able to tune the piano and, since there were no professional technicians other than the builders, to make necessary adjust-

---

*This probably means blocking, where the hammer sticks at the string, damping it with a thud.

ments. Mozart's letter demonstrates some of the problems players had with pianos: the hammers tended to block, that is, to jam up against the strings instead of falling away; they bounced back to the strings after falling away; dampers did not damp but allowed audible vibration to continue; knee-levers did not bring the dampers back fully to the string with the same effect; soundboards cracked and warped, inhibiting the even resonation of the tone; actions were uneven, so that the same pressure on different notes produced too loud or too soft a tone, or even no tone at all. Mozart did not mention another problem, probably assuming that it could not be remedied: strings broke. Of course, Mozart himself seems to have been a very quiet player. The day of the crashing chord and thundering octave was still in the future. Even so, strings broke, sometimes in the middle of a performance.

Mozart also gives an interesting picture of the craftsman in the shop. The manufacturing technology of this entire period—indeed, until far into the nineteenth century—was exclusively that of the artisan working with hands and hand tools. The shop was part of the artisan's home, and the apprentices, learning to do exactly what the master did, usually lived in that home. The sons and sometimes the daughters often worked as apprentices. This manufacture was a craft, and as one would expect, no two of the instruments produced were identical. To be sure, those who have made it their business to know can recognize the distinctive marks of a particular master's technique even if an instrument is unsigned. The shape of a leg, the curve of the case, the design of bridge or string plate, will suggest a particular maker. But some apprentices were good imitators, and they carried on the master's technique when they had gone out on their own.

Stein did everything in manufacture himself, so far as we can tell from Mozart's letter, though he had apprentices as well. Johann Schmidt was one of them, and Stein's own son and daughter learned piano making from their father. The establishment was probably quite small. Doubtless Stein bought strings from a wire-drawing foundry. The lower strings were ordinarily of brass (in Schmidt's grand, from FF–G), the rest cold-drawn wrought iron, as had for a long time been the rule with harpsichord strings as well. Stein did all his work with hand tools, and he used natural means to cure the soundboard and the other parts that needed curing.

There was, indeed, a considerable difference between Stein's instruments and the ones made in Vienna and used by pianists such as Mozart. (For all his earlier praise of Stein, Mozart later owned a grand made by Anton Walter, which is now in the Mozarteum in Salzburg.)[29] Stein's soundboards and bridges were thinner than those of the Viennese makers of the time,[30] a feature that made his instruments more responsive, perhaps a bit clearer in tone, but also considerably softer in volume than, for example, a Walter. This fact is noted in a contemporary account of the differences between the Viennese makers in the Stein tradition, principally his children, Nannette and Matthäus Andreas, and those like Walter who apparently followed an earlier Viennese tradition.* The writer described Walter's pianos this way:

His fortepianos have a full, bell-like tone, distinct articulation, and a strong, full bass. At the beginning, the sound may be somewhat dull, but if the instrument is played for a time, the treble especially becomes very clear. But if it is played a great deal, the tone soon becomes sharp and metallic [*eisenartig*, "iron-like"], which can be repaired by new leathering of the hammers. Often a flaw shows up in the instruments of this master, which one should consider when selecting one, namely that the treble and bass do not in all of them have the best relation to one another. With some the bass is too full for the treble, with others it is too strong, and with still others it is metallic.[31]

Compared with Walter's pianos, those of Nannette Streicher, who had moved to Vienna in 1794, lacked strength, the writer felt, "but for even balance of tone, purity, charm, grace, and softness, they are unmatchable. Their tones are not aggressive but gentle, the touch demands a light hand, elastic finger work, and a sensitive heart."[32] The Stein-Streicher tradition, then, was characterized at that time by soft purity of tone, and the writer, Johann von Schönfeld, recommended its exemplars to pianists who sought "sustenance for the soul" and who love "not only distinct but also soft, gentle playing."[33]

Making a piano was a long-term affair. We do not know how

---

*Nannette Stein married Johann Andreas Streicher, a pianist and composer, who joined her in making pianos. A Streicher grand is discussed in Chapter Three.

many instruments Stein made in his 40 years or so in the trade, since, like most German and Austrian makers, he did not give them serial numbers. One estimate puts the total at about 700, an average of 17 or 18 yearly; another gives a figure of 20–25 per year.[34] Stein's high reputation is proved not only by the quality of the few instruments of his that remain, but also by the fact that many makers imitated his designs and inventions (patenting was less an issue in those days than these, and the political fragmentation of Germany meant that patents did not apply widely in any case), and some of them apparently even put fake Stein labels in their instruments. One beautiful Viennese instrument in the Smithsonian Institution (catalog no. 303,537) with a 1773 Stein label on the soundboard was for years assumed to be genuine. When the piano was disassembled for restoration, the signature of Louis (Ludwig) Dulcken of Munich was discovered on the soundboard. There seems to be no way of being certain whether Dulcken attached the Stein label himself or whether some later dealer did so to drive up the price.

We now turn to the other type of classic grand, the English. The beautiful grand by Robert Stodart pictured in Figure 2.15 is a good example of the classic English grand, made only a few years before some extensions and innovations would be introduced.

The range is the same five octaves as in the Schmidt, a range into which practically all classic piano music falls. Mozart never exceeded the FF–f³ compass, nor did Haydn until his late C-major Sonata, H.XVI, 50, written during his second visit to England in 1794–95. One of the standard features of classic pianos and their music is this five-octave range. A few Viennese grands went to g³, a whole tone higher, and some to a³. Even Beethoven wrote higher than f³ only four times before 1803, though several passages show that he clearly wished he could write beyond that.

The Stodart's stringing is standard for English grands: it is triple-strung with plain wire over the entire range. German and Austrian pianos at this time had triple-stringing, if at all, only in the very highest notes. The more strings there are, of course, the more volume the instrument gives, for three strings generate more

FIG. 2.15. *Grand piano, Robert Stodart, London, 1790.* Inscription: "Robertus Stoddart et Co., Londini, fecerunt 1790 / Wardour Street Soho." Action: English grand action, over-dampers; leather-covered hammers. Stops: 2 pedals: una corda, dampers. Range: FF–f³. Stringing: Triple-strung, no wound strings; FF–F brass, F♯–f³ iron; FF 170.5 cm, c² 28 cm, f³ 10 cm. Framing: Wood, with 3 gap-stretchers. Case: Mahogany veneered; 225 cm long, 94.8 cm wide. Location: Smithsonian Institution, Washington, D.C. Catalog no. 303,526.

vibrating energy than two, unless the double-strung wires are of considerably greater mass. One of the boasts of the English makers was that their pianos had strength of tone.*

That strength required the adjustment of the framing. Stodart retained the wooden string-plate that all of his contemporaries had. But the added tension in the triple-strung English pianos led

---

*The amount of increase in volume is not as great as it might seem. Acoustic studies have shown that two strings give 30 percent more volume than one, and a third adds 17 percent of volume. Thus a triple-strung note will be not quite half again as loud as one single-strung with the same gauge of wire.

their makers to introduce a new kind of brace, which has come to be called a gap-stretcher. The hammers of a grand rise to the strings through the opening between the pin block and the sound-board. It is a point of notorious weakness, for if the soundboard is not carefully braced, the string tension can simply tear it out of its rear moorings. The string-plate and the wooden braces connected to it underneath the soundboard are part of the bracing. Attached under the front end of the soundboard is a stout brace called the belly rail, which runs across the width of the case and is anchored at both sides. A number of English makers weakened that rail by making it composite, with a thinner plank at the bottom (I myself have seen this only in Broadwoods). To take up some of the strain, English makers began at least as early as 1772 to bolt an arch-shaped piece of iron to the belly rail at one side and the pin block at the other, spanning the gap and holding it open against the string tension. These gap-stretchers were the modest forerunners of the complete cast-iron frame that we saw in the modern piano in Chapter One.

The English classic piano shows another difference from the Continental one. The stops came in England to be controlled by pedals rather than by the hand-stops we saw in the Zumpe square and the Schmidt or by the knee-levers that Schmidt used for the dampers. There is some question about when pedals were intro-duced. Broadwood patented them in 1783 (English patent no. 1379). The Händel-Haus Collection in Halle claims that one of its instruments, a square by Adam Beyer of London, dated 1777, is the earliest known piano with a damper pedal.[35] But a grand made in London in 1772 by Americus Backers, now on loan to the Rus-sell Collection at the University of Edinburgh, has what seem to be original pedals.[36] (This Backers grand is certainly the earliest piano with iron gap-stretchers.) There is a great difference in the ease with which pedal stops can be worked as compared with hand-stops. The pianist need not stop playing or hire an assistant to work the pedals. The same can be said of the Continental knee-levers. The knee-levers have the advantage of being a little less conspicuous, for pedals must either protrude from the front legs, as they do on the 1772 Backers and on a number of later Broad-woods, or have a support in the front center of the case. The support was later the occasion for fancy decorations, including the not very subtle use of lyre shapes to the point where the frame that holds the pedals and their rods is now technically called the lyre. Pedals finally won the day, and pianists who play Viennese forte-pianos with the knee-levers must adjust their minds and muscles to get used to them.

The stringing patterns, the gap-stretchers, and the use of pedals are not the most important differences between the English and the Viennese classic pianos. The two types are most significantly distinguished by their actions. As we have seen, the English piano industry was established by craftsmen trained in Gottfried Silbermann's shop. Silbermann had copied the Cristofori action, and when his apprentices came to England, they brought with them the Cristofori principle of mounting hammers on a rail. From that model the English grand action was developed.

Figure 2.16 makes evident the derivation of the action from Cristofori's. The hammers are hinged on a stationary rail, and the jack, mounted on the key, propels the hammer to the string. Two important differences are to be noted. In the English grand action,

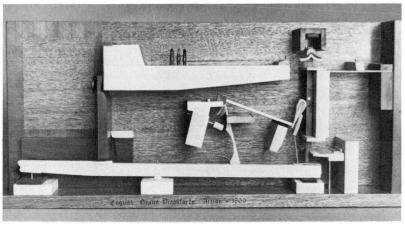

By courtesy of Ronald V. Ratcliffe

FIG. 2.16. *English grand action*.   The jack, mounted on the key, strikes a notch in the butt of the hammer. As the jack moves upward, its projecting point on the left is forced to the right by the round button against it, so that the jack does not strike the notch in the hammer butt when the hammer descends—a form of escapement. Model by Ronald V. Ratcliffe.

the jack works directly on a notch in the butt of the hammer, whereas Cristofori had introduced an intermediate lever between the jack and the hammer butt. It is a nice question whether the intermediate lever, which returned in actions of grands of the nineteenth century (and even earlier in squares), allows more subtlety and better control than this direct-blow action.

The second difference is that the jack's escapement now works differently from Cristofori's. The jack is positioned against an offset escapement button, adjustable by a screw through the hammer rail. As the jack moves up, its surface slides against the escapement button, which forces it to move out of range of the notch in the hammer butt when the hammer falls back from the string, to be caught by the back check. The spring from jack to key, unlike the one in Cristofori's 1726 action, helps the escapement button to push the jack out, and the jack returns to its starting-point by the gravity of its backward-leaning position when the key is released.

The adjustable escapement button is new. It adjusts the jack's movement to determine the point at which the hammer flies free from the jack. The touch is thus somewhat adjustable. If the hammer is released from the jack at a point too close to the string, the touch feels heavy and is hard to control because the key must be pushed far down to produce a sound. If the release point is too far from the string, the touch feels light because a shallow motion of the key does all the work; a very soft blow may not have enough energy to move the hammer to the string at all. To be sure, the English action typically had a deeper key movement ("dip") than the Viennese action.

The damper mechanism is the same as Cristofori's, with the damper positioned on top of the string and lifted from it by a wooden jack over the end of the key. The jack is considerably shrunk from the standard harpsichord jack that Cristofori used. All surfaces that touch other surfaces are covered with soft material to make them noiseless, usually soft leather, sometimes thin felt or wool cloth. The tip of the jack, the notch in the hammer butt where the jack strikes, the rail on which the hammer shank rests, the back check, and the facing on the key under the damper lifter are all covered with noise-reducing material.

This is an elegant, simple action with few weak places to fail the performer at crucial times. It was devised mainly by Americus Backers, a native of Holland whom I have previously identified as one of the "twelve apostles," with help from John Broadwood, whose name we will see again, and from Robert Stodart, who built the piano under discussion. This improvement on the Cristofori-Silbermann design was apparently complete in about 1776, and Stodart had been instrumental enough in the work to warrant his taking out the patent on the new action in 1777 (English patent no. 1172). It is interesting that in connection with this patent, Stodart was the first to call this shape of piano a "grand" piano, by which he meant no more than "large." The affection in which the English makers held the Backers-Stodart-Broadwood action can be seen in the fact that we still find it, unchanged except for the addition of weight to move heavier hammers to heavier strings, in Broadwood grands in 1895.[37]

The two types of classic grands, the English and the Viennese, achieved quite stable forms early in the 1770's and retained them for more than 20 years. Both types of action mechanisms, modified only by the addition of weight, were still to be found in pianos made well over a hundred years later. To be sure, by then both actions were holdovers—or holdouts—from a new, more complex action. But other modifications in the entire system forbid us to identify as classic pianos the 1895 instruments with the English grand action or the Austrian grands with the Viennese action. The action may have been classic in origin, but added weight is a greater alteration than it might seem in view of other changes that were being made.

Make no mistake: the development of grands was by no means the focus of piano makers' principal energy. That was lavished on squares. Zumpe never made a grand in his life. Why should he? He had more orders for squares than he could fill himself, and squares were the more convenient, if more modest, instrument for the home. At the end of the century, the piano was already displacing the harpsichord as the home instrument, and clavichords, though they continued to be made after the harpsichord was abandoned, were never really big business.

The piano became big business because the late eighteenth century witnessed an extension of the economic power of the middle class, sooner in England than on the Continent, an economic power that put money in the pockets of families and led them to aspire to cultural goods previously limited to the aristocracy. People could afford to buy pianos to replace harpsichords or clavichords, even if, like Zumpe's little squares, they were relatively expensive. The squares could be sold in quantity and were therefore made in quantity. Surviving squares from the eighteenth century outnumber surviving grands by a good margin (in absolute terms, that is to say; because museums and collectors have tended to be more interested in grands, and because grands were usually more carefully made, they have had a higher survival rate in terms of the numbers produced). At a fair estimate, about 10 squares were made for every grand.*

Why were grands made at all? There certainly was demand for them. The aristocratic homes that had held expensive harpsichords would hold expensive, harpsichord-shaped pianos. Professional musicians like Haydn and Mozart preferred grands because they were the best instruments, and makers very soon discovered that the possession of their pianos by well-known musicians was a selling point. They might even offer a musician the free use of an instrument and a commission in return for recommendations to friends and inquirers.

Moreover, the day of the public concert was beginning to arrive. Performing musicians in eighteenth-century Europe were not free-lancers. They were employed by the Church, the Court, aristocratic families, and governments. Performances were mostly either given for the private pleasure of the performer's employer and the employer's guests or commissioned for some ecclesiastical or civic occasion. The eighteenth century saw the formation of associations for the purpose of sponsoring performances, to which only members of the club had access. But with the rise of a moneyed middle class, especially in England, began the practice of public performances to which anyone possessing the price of a ticket would be admitted. The concert in 1768 at which Johann Christian Bach played the first piano solo in public in England was

---

*The estimate is of total production. Some houses like Broadwood made a disproportionate number of grands. One figure for about 1800 is 300 squares and over 100 grands yearly, the highest annual production in the world at the time (Cyril Ehrlich, *The Piano*, p. 18). Most makers produced no grands at all. But the 10:1 ratio is only a guess.

probably such a concert. The first musician who tried to break free of employment by Church, Court, or aristocracy, and to make a living by publishing compositions and performing them in concerts, was Mozart. And he failed to make it, dying in 1791 in abject poverty at the age of thirty-five.

Such concerts were usually performed on the player's own piano, which was transported to the concert room. A local piano maker might offer the use of one of his best grands in order to profit from the advertising. A grand it would be, since the programs always included one or more concerti with orchestra. No square could stand up to an orchestra, and even the competition between a grand and an orchestra in those days was rather severe. The balance between a silvery-toned little instrument like the Schmidt and a band of perhaps 30 players is altogether different from the balance between a modern, nine-foot black dragon and a full orchestra. The modern concert grand can outshout a full orchestra, or can at least compete on even terms. When a Mozart concerto is played today on a concert grand with a reduced orchestra of only 40 to 50 players, as is a frequent custom, the impression of the forces in the original is quite reversed. Mozart's piano could not dominate the orchestra, even though the orchestra against which Mozart was playing was smaller in size and softer in volume than that of today. Indeed, that sense of a struggle between two forces, one at something of a disadvantage to the other, is a musical element in the classic Mozartean concerto, a struggle that seldom surfaces with today's instruments.

Another aspect of the relation of the fortepiano to classic music is similar. Mozart, Haydn, and early Beethoven, played on a modern piano, sound easy to the unwary ear. Any pianist will emphatically testify to the contrary. Those works are difficult to play with the control, nuance, and clarity that they demand. The reason they sound easy is that, unlike many of the works of Claude Debussy, Béla Bartók, and Sergei Prokofiev, classic piano music does not demand the full resources of the modern piano. A crashing chord is stylistically out of place in Mozart. In classic works, the modern instrument, in distinction from the player, is not taxed to its utmost. Listen to the same works on a piano contemporary with them, and you hear both performer and instrument stretched to the limits of their capacities of tone, of volume, of range, and of nuance. The musical textures take on different balances and relationships with one another.*

By the close of the eighteenth century, the piano nearly everywhere had decisively displaced the harpsichord as the principal keyboard instrument. ("Like the Bronze Age," says Sibyl Marcuse, "the harpsichord age lingered longer in Ireland than elsewhere in Europe." John Southwell of Dublin was still making harpsichords in 1822.)[38] In 1790, Haydn advised a friend to sell his harpsichord and buy a piano. In 1793, Burkat Shudi the Younger, John Broadwood's partner, made his last harpsichord, and in the same year a piano replaced the harpsichord in the performance of the annual birthday ode to the King. In 1797, the *Pianoforte Magazine* began to be published in London, containing pieces for amateurs to play at home. The year 1798 was the last in which the Paris Conservatory gave a prize for the harpsichord. In 1799, it began awarding one for the piano, and also named François Adrien Boieldieu as the first professor of piano. The old order passed, and the piano entered new stages of experiment and development.

---

*Cyril Ehrlich (*The Piano*, pp. 24–25) scorns this argument, as if anyone who makes it "ignores the late nineteenth century's rejection of the old technology, or regards it implicitly as an aberration." Ehrlich does not deal with the fact that the rejection of the old technology in the late nineteenth century was accompanied by a new aesthetic, or with the fact that the old instruments with what he calls their "manifest inadequacies" were not necessarily perceived as flawed by those who wrote for them.

3

Beethoven and the Growing Grand

Beethoven looms over the pianos of the years 1800–1825 as he does over the music of those years. Though it would be claiming too much to argue that he himself caused the changes that were taking place, he, perhaps better than any other pianist of the day, represents and reflects them. Many pianists were taking concert tours or were moving from one country to another. Beethoven, staying close by Vienna (he thought more than once of accepting invitations to go to England but never did so), nevertheless owned and played several kinds of pianos that show in a very interesting way the developing state of the craft in all of Europe during those years.

Of the four instruments I will discuss in this chapter, one belonged to Beethoven, another is an identical twin of an existing piano that he owned, a third is exactly like one we can be nearly certain that he owned, and the fourth was built by the maker of his last piano. Two of the instruments were made in Vienna, one in Paris, and one in London.

The two types of actions from the Classic period continued in use in the grands of this period, though some experiments aiming toward something else were going on. The main factor now was the growth of the instrument beyond the five-octave grands that we saw in Chapter Two. Even before the years we now take up, extensions of range were being tried. By the time of the last piano in this chapter, at least one maker had achieved—but not really successfully—a range close to that of the modern piano.

This chapter will deal with grands, the pianos of artists and concert performances. In the next chapter I will take up pianos made for use in the home rather than for public performance. There, growth was one development, but shrinkage was another. With grands, we see an almost constant expansion in size, together with modifications of several kinds that must accompany any growth of the instrument.

The most obvious point of this growth lay in the expanding range. Here Beethoven is especially interesting, because his published piano music nicely illustrates the development. Until 1803, Beethoven's music remained within the classic five octaves, with a few excursions as high as g^3. Those breakings of bounds are not totally unexpected, since Beethoven owned a piano by Anton Walter in the last years of the 1790's,[1] and Walter not infrequently built pianos with the range FF–g^3. In 1803, Beethoven began to use an FF–c^4 range, and from about 1808 we see him regularly using the six octaves from FF–f^4. Finally his piano music began to demand even lower notes, coming in 1818 to its widest compass with the Sonata in B-flat, op. 106 (the *Hammerklavier* Sonata), which takes six octaves and a fourth, CC–f^4.

It is sometimes implied that Beethoven forced piano makers to widen the range by writing music that exceeded what people could play on their instruments, banking on his genius to have this "futuristic" music accepted. This is certainly a false conclusion. Beethoven had a very high opinion of his originality, but he was also extremely anxious to have his music both published and played. And he was in chronic need of money. It would not have served his ends to bull his way ahead, writing what his muse dictated without any concern for economic reality. A perusal of Beethoven's letters will persuade even the most enthusiastic adulator of his musical greatness that the pursuit of money was a subject frequently uppermost in his mind.

The fact is that Beethoven's piano music reflects the instruments of his day, and the extensions of range in it exactly parallel the extensions of range in the pianos that he—and his potential customers—possessed. I know of not one shred of evidence that Beethoven influenced any piano maker, directly or indirectly, to enlarge the range of any piano. The problem of the relations between pianists or composers and piano makers is an intricate one. In some instances, musicians apparently influenced makers (the Bohemian virtuoso Ignaz Moscheles influenced Erard, for example), and in some instances the influence went the other way (Stein on Mozart, perhaps). But Beethoven is not one of those who influenced piano makers.*

The builders, however, were usually happy to have him play their products. To be sure, Beethoven was known as a powerful player, and he seems to have been hard on pianos. But the idea of the big name for advertising one's wares was not foreign to the piano merchants of the 1800's. The Erard house in Paris even sent Beethoven a piano all unsolicited, the instrument pictured in Figure 3.1. It was presented to him on August 6, 1803,[2] and he used it extensively for seven years or so. Indeed, he gave it such hard use that in 1810 we find him complaining to Johann Andreas Streicher that the Erard was worn out and useless to him.[3] Though he seems not to have played it after that time, he kept it until about 1824, when he gave it to his brother Johann. Johann in turn presented the instrument in 1845 to the Oberösterreichisches Landesmuseum in Linz, which later loaned it to the Kunsthistorisches Museum in Vienna.[4]

Sébastien Erard, the maker of this instrument, was a survivor. As a young cabinetmaker, he came to Paris from his native Strasbourg in 1768 and soon changed his name from its German-sounding original, Erhard. He was apprenticed to a series of harpsichord makers, but his native gifts quickly made him their superior, and he was soon able to set up on his own. Erard turned early to pianos, making his first, a square, in 1777 and continuing under the aristocratic support of the Duchesse de Villeroi. He became so successful that he posed a threat to the instrument makers' guild, whose campaign to close down his shop by reason of his non-membership in the guild was foiled only by a decree from

---

*That is not the story we hear from the composer and critic Johann Friedrich Reichardt. In a letter of Feb. 7, 1809, from Vienna, he said, dilating on the pianos of Johann Streicher: "Streicher has left behind the weakness, too easy yielding, and bouncing roll of the other Viennese instruments, and, with Beethoven's advice and desire, has given his instruments more resistance, elasticity. . . . Thereby he has provided his instruments with a larger and more varied character, so that more than any other instrument they must satisfy the virtuoso who seeks not merely flashy brilliance in playing. His whole effort is thus for a rare excellence, worth, and durability." (*Vertraute Briefe*, 1: 311.) Reichardt makes it sound as if Beethoven hung around the Streichers' workshop telling them how to improve their pianos. A very different picture is presented in Beethoven's letter of July 7, 1817, to Nannette Streicher, in which he said: "Perhaps you are not aware that, although I have not always used one of your pianos, since 1809 I have always had a special preference for them." (Anderson, *Letters of Beethoven*, 2: 686.) Had Beethoven been the prime influence on the Streichers, he would not have had to reveal his preference in that way.

King Louis XVI in 1785.⁵ Royal and aristocratic protection, however, meant trouble in those revolutionary times. In 1786, apparently seeing potential disaster ahead, Sébastien fled to London,
where he had opened a sales branch several years earlier, and left
his brother, Jean Baptiste, in charge in Paris.*

In 1796, when things in Paris had quieted, Sébastien returned
with some new ideas gained from observation in England. He had
not wasted his time there, expanding the sales establishment into
a manufacturing shop, which remained one of the larger piano
manufacturers in London until 1890, when it was closed. Erard
had seen and adopted the English styles of action and used them in
his squares and in his first grand, made in 1796. It was not long
before the Erard name became even more prominent. The survivor was a shrewd judge of business opportunity, and his competition in Paris for the time being was not heavy (English pianos,
indeed, were more popular in Paris than the French ones). Shortly
after the turn of the century, Erard began to place his instruments
in high places, both of society and of musical art. The company
made grands for Napoleon Bonaparte and Haydn in 1801, presented the one in Figure 3.1 to Beethoven in 1803, and made a
grand for Louis Bonaparte, then in his brief reign as King of Holland, in 1808 (the piano is now in the City Castle in Amsterdam).

Johann Friedrich Reichardt, writing from Paris to Germany in
November 1802, gave an interesting, though brief, account of the
manufacturing establishment.⁶ According to him, everything that
went into the pianos was made on the Erard premises, and
Reichardt was impressed with the large size of the work force:
"Not only do the actual instrument maker, joiner, turner, fitter,
and steelworker have their completely equipped workshop there,
but also the bronzer, the painter, the lacquerer, the worker in
ebony and enamel, the gilder, the wire drawer, and who knows
who else work there in spacious, well-equipped workshops." It is
interesting that the job of instrument maker is not broken down
into a number of tasks, showing that each worker built the entire
instrument rather than dividing the labor into separate special-

---

*Jean Baptiste must have been a survivor too. People were guillotined in the Terror for
less than having a brother who had enjoyed the protection of the King and a duchess and
who sold pianos to the same gentry. Indeed, of the 20 French pianos confiscated from the
estates of beheaded or decamped French aristocrats during the Terror, 12 were Erards
(Loesser, *Men, Women, and Pianos*, p. 324). But Jean Baptiste lived through it all and kept the
shop in good condition.

Fig. 3.1. *Grand piano, Erard Frères, Paris, 1803.* Serial no. 133. *Action:* English grand action; leather-covered hammers. *Stops:* 4 pedals: lute, dampers, buff, una corda. *Range:* FF–c⁴. *Stringing:* Triple-strung, no wound strings; FF–g♯ brass, a–c⁴ iron; FF 171.2 cm, c² 27.8 cm, c⁴ 7.2 cm. *Framing:* Wood, with 4 gap-stretchers. *Case:* Mahogany veneered with brass stringing; dust cover over strings; 222 cm long, 109 cm wide. *Location:* Kunsthistorisches Museum, Vienna. On permanent loan from Oberösterreichischen Landesmuseum, Linz, Austria.

ties. The specialists were those who had to do with the cases and the decoration or with wire drawing (what the steelworker did I am uncertain). And over the whole Sébastien Erard presided, overseeing the instrument making and putting the final touches on each piano himself.

Erard was a craftsman of the highest order, who made a number of critically important improvements in the piano. Most of those we will discuss further on, since they followed this instrument. One, which has long been overlooked, was a new method of hinging the hammers on the hammer rail in the English action. Broadwood and other English makers attached the hammers to the rail in groups of six to eight, with a single pin through the flanges. It was an inconvenient way to hang the hammers, which tended to have a certain amount of sideways play on the pivot pin. If a hammer became in the slightest warped or out of adjustment on the pivot, it would not strike the strings correctly. To repair one, the entire group of hammers on the single pin had to be removed, and it was a matter of guesswork whether the offending hammer would be fixed. Erard attached his hammers singly to the rail, and provided each with an adjustment screw so that it could be precisely adjusted without disturbing the others.*

The action of the Erard is the standard English action, like the one pictured in Figure 2.16 (p. 63). Beethoven's opinion of the Erard was not entirely favorable. Johann Streicher used this as a reason to reject the idea that he might switch to the English action in his pianos. Writing to the publisher Gottfried Christoph Härtel in Leipzig in 1805, Streicher said that Beethoven, strong as he was, found the Erard too stiff to manage and had tried twice to have the action lightened, but without improvement.[7] It is an extraordinary comment on pianists' expectations that Beethoven of all people, who had such a reputation as a hard player, should find the Erard too stiff—an action that a modern pianist would find so light as to be nearly unmanageable without hours of practice. Yet Reichardt, on his visit to the Erard workshop, found Erard pianos much preferable in lightness to the English instruments.[8]

The Erard is a first-rate exemplar of an English-style grand. It is triple-strung throughout, without wound strings, and it carries the English type of arched iron gap-stretchers between the pin block and the belly rail. Somewhat unusually, Beethoven's Erard has four pedals, unconventionally arranged. From left to right, they are a lute stop, which gives a pizzicato-like sound; the usual damper pedal; a buff, which introduces tongues of leather between the hammers and the strings; and the una corda.

---

*This arrangement, which has not been noted in any of the sources I have consulted, was pointed out to me by Bjarne B. Dahl of Sunnyvale, California.

In one respect, the one that is the subject of this chapter, the Erard represents a first step forward. Its range, FF–c⁴, goes higher by a fourth than any music Beethoven had written before 1803.* With the arrival of this instrument, he began to write works demanding its upper range: the Trio, op. 38, arranged from the Septet, op. 20 (1803); the *Waldstein* Sonata, op. 53 (1804); the Triple Concerto, op. 56 (1804); the *Appassionata* Sonata, op. 57 (1805); and a number of others through the G-major Sonatina, op. 79 (1809). After that, ranges higher than c⁴ become the rule, though even before 1809 a few works go higher than the top of the Erard.

Extensions of range were being made well before Erard made Beethoven's grand in 1803. The Czech pianist Jan Ladislav Dussek, who was living in London during the 1790's, persuaded Broadwood to give him more notes to play with; and in 1790 or 1791, the company began to bring out both squares and grands with the FF–c⁴ range.⁹ As early as 1796, Broadwood made a grand on special order, designed by Thomas Sheraton, for the Spanish minister, Don Manuel de Godoy, to give as a present to his Queen, María Luisa; as the invoice shows, it had a six-octave range, CC–c⁴.¹⁰ In 1795, Johann Jakob Könnicke of Vienna made an experimental six-octave piano, with *six* keyboards, tuned so that one could play in all keys with "just" tuning;† it is said that

---

*In four earlier works, Beethoven exceeded the standard f³ top of the classic piano. He required f♯³ in the C-major concerto, op. 15, and the Sonata op. 14, no. 1, and g³ in the Trio op. 1, no. 2, and the very early Trio in B-flat, WoO 38. Viennese pianos ranging to g³ were known; one by Anton Walter of 1785 is in the Kunsthistorisches Museum (inventory no. 454), another by Louis (Ludwig) Dulcken of the 1790's is in the Smithsonian Institution (catalog no. 303,537), and others are extant.

† Tuning systems were a very intricate problem in this period. Just tuning was a way of allowing keyboard instruments to be in tune for certain frequently used keys, such as C, F, G, D and B-flat. In other keys, the instrument would sound somewhat out of tune. The tuning of musical intervals is strictly related to the specific keys in which they occur. As any violinist will testify, F♯ and G♭ are not the same pitch, F♯ being, as the violinist hears it, slightly lower than G♭. In just tuning, the piano's F♯/G♭, being the same note, will be tuned to F♯, which means that chords and intervals of any key that requires G♭ are out of tune. The earliest existing Zumpe piano, a square of 1766, had split black keys so that notes can be tuned to both pitches implied by them. Systems of "equal temperament," a compromise acceptable to the ear, began to be used in the eighteenth century, though it was well into the nineteenth before the use of equal temperament became fairly general. This compromise tuned the 12 half-tones in an octave so that they were equidistant from each other in frequency; all intervals except octaves are out of tune to an extent that the normally trained ear is not troubled by it. The origin of equal temperament is often attributed to Andreas Werckmeister in 1691, though he was only one of a number of theorists who proposed it. For a discussion of the entire subject, see J. Murray Barbour, *Tuning and Temperament*.

Beethoven, Haydn, and other musicians played this instrument in Vienna in 1796.[11] Könnicke seems to have been the earliest in German-speaking Europe to take the range beyond five octaves and a third.

The Smithsonian Institution has a grand by Carl Hannsen of Bamberg (catalog no. 299,852) with the FF–c⁴ range, which is dated c. 1785 in the checklist,[12] and a little square by "Jn" (Jean?) Nägelé of Paris (catalog no. 315,755) with the range of six octaves, FF–f⁴, and the date 1785 on the nameboard. However, I confess to some suspicion about both of these instruments. An FF–c⁴ grand in 1785 is very surprising, but a six-octave square in that year is absolutely astonishing, especially when I can find no reference to that maker in Paris in 1785 or in any other year. The date of the Hannsen grand is probably the estimate of Hugo Worch, from whose collection the instrument came to the Smithsonian, and he may simply have been mistaken. As for Nägelé, the name looks more Swiss than either French or German, but the nameboard clearly says "Paris, 1785." (I have seen only photographs of both instruments.) If the Nägelé is not a forgery (perhaps an American-built square from the early nineteenth century whose builder attached a false Paris label in order to ensure a quick sale), it is an exceedingly important instrument.*

Broadwood was probably the first to experiment with adding notes to the top range. It is said that Dussek first performed on one of the enlarged Broadwood grands in 1794,[13] but I have been unable to verify his performance. In about the same year, Haydn, then visiting London, made use of notes above f³ for the only time in his career, using a³ several times in the third movement of the great Sonata in C major, H. XVI, 50. Dussek arranged for Haydn to have the use of a new grand from Broadwood during the 1794–95 visit, and it surely contained the extra notes.

As we see, even before Erard presented his grand to Beethoven, the range was being extended not only to FF–c⁴, but even farther in some experimental pianos. In squares, as we will see in the next chapter, the addition of notes at the top entailed a modification of

---

*Two squares in the Neupert Collection in the Germanisches Nationalmuseum, Nuremberg, one by Charles Käfferle of Ludwigsburg, dated 1784, and the other by Martin Steinbacker of Bamberg, dated 1793, listed in the checklist of that collection as having six octaves (J. H. van der Meer, "Die klavierhistorische Sammlung Neupert," p. 263), actually have only five octaves, as a letter from Dr. van der Meer assured me.

the action frame. The enlargement of the instrument was affecting the modest instruments made for the home fully as much as the grands that artists and rich amateurs played.

———————◄◆►———————

I reverse the chronological order of the next two pianos in order to maintain the correlation of the growing grand with Beethoven's career. The 1814 Streicher pictured in Figure 3.2 is, we may suppose, very like several that Beethoven owned during the years between about 1810, when he complained that the Erard was worn out, and 1817, when he was writing music that necessitated a still greater range that the FF–f⁴ of this piano. That Beethoven actually owned a Streicher like the one pictured seems probable on the face of it, but no records show indubitably that he did. He was, of course, a close friend of Johann Andreas and Nannette Streicher, and the volumes of his letters are full of notes to Nannette, though most had to do not with music or pianos, but with getting his laundry done or complaints about his nephew or requests for help in finding a new servant. Nannette Streicher seems to have been very patient about all this. What she said to her husband in private has not been preserved.

We have already met Nannette Streicher, the daughter of Johann Andreas Stein whose pianos so aroused Mozart's enthusiasm. Shortly after Stein's death in 1792, two significant things happened to his heirs: Nannette married Johann Andreas Streicher in 1793, and in 1794 the newly formed Streicher family and Stein's son, Matthäus Andreas, moved the business to Vienna. Both had learned the trade from their father, and it is worth noting that Nannette Streicher is the only woman who has made an important, independent reputation as a piano maker. The siblings continued in partnership as Frère et Soeur Stein until 1802, when Matthäus Andreas broke away to go into business for himself. The Streichers continued under the name Nannette Streicher, geb. (for *geborene*, "born") Stein: the connection with the famous old Stein name had to be capitalized on. Sometimes, as with the Streicher in Figure 3.2, the genealogy was not stated on the instrument; the nameboard simply says "Streicher à Vienne," and on the soundboard, written in ink, is "Nr. 1031 / von STREICHER in / Vienne 1814." Johann Andreas Streicher, a boyhood friend and schoolmate of the famous German poet Freidrich von Schiller, was a composer and piano teacher, but he took up piano making as well.

Production in the Streicher establishment was not large. Unlike many Viennese makers, the Streichers used serial numbers, and these extended from 804 in 1809 to 1031 in 1814, an average of about 45 pianos a year.* By 1816 the serial number 1152 had been reached, pushing the average up to about 60. A number like that suggests that more people than the husband and wife were at work, but it is difficult to estimate how many workers there might have been. Austria was still under an apprenticeship system, and it is probable that there were a few journeymen and a handful of apprentices. It was not yet a factory.[14]

That Streicher was the leading firm in Vienna was commonly agreed, it seems, though other makers, such as Anton Walter, who was still in business, Conrad Graf, and Josef Brodmann, would not have joined that consensus. Perhaps Beethoven's preference for Streichers, as avowed in his letter to Nannette, has made later generations assume that they were more generally appreciated than they were. As I said above, there is no clear record that Beethoven ever owned a Streicher. He wrote several letters in the year 1810 requesting that Streicher send him a piano; in the last one, written in mid-November, he complained that he had not yet received it and lamented that the Erard could not be played.[15] In 1814 he sold a Vogel to another maker,[16] and in 1815 he recommended a Schantz to a prospective buyer, saying that he had one himself, but complaining in another letter how poor it was.[17] Clearly the letter to Nannette Streicher in 1817, asking for the loan of a piano until he could afford to buy it† and expressing his preference for Streichers since 1809, is accurate in saying, "I have not always used one." But it also clearly implies that he *had* used one at some point, and he certainly remained on good terms with the Streichers.

*The serial numbers of Streichers given in the *Pierce Piano Atlas* (7th ed., p. 269), are completely mistaken. Anyone who has used the book knows how helpful it often is and also how frequently wrong. Unfortunately, Herzog's *Europe Piano Atlas* (4th ed., p. 76) simply repeats the error.

†Streichers were expensive. In 1796, when Schantz's pianos started at 40 ducats and Walter's at 50, Nanette's cheapest instruments were 66 ducats (J. F. von Schönfeld, *Jahrbuch*, pp. 88–90).

FIG. 3.2. *Grand piano, Nannette Streicher, Vienna, 1814.* Serial no. 1031. *Inscription:* "Streicher à Vienne." *Action:* Regulatable Viennese action, leather dampers, leather-covered hammers. *Stops:* 2 knee-levers: bell, drum (Janissary music); 4 pedals: una corda, bassoon (stop missing), dampers, moderator (lyre and pedals missing). *Range:* FF–f⁴. *Stringing:* FF–BB♭ double-strung plain brass, BB–f⁴ triple-strung plain iron; FF 177 cm, c² 26.6 cm, f⁴ 4.9 cm. *Framing:* Wood, with 2 iron braces between pin block and belly rail. *Case:* Cherry veneered; 224.5 cm long, 116 cm wide. Legs missing. *Location:* Neupert Collection, Germanisches Nationalmuseum, Nuremberg. Catalog no. MINe 118.

The instrument itself is a typical Viennese grand of the period. Its cherry-veneered case is like many others to be seen before and after, but since the legs and pedal lyre are missing, it is difficult to be sure how the underpinnings looked. In this instrument, the Streichers, along with Nannette's brother the heirs of the Stein tradition of the developed Viennese action, have gone beyond what Stein had done. The action has a back check, which Stein never used, and it also has a mechanism that permits the regulation of the touch. The screw through the regulation rail, as shown in the diagram in Figure 3.3, rests against the lower face of the escapement rail. Moving it farther in or farther out changes the placement of that rail, thus changing the point where the hammer in its upward arc flies free of it. When the rail is permitted to lean farther in by the regulating screw, the let-off point for the hammer

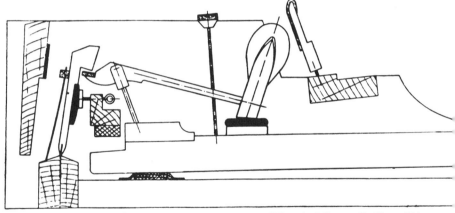

By permission of Das Musikinstrument, publishers of trade literature, Frankfurt am Main

FIG. 3.3. *Viennese action with regulating screw*. Early 19th century. The screw, which regulates the position of the escapement rail, can be seen just under the tail of the hammer at left. Diagram from Walter Pfeiffer, *The Piano Hammer*, tr. J. Engelhardt (Frankfurt am Main, 1978).

is farther up toward the string. Conversely, if the rail leans farther back, the hammer flies free of it sooner. But this also affects the touch of the instrument. For one thing, the placement of the rail determines the amount of resistance the tail of the hammer encounters when it bumps against the top of the notch. For another, the let-off point of the hammer marks the distance the key must travel to propel it. When the rail leans farther in, the touch feels harder because a heavier blow is required to move the hammer to the let-off point. When it leans farther back, the touch is lighter. The danger, of course, is that one may not hit the key hard enough to produce a sound at all.

The range is now extended to six octaves, FF–f⁴. This was the typical six-octave range of German and Austrian pianos in the period, and when Beethoven remained within a six-octave range, as he did for the most part between 1808 and 1817, it was usually this one. The piano works of Franz Schubert also assumed this range.

We still do not have wound strings in the bass of this instrument, and they seem not to appear in grands for a decade or so yet. But we do have brass strings in the bass and iron ones for the rest of the range. The strings in this particular piano are almost certainly not original, but the pattern is doubtless the same. Only in the bottom fourth, FF–BB♭, is there now double-stringing, with all of the rest triple-strung. The earlier Viennese makers tended to triple-string only the top few notes, but already we see in the stringing pattern the assumption that more sound is needed than Johann Schmidt's grand of the 1780's put out. When we add to the extra fourth in the top range the addition of triple-stringing over most of the range, the added tension on the strings puts a great deal more force on the framing than with earlier pianos.

The added weight of tension is compensated for in two ways. The first is by an increase in bracing, which shows in this instrument especially in the thickness of the wooden string-plate (1.50 cm at the bass end, 1.81 cm at the treble, i.e. between 0.6 and 0.7 of an inch). Doubtless the bracing inside the case was also strengthened, but I have been unable to get information about it. Viennese pianos were still built mostly in cases with closed bottoms. But it is at about this time that Viennese grands began to have deeper cases, a change surely brought about by the need to accommodate heavier interior bracing. The second way in which tension is taken up is by the addition of two small iron gap-stretchers, not arched as in the English pianos, but straight wrought iron bars that cross under the strings from the pin block to the belly rail.

By the time this piano was made, the six-octave range was no longer experimental. I noted above the unusual Könnicke with six keyboards made in 1795 (it has not survived). Beyond that, Arthur

Loesser claims to have found an advertisement for a six-octave German grand dated October 1799; Rosamond Harding pictures an unnamed Viennese-type grand, made in about 1800, with the FF–f⁴ range, which belonged to Dr. Johann Kanka, a lawyer who once represented Beethoven; and William S. Newman says that by 1803 the Streichers were making six-octave grands.[18] I have not discovered evidence of Streicher grands with this range so early, though a six-octave Matthäus Andreas Stein grand in the Colt Clavier Collection (Bethersden, Kent, England) is dated about 1802.[19] Six-octave grands from about 1808 and after are to be found in various museum collections. Beethoven certainly had access to grands with that range as early as 1808, when he required it in the Trio, op. 70, no. 2; and nearly all of his works involving the piano written in 1809–10 call for these six octaves.

On June 18, 1818, a new piano arrived in Vienna for Beethoven, sent from John Broadwood & Sons in London by way of Trieste, its condition none the better for its having been brought by cart over the Alps.[20] For the time being it was kept by the Streichers, who with the help of Cipriani Potter, an English pianist and friend of Beethoven's, worked to put it in condition.[21] Thomas Broadwood, John's son, who now headed the firm, expected the English technician and harp maker Johann Andreas Stumpff to put the instrument in playing condition, but Stumpff apparently did not get to Vienna at that time.[22] Beethoven may have been a bit crusty and paranoid about his gift. When Potter told him that it was out of tune, he replied, "That's what they all say; they would like to tune it and spoil it, but they shall not touch it."* But soon the instrument was in condition and delivered to Beethoven. It is not clear that he sat right down to it to compose a masterpiece, as he had promised Thomas Broadwood he would do.[23]

Beethoven kept the Broadwood for the rest of his life. At his death, the publisher Anton Spina bought it from his estate. Later,

---

*Alexander W. Thayer, *Life of Beethoven*, p. 675. Legends about the Broadwood came very soon into circulation. A fascinating one was translated from an unnamed German newspaper in the June 3, 1820, issue of a short-lived Boston musical journal, *The Euterpiad* (1.10: 40): "To give a just idea of the superior construction of this instrument, it will be sufficient to state the fact that after being transported from London to Trieste, and thence on wheels to Moglin [Mödling], it was opened and found to be in perfect tune, all ready for the touch of the *Mighty Musician*" (italics in the original).

FIG. 3.4. *Grand piano, John Broadwood & Sons, London, 1811.* Serial no. 5170. *Inscription:* "John Broadwood & Sons / Makers to His Majesty & the Princesses / Great Pulteney Street   Golden Square / London." *Action:* English grand action, cloth over-dampers; leather-covered hammers. *Stops:* 2 pedals: una corda, dampers (split pedal: left, dampers to b; right, dampers c^1–c^4); due corde slide on right cheek block. *Range:* CC–c^4. *Stringing:* Triple-strung, no wound strings; CC–A♭ brass; A–c^4 steel (originally iron); CC 192.9 cm, c^2 26.4 cm, c^4 7.3 cm. *Framing:* Wood, with 5 iron gap-stretchers. *Case:* Mahogany; 245.9 cm long, 114 cm wide. *Location:* Department of Music, Stanford University. Restored by Bjarne B. Dahl. Photography by Margaret Straka.

the Princess Caroline Sayn-Wittgenstein, Franz Liszt's last mistress, bought the piano from Spina and gave it to Liszt, and at his death it came to the Magyar Nemzeti Muzeum in Budapest, where it still is.

The instrument pictured in Figure 3.4 is not Beethoven's Broadwood, but it is an identical twin to it, made in 1811. Like the Erard, the Broadwood is triple-strung throughout the range, and like all the grands we have seen so far, it has no wound strings. The strings that are now in this piano are not, of course, the originals, which would have been of brass and wrought iron; these are of brass and of a mild steel with the same density as the iron. It has a feature Broadwood used in many grands: a split damper pedal, with which one can separately control the dampers from c^1 up and those from b downward. Putting the foot on both halves at once brings all the dampers up from the strings. This piano has a true una corda pedal, which moves the keyboard and action to the right so that the hammers strike but one of the three strings of each note. It can be judiciously depressed (the feat takes a good deal of practice) so that the hammers strike two of the three strings, or one can use a little *due corde* (two-string) slide that Broadwood often installed on grands at the upper end of the keyboard. Pulled up, the slide moves a block into place that stops the keyboard at the point where the hammers strike two strings when one uses the una corda pedal. (This slide was certainly devised mainly to aid in tuning.)[24] The una corda stop precisely meets what Beethoven wrote in such passages as the transition between the third and fourth movements of the A-major sonata, op. 101. The third movement is marked "Mit einer Saite" ("on one string"). At the cadenza that closes the movement, leading into a reprise of the beginning of the first movement as transition to the fourth, Beethoven writes "Nach und nach mehrere Saiten" ("progressively more strings"), until, with the return of the first movement tempo, he calls for "Alle Saiten" ("all strings"). The effect that is wanted is to move slowly from an una corda timbre through two strings until at last, with the familiar strains of the earlier movement, the hammers are striking all three strings.* It is a remarkable transition, not in loudness but in tone quality, a transition, moreover, that the modern piano is incapable of reproducing since it does not possess a true una corda stop.

English pianos had a reputation for a big tone. It is a thicker sound that that of a Viennese grand—some called it muffled—with a more powerful bass but often a weaker treble. English (and French) pianos had a tendency to a rather "woody" tone in the

---

*The effect can be heard most clearly in a passage similarly marked in the second movement of Beethoven's Fourth Piano Concerto, op. 58, in the recording by Paul Badura-Skoda with the Collegium Aureum, BASF KHB 21510. The piano is a Conrad Graf grand of 1820, and the orchestral instruments are also authentic.

highest registers. This could be in part because the English pianos probably had heavier wire, at least in the treble, and the speaking lengths of the strings in that range tended to be longer than in the Viennese grands. The Broadwood's c^4, for example, is 7.3 cm, compared with 6.2 cm in the 1814 Streicher. Thus the tension in the Broadwood must be greater, and it may pass the point where increasing tension provides increasing elasticity. In addition, the English action was considerably stiffer than the Viennese, and it typically had a deeper dip of the keys. All of that makes for a heavier touch on English pianos.

The bigger sound of the English grand was probably in Thomas Broadwood's mind when he sent the piano to Beethoven. The composer's deafness was well known, and the manufacturer almost surely thought that a piano with a stronger sound might be audible to him. It was neither the first time nor the last that Beethoven's deafness set piano makers to work. He himself had asked the Streichers to make a piano as loud as possible in 1817.[25] Attempts to improve audibility continued almost to Beethoven's death, with makeshift ear trumpets attached to the soundboards, what were supposed to be resonance plates placed under the piano, and even, in Beethoven's last piano, a grand by Conrad Graf, quadruple-stringing from D to the f^4 top. (I will discuss this instrument later.)

Nothing worked, of course. By the time Beethoven received the Broadwood he had for all practical purposes lost his hearing.[26] In 1817, he began to ask all his visitors to write their remarks in conversation books because he could not hear speech. That he ever heard his Broadwood in anything like a normal sense of the term is therefore not only doubtful but nearly impossible. A firsthand report shows that in 1825 he could not hear it. Ludwig Rellstab, later a famous critic, visited Beethoven in that year and reported an incident in which the composer played the Broadwood. He was proudly showing it to his visitor, as Rellstab told the story:

"It is a handsome gift," he continued, stretching his hands towards the keys, yet without ceasing to hold my eyes. He gently struck a chord. Never again will one penetrate my soul with such a wealth of woe, with so heart-rending an accent! He had struck the C-major chord with his right hand, and played a B to it in the bass, his eyes never leaving mine; and, in order that it might make the soft tone of the instrument sound at its best, he repeated the false chord several times and—the greatest musician on earth did not hear its dissonance![27]

Regrettably, a good deal of nonsense has been said about the Broadwood's influence on Beethoven. Derek Melville claims that the "impressionistic" use of the piano in Beethoven's last three sonatas is traceable to the Broadwood's tonal characteristics.[28] The allegation runs afoul of two facts: (1) that Beethoven could almost certainly not hear this or any piano well enough to distinguish its tonal characteristics from those of another instrument, and (2) that only one of the last three sonatas can be played as Beethoven wrote it on the Broadwood. The sonatas in E major, op. 109, and C minor, op. 111, exceed the CC–c^4 range of the Broadwood; only the A-flat major sonata, op. 110, stays within that compass. As a matter of fact, of the nine works involving the piano that Beethoven wrote after receiving the Broadwood in 1818, only this sonata, the Diabelli Variations, op. 120, and the Bagatelles, op. 126, can be played on that piano. All of the others exceed its upper range.

The Broadwood's six octaves are CC–c^4, whereas the typical Viennese six octaves, as we saw with the Streicher, are FF–f^4. Broadwood had begun to make pianos with the range of this one in the 1790's, on some accounts as early as 1794.[29] The earliest of which I have found certain evidence was the 1796 instrument mentioned earlier, the piano that Godoy presented to the Spanish Queen. Since Broadwood was the leading English maker, other London houses soon followed the lead in extending the range downward. As we have seen, the Viennese and German makers generally extended the range upward, from c^4 to f^4. Beethoven had been accustomed to using those uppermost notes since at least 1808, and Newman is probably correct when he says that the Broadwood, with its CC–c^4 range, "probably struck Beethoven not as a new widening of the horizons, as generally has been stated, but as a disappointing limitation."[30] When, in 1823, the pianist Ignaz Moscheles asked Beethoven for the loan of his Broadwood for a concert in Vienna, the composer is said to have suspected Moscheles of some kind of financial speculation, "since the piano had too short a keyboard to be of use to him."[31] Beethoven was certainly proud of the Broadwood, but the reason probably had more to do with its prestige than with its musical qualities, which Beethoven was never in a position to appreciate. When the mood struck him, he could even insult it. The English harp maker and piano technician Johann Andreas Stumpff, visiting in 1824, was told by the composer, "I myself possess a London instrument, which, however, does not live up to my expectations." When Stumpff saw the piano, as he wrote, "What a sight confronted me! The upper registers were mute and the broken strings in a tangle, like a thorn bush whipped by the storm!"[32] Beethoven had at least played the Broadwood, and by the next year, when Rellstab saw it, he had had it repaired.

The extension of the range down to CC had an untoward effect on the instrument, which shows very clearly in the picture of Stanford University's Broadwood in Figure 3.4. The corner of the case, where the bent side begins its curve, is alarmingly distorted with "cheek disease." The use of triple-stringing over the entire range, added to the extension of the range in the bass, put a tremendous amount of strain on the framing. There are, to be sure, those typical Broadwood arched gap-stretchers between the pin block and the belly rail. On the whole, the tension in the bass strings is greater than that in the treble strings in total force. Thus it is precisely the added notes in the bass that put the extra strain on an inadequate frame; the evident effect is at that corner on the treble side because just there is a joint in the case and frame that is difficult to strengthen.

This cheek warp was especially to be found in English and French pianos because of the triple-stringing and inadequate interior bracing, and it can be seen in many photographs of instruments built throughout the late eighteenth and early nineteenth centuries. The builders attempted to strengthen the interior bracing. The photograph of the interior of a 1798 Broadwood grand in Figure 3.5 shows how the braces run every which way inside the case, and in this particular instance, they look quite higgledy-piggledy. It was a noble if not a frantic effort, but it did not work. During the first decade of the nineteenth century, Broadwood began to try to meet the problem by placing metal tension bars above the strings in grands. The effort was unsuccessful at the time, apparently because the firm could not find a satisfactory way to attach the bars.[33] The difficulty was well known, and solutions would soon be forthcoming. In squares, the

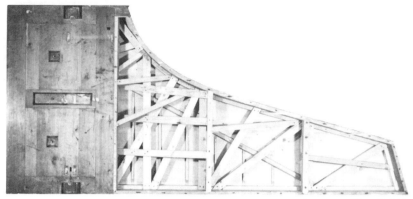

FIG. 3.5. *Interior bracing of a Broadwood grand, 1798.* The case is shown with the bottom removed.

tension warp shows up in a slightly different way. Since the strings in a square run more or less diagonally from corner to corner, with the bass strings, which exert the heaviest pull, occupying the middle of that line, the right front and left rear corners were often pulled upward out of line with the other two. It was the same problem, and it would require the same kind of solution.

In the meantime, grands were growing still bigger, as the Conrad Graf pictured in Figure 3.6 shows. Made in about 1825, this instrument covers six octaves and a fourth, CC–f⁴. It goes as low as the English six-octave pianos and as high as the Viennese six-octave ones, combining both extremes. To be sure, by the time this instrument was built, some makers had attempted seven octaves. The Streichers are said to have made some seven-octave pianos in 1816 or 1817, no examples of which survive,[34] nor have I discovered information on their exact range. In 1823 or 1824, Sébastien Erard began to produce seven-octave grands, range CC–c⁵; the thirteen-year-old Liszt played one at his Paris debut in 1824.

But it is important to recognize that the instruments with these ranges were experimental. Very few of them were made, and the older sizes continued to be built for another 15 years or so. Indeed, as late as about 1820 one even finds five-octave squares (one made by John Haberacker of Reading, Pennsylvania, is in the Smithsonian Institution), and in the early 1830's, squares were still made with the old FF–c⁴ range (the Smithsonian also has one of these, made by Alpheus Babcock in Philadelphia between 1831 and 1833). But in the 1820's the most common size among survivors is the six-octave piano, either in the typical English or in the typcial Viennese range. As the 1830's wore on, ranges like that of the Graf became much more common, and extensions were made up to g^4 and a^4 in a number of cases. The acceptance of novelty in piano making was slow; that someone did something new at a certain time is no indication that from that moment on it was adopted by everyone.

Who first attempted the six and one-half octaves that the Graf

By courtesy of Händel-Haus, Halle, GDR

FIG. 3.6. *Grand piano, Conrad Graf, Vienna, c. 1825.* Serial no. 1065. *Action:* Viennese action; leather-covered hammers. *Stops:* 4 pedals (mechanisms missing): una corda, bassoon, buff, dampers. *Range:* CC–f^4. *Stringing:* CC–DD double-strung wound, DD♯–EE double-strung plain, FF–f^4 triple-strung plain; CC 193 cm, c^2 27.3 cm, f^4 5.4 cm. *Framing:* Wood. *Case:* Mahogany veneered, with bronze ornaments on nameboard and cheek; 242 cm long; 121.5 cm wide. *Location:* Händel-Haus, Halle, GDR. Catalog no. MS-38.

has is not known. As far as I can tell, the earliest piano with this range whose date is beyond question is another Graf, dated about 1811, in the Neupert Collection at the Germanisches National-museum in Nuremberg (catalog no. MINe 136). The same collection has a Nannette Streicher grand with the same range that is given the date of 1807 with some suspicion (van der Meer's checklist says, "ostensibly 1807"); and N. E. Michel has a picture of a six-and-a-half-octave Streicher in his book that he dates in 1803 (a date that, like much of what is presented as fact in that work, deserves profound skepticism).[35] The second decade of the nineteenth century saw more of the larger range; survivors include a pedal grand by Josef Brodmann of 1815 in the Kunsthistorisches Museum in Vienna and an 1816 Nannette Streicher grand in the Yale University Collection of Musical Instruments.

Beethoven must have had one or more pianos with this range. Indeed, some facts about his works suggest that he might have had one quite early. Consider the ranges of the following works (numbers in parentheses are dates of publication):

1808	Trio, op. 70, no. 1 (1809)	$EE-c^4$
1811	*Archduke* Trio, op. 97 (1816)	$EEb-eb^4$
1816	Sonata, A major, op. 101 (1817)	$EE-e^4$
1818	Sonata, Bb major, op. 106 (1819)	$CC-f^4$
1818	Ten Varied Themes, op. 107 (1819–20)	$EEb-e^4$
1820	Sonata, E major, op. 109 (1821)	$DD\sharp-c\sharp^4$
1822	Sonata, C minor, op. 111 (1822)	$CC-eb^4$
1826	Grosse Fuge, transcribed by Beethoven for piano 4 hands, op. 134 (1827)	$DD-eb^4$

The first of these works, the Trio, might presuppose a piano with the $CC-c^4$ range. But the ranges of all of the other works listed indicate the availability of pianos that went both below the FF bottom of the Viennese six octaves and above the c^4 top of the English six octaves.* Though these are not the only works that Beethoven wrote during those years, they suggest that he and those who bought his music had access to pianos with the $CC-f^4$ range. To be sure, only one of these works, the huge *Hammer-klavier* Sonata, op. 106, requires the entire range, but Beethoven

---

*Beethoven's last five sonatas, op. 101, 106, 109–11, are recorded by Paul Badura-Skoda on a Conrad Graf grand of about 1824, like Beethoven's own, on the Astrée label, AS 47–49.

was approaching completion of that work when the Broadwood arrived from London in 1818.*

Unfortunately, we simply do not know what instruments Beethoven had in his rooms besides the Erard and, after 1818, the Broadwood. As we have seen, in the summer of 1817 he was asking for as loud a Streicher as possible and talking wistfully of borrowing one until he could afford to buy it. He was apparently thinking of a new model of some kind—perhaps one with the CC–f^4 range—when he said, in the same year, "Your patent piano certainly does not need my approval, but for my own sake I have long desired to make its acquaintance."[36] But we cannot say confidently, with Ernest Closson and Alfred Dolge, that Beethoven had a six-and-a-half-octave Streicher in 1817.[37]

Only in 1824 do we know that he had a grand with that range. At that time—when Beethoven passed the old Erard on to his brother, perhaps to make way for a new piano—Conrad Graf put at his disposal a six-and-a-half-octave grand, which was with him until his death. It was not like the instrument pictured in Figure 3.6, but was a special model with triple-stringing from CC to C♯ and quadruple-stringing from D to the f^4 top. The piano was doubtless given to Beethoven on the assumption that the quadruple-stringing would make it audible to him, though it is not true, as some have said, that Graf devised the stringing in order to make a piano that Beethoven could hear. Graf had made a piano with such stringing as early as 1820—it is mentioned in one of Beethoven's conversation books—and one report has him thinking of it as early as 1812.[38] Indeed, if the idea was to increase the volume, it did not work. The added strain on the framing introduced by the fourth string over so much of the range necessitated the use of smaller-than-usual wire gauges, and the sound of the Graf was no louder than that of ordinary pianos of the day.† Bee-

*That only one work makes use of the entire range, though a number of others seem to imply it, shows that the frequent assumption that Beethoven *always* used the entire scope of what was available to him, indeed, always wanted more than was available, is simply mistaken. Even the meticulous Donald Francis Tovey is caught in that misstatement—rare for Tovey—when, in the preface to his edition of the Beethoven sonatas (1931), he says (p. 7): "The compass of the piano hampered Beethoven in all his works for it." The compass of the piano did hamper Beethoven in *some* of his works for it, but most of them fit quite comfortably within what was available.

†Derek Melville, "Beethoven's Pianos," p. 46. At Beethoven's death, Graf took the piano back, and it was sold elsewhere. The instrument has been restored (on some accounts, not very accurately) and is now in the Beethovenhaus in Bonn. Two photographs of

By courtesy of Eugene M. Schachter

FIG. 3.7. *Interior bracing of a Graf grand, c. 1824.* The different shades of wood show the laminations, which interlock with each other. Alternating laminations in the cross brace and the longitudinal braces pass all the way through. The result is a very powerful frame that disperses the strain, needing no iron to resist the tension. The piano pictured, shown in process of construction by Eugene M. Schacter, is an exact copy of an instrument in his possession.

thoven probably did not use the Graf much. The only work he wrote for piano after getting it was the four-hand transciption of the Grosse Fuge, originally for string quartet, and the indications are that he was playing very little even for himself in the last three years of his life.

The Graf pictured in Figure 3.6 is interesting on two counts. First, this is one of the earliest grands I know of that has any wound strings. They had been standard on squares from the beginning, because they had been commonly used in clavichords. Plain strings had been the rule in grands, but from now on wound strings rapidly became universal in the bass. But only the lowest three notes of this piano have wound strings. Second, though the Graf's range is so wide, its framing is entirely of wood, with only a little iron gap-stretcher between the pin block and the belly rail. Graf built up his interior bracing—which he made of oak—in a way peculiar to him, using a kind of lamination and interlocking joints that made an extraordinarily stable framing (see Fig. 3.7).

it are in Franz Josef Hirt, *Stringed Keyboard Instruments*, p. 49; and Jörg Demus has recorded it in Beethoven's sonatas in E major, op. 109, F-sharp major, op. 78, and A-flat major, op. 110, the G-major Rondo, op. 51, no. 2, and the Bagatelles, op. 126, on BASF KHF-20328.

Though he used so little iron, the case shows no signs of the arthritic joints at the cheek that the 1811 Broadwood has.

Conrad Graf, like many of his piano-making colleagues, started as a cabinetmaker. He had enlisted in the army in about 1800, when he was eighteen or so, but was mustered out with a foot injury and decided to switch to piano making. His apprenticeship was served with a man named Schelkle. On Schelkle's death in 1804, Graf took over both the shop and his widow (perhaps in reverse order). The business expanded relatively rapidly, and in 1809–10 he was already employing 10 workmen. Moving inside the city of Vienna in 1812, he continued to work at improvements. According to the 1835 report from which most of this information comes,[39] he devised especially strong means of interior bracing, used a new way of leathering hammers, employed steel pins in the bridges to improve the tone, and as we have seen, tried quadruple-stringing. In 1824 he received the formal designation, as the nameboard on a grand of that year in the Badura-Skoda Collection (Vienna) says, "Kaiserl. kön. Hof-Fortepiano-macher."* By 1826, Graf employed 40 workmen. The business went on growing, as demonstrated by the fact that the piano here discussed, serial no. 1065, was made in 1825, showing that since 1804 Graf had averaged about 50 pianos a year. In Chapter Six, we will look at a Graf grand of 1839, which has the serial number 2616. Assuming that Graf numbered all of his pianos seriatim, that would mean that between 1825 and 1839 he averaged about 110 pianos a year. That is not a terribly high output for a 40-person shop, about 2.75 instruments per worker per year.† The rate is fairly standard: Erard, the largest French maker, with 150 workers, was making 400 pianos a year about then, for an average of 2.67. The largest house of all, Broadwood, manufactured about 1,650 instruments annually at that time.[40] Graf's factory methods, then, whatever they were (no information on them survives, at least where I could find it), were about the equivalent of Erard's for the time being, though

---

*"Imperial Royal Court Fortepiano Maker." The piano is the one Badura-Skoda plays in the last five Beethoven sonatas (see footnote to p. 90, above), and the nameboard is pictured on the jacket of Astrée AS 47.

†According to the report of the 1835 Vienna exhibition (*Bericht über die Gewerbs-produkten-Ausstellung*), Graf had produced a total of 5,000 pianos. That would mean that in the 10 years after no. 1065 was made, the company had built nearly 400 pianos a year, a very high output for that time. The serial number of the 1839 Graf is sufficient disproof of the claim.

as we will see, some later figures suggest that, before too long, the efficiency of French manufacturers rose, while that of the Austrians fell.

William S. Newman wrote an article in 1970, attempting to demonstrate that Beethoven's ideal of piano sound was always that of the Viennese piano.[41] As a corrective to earlier, mistaken estimates, especially of the importance of the Broadwood to Beethoven, it is a valuable collection of information. There is, however, one remark of Beethoven's that suggests that his ideal of piano sound was locked inside his own head and remains quite inaccessible to our analysis. His friend Karl Holz reported that Beethoven said, "The piano is and remains an inadequate instrument."[42] Is that simply the outburst of a deaf, frustrated musician? We cannot be sure. It throws a shadow, however, over every effort to reach a definitive conclusion about Beethoven's role in the development of the piano. His part of the story of this chapter, then, comes out to ambiguity.

The piano's part of it points forward. The expansions of the grand's range that I have described were at once a step toward the new expressiveness in the early Romantic composers, in which new tonal colorations and textures loomed larger, and a new technological problem that had to be addressed. The tendency was not only toward greater range, but also toward greater volume and higher pitch. The increased volume was demanded by the fact that, as concerts became more popular, concert rooms were built larger. Higher pitch, with all that it implied of greater tension on piano strings, was imposed on pianos largely by orchestral instruments. Higher-pitched wind and stringed instruments gave more brilliant tone, and pianos simply had to reach for that tone. Strength, then, and brilliance were becoming important aspects of piano sound, and this meant that the instrument had to be built proportionately stronger. Yet it was not merely strength that was wanted, but flexibility—the capacity to play louder and also softer, the responsiveness of the instrument to a different kind of affective expression. I do not mean that Romantic music was expressive and classic music was not. But beginning with Beethoven, the Romantics wrote music differently, bringing emotions out to overt, sometimes excessive, expression, rather than depending on more subtle associations. The pianos had to be able to produce what was wanted, and added strength in stringing and framing was the only way to ensure it. The piano began to compete with the orchestra on more nearly even terms and to be conceived as a kind of living-room substitute for it.

The technological problem had not yet been solved, though Graf's success in widening the range along with devising an interior bracing system that did not buckle under the tension, as Broadwood's sometimes did, indicates that the solution eventually adopted was not the only possible one. Before we turn to that solution, we must return to the same years we have just covered from a different angle. Grands were important as the instruments of artists and of the rich. But piano makers earned their incomes from pianos that sold in much greater quantity than the grands, pianos designed to be used by amateurs at home.

4

Pianos for Early-Nineteenth-
Century Homes

The piano business has always depended far more on the amateur
pianist than on the professional, on the music lover than on the
musician. The reason is not far to seek: there are many more
amateurs than professionals, always have been, always will be.
Business insists on being economically successful, and the maker
of pianos who caters only to the professional musician will make
no decent living. In paying more attention in these first chapters to
the development of the grand piano, I have skewed the actualities
of the instrument's manufacture, at least so far as the bulk of the
manufacturers' concern goes.

At the same time that piano makers made a great many more
instruments for the home than for the concert hall, the technology
used for, and the experience gained in, the concert hall had its effect on the instruments made for the home. In this respect, the
story may not be as lopsided as it may seem. Certainly most of the
influence exerted from one type of piano to another went from the
concert or professional instrument to the amateur, not in the other
direction. What Broadwood learned from building grands affected his squares, not vice versa. But it was the squares that kept
bread and meat on piano makers' tables, and the grands, if they
added to income rather than detracted from it, provided cake and
sweets.

I do not mean that the pianos made for home consumption were
so inferior to those made for professionals as to be of doubtful
technological interest. Quite to the contrary. The challenge to a
designer of devising a responsive action for an upright piano was a
very great challenge indeed, one to which, it can be argued, a re-

ally satisfactory solution has yet to be found. The challenge of designing a square that produced volume of sound as well as subtlety
of declamation occupied some of the best talents in the industry.
And the technological know-how entailed in producing instruments of acceptable quality within an acceptable price range
marked off the good technologist from the poor one. In that respect, if in no other, men like John Broadwood, Matthäus Andreas Stein, and Alpheus Babcock were shining lights in their
generations.

The homes for which such pianos were intended certainly varied a great deal. Some were destined for rather modest homes,
whereas others, like the large uprights of Stein, doubtless graced
the drawing rooms of the rich. These were, nevertheless, pianos
to be played by amateurs and to be comfortably ensconced with
the rest of the furnishings of the early-nineteenth-century home.
In a way more centrally important for these instruments than for
those made for concert rooms and musicians' lodgings, they were
social artifacts, as Arthur Loesser has so vividly described them.
One of their social effects was to allow viable piano industries to
flourish in their societies.

The square by George Astor of London pictured in Figure 4.1 is
typical of the technology of the turn of the nineteenth century,
though in a couple of respects, as we will see, it is conservative.
But the action in this instrument is the one we would expect to find
in any English, French, or American square made during the first
half of the nineteenth century, and its extended range demonstrates again what we have seen happening in the grands of the
same time.

The standard five octaves, FF–f^3, has been increased by the
interval of a fifth, to FF–c^4. As we saw in Chapter Three, such
extensions of range were being made in England, France, and
Germany. Astor, like most makers of squares for some time, has
arranged the added fifth at the top in accordance with a patent
granted to William Southwell in London on October 18, 1794
(English patent no. 2017). Not wishing to eliminate any part of the
soundboard, lest the volume be diminished, he divided the action
frame into two sections. The top section, which slides out sepa-

FIG. 4.1. *Square piano, Astor & Company, London, c. 1800.* Serial no. 2752. *Inscription:* "New Patent / Astor & Comp.^{y} / N°, 79 Cornhill, London." *Action:* English double action; leather-covered hammers. Damper wires glued to backs of keys. *Stops:* 2 pedals: dampers to d^3; "nag's head" swell. *Range:* FF–c^4. *Stringing:* Double-strung; FF–E♭ wound brass, E–c^4 plain iron; FF 141.6 cm, c^2 29.3 cm, c^4 7.6 cm. Tuning pins at right side of case. *Framing:* Wood. *Case:* Mahogany with cherry and greenwood banding; 165.1 cm long, 59 cm deep. *Location:* Museum of Fine Arts, Boston, Mass. Gift of Clement R. D. Meier in memory of his wife, Dorothy Niedringhaus Meier.

rately, contains the seven keys of the added range. Their hammers strike upward through a slot at the side of the soundboard called the extra keys slot. For several years, until they became the dominant type, pianos with the FF–c^4 range, especially squares, were known as pianos "with the extra keys."

One might wonder why makers did not extend the soundboard in squares to cover the keys. The reason is that with tuning pins or hitch-pins at the back and the striking points of the hammers on the strings near the back, there was no place to put the belly rail, the brace underneath the edge of the soundboard that kept it in place. Dividing the action frame into two sections allowed space for the belly rail between them. Some makers, however, did not bother with the "extra keys slot." In a little square of 1798 by Charles Albrecht of Philadelphia in the Smithsonian Institution (catalog no. 315,682) with FF–c^4 compass and Viennese action, the soundboard does not cover even the top seven keys.

Astor's square has an action we have not seen before. The mechanism came to be called the grasshopper action after the jack, or hopper (short for grasshopper) as the English called it. Unlike Zumpe's very simple action and similar ones in England and France, this action reintroduced Cristofori's intermediate lever between the jack and the hammer butt, as the diagram in Figure 4.2 shows.

This action was patented in 1786 by John Geib, one of the "twelve apostles" and at that time a workman in the shop of Longman and Broderip in London. At about the time of his patent, Geib seems to have gone independent. He and his sons, Adam and George, moved to the United States shortly after 1800, where a series of companies with the Geib name can be traced. This simple action had more leverage control than the single ac-

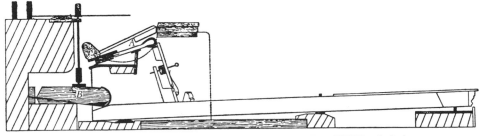

By permission of Gresham Books Ltd., The Gresham Press, Old Woking, England

FIG. 4.2. *English double action.* This is the action for squares patented by John Geib in London, 1786. The escapement (familiarly called the grasshopper, shortened to hopper) is the elaborated jack, resting on the key, which pushes against the intermediate lever (*A* in the diagram) to propel the hammer to the string. Diagram from Rosamond E. M. Harding, *The Piano-Forte: Its History Traced to the Great Exhibition of 1851*, 2d ed. (Old Woking, Eng., 1978).

tions of Zumpe (see Fig. 2.7, p. 46, above) or Broadwood. For a considerable time to come, the grasshopper action was the one to be expected in English, French, and American squares. It was durable, adjustable, and serviceable, though it was never as satisfactory as the direct-blow jack action of the English-type grand.

Astor has introduced a serious flaw into the action, however. The damper mechanism has the disadvantage that the lifter wires are glued to the surfaces of the keys, doubtless to avoid the noise of their falling back. This was the reason urged by William Southwell, formerly of Dublin and from 1794 in London, in his 1794 patent for what came to be known as the Irish damper.[1] Southwell's patent calls for the damper wires to be screwed into wooden sockets attached to the keys, an arrangement I myself have seen only in a Clementi square. It has at least the relative advantage that the damper wires can be screwed out if the action must be removed from the case for repair or adjustment, though unscrewing and rescrewing 66 wires individually is not exactly a pleasant task. In Astor's piano, the glue joint must simply be broken if the action is to be taken out. It is a nearly fatal flaw so far as the ease of repair is concerned.

As I have said, in two respects this instrument is conservative. The tuning pins are at the right side of the case, with the pin block taking up vibrating space from the soundboard. This placement of the pins characterized the Zumpe square that we examined in Chapter Two, as it characterized all virginals and clavichords. In 1783, John Broadwood, seeing disadvantages in the arrangement, shifted the tuning pins and their block to the back of the case, with the hitch-pins now on the soundboard side. Broadwood explained his purpose in the patent specifications (English patent no. 1379, dated Nov. 15, 1783) as giving "room to fix the strings without being crowded on one another, which otherwise make a great jarring on the said rist [wrest, i.e., tuning] pins when placed on the right side of the instrument, & also gives a more regular pressure on the bridges, and produces a more regular tone." The point about the bridges is the more important one. Rosamond Harding says that the purpose was to equalize the tension on the two bridges,[2] but I believe that by "more regular pressure" Broadwood meant something like "regulatable." This requires some explanation.

Part of what affects the tension on, and the elasticity of, the string is its down-bearing on the bridges, that is, the angle at which the string goes from bridge to pin (see Fig. 1.5, p. 11, above). Tension and elasticity in their turn affect the tone. If the angle of down-bearing is too slight, the string may too easily move up from the bridge's surface; this weakens the tone, which cannot be properly resonated by the soundboard unless the string constantly touches the bridge. If the down-bearing angle is too great, the elasticity of the string may be adversely affected and the tone go dead. In the old arrangement, with the strings running from tuning pins on the right directly to the soundboard bridge, the angle of down-bearing was determined by the place on the tuning pin where the string's wrapping was done. In order that the angle of down-bearing might be precisely the same for all strings, all of them had to be wrapped around the tuning pins at precisely the same level, a very difficult maneuver to execute. The hitch-pins, in contrast, are angled so that the strings naturally loop on them at the same level. Thus the angle of down-bearing is more easily regulated by the height of the bridges if the hitch-pins are at the right, giving "a more regular pressure on the bridges." The explanation may be mildly tedious, but it is not nearly so tedious as trying to regulate down-bearing by wrapping wires around tuning pins.

Another advantage of the shift of the pin block away from the soundboard was that a greater area of soundboard was freed to resonate the tone. A number of British makers took up Broadwood's idea, but even around 1800 Astor had not yet done so. Before many years, however, in English-type squares, which included nearly all French and American ones, the tuning pins were almost universally at the back, and they remained there until the square became obsolete. The latest square I have seen with tuning pins at the right is a lovely instrument made by Robb and Mundy of New York, dating from about 1825, owned by Hans Groffie of Palo Alto, California.*

Astor's other conservative—perhaps even eccentric—arrangement is an odd function of the right pedal. It operates a lid-lifter, or what was sometimes called a "nag's-head" swell, a lever

*Claude Montal, *L'Art d'accorder* (1836), gives a plan view of a six-octave double-strung square (Fig. 5) and shows the stringing of the top octave of a triple-strung square (Fig. 12), both with tuning pins at the right.

that lifts the flap of the lid to the player's right over the part of the case in line with the keyboard (the lifter is the white knob just to the right of the keyboard in Figure 4.1). The effect is the same as lifting the lid on a grand: it allows more sound out of the box when the main lid of the square is down. The pianist could use it in the same way an organist uses the swell pedals, to give a temporary dynamic rise and fall to the music by raising and lowering the lid. The nag's-head swell seems to have been the invention of Jacob Kirckman of London as an answer to the inexpressiveness of harpsichords. It is to be found on a Kirckman harpsichord as early as 1754.[3]

Why a piano maker even thought such a device desirable on a piano escapes comprehension, since the piano mechanism, unlike that of the harpsichord, allowed the player to make dynamic changes with the fingers. But no builder seems to have thought of the use one young pianist is said to have made of the nag's head. Right around the time of this Astor there was a considerable vogue for descriptive battle pieces for the piano, complete with imitations of drums, marching feet, the cries of the wounded, and the roaring of cannon.[4] It is said that this imaginative performer produced a more realistic cannon shot by suddenly releasing the nag's-head pedal, whereupon the lid fell with a bang.[5]

George Astor had a brother who moved to New York to engage in the American trade. He imported his brother's pianos and other instruments for some years until he discovered that less fortune was to be made in pianos than in furs. His name was John Jacob Astor.

<hr />

In 1795, it is said, Joseph Haydn, visiting England for the second time, went to the shop of William Stodart, the son of Robert Stodart, and saw his new patent piano, a large upright made, as Stodart said, "in the form of a bookcase."[6] Haydn, the story goes, was pleased with the design, which saved floor space without losing soundboard area. The Stodart piano pictured in Figure 4.3 is like the one Haydn saw, except for its wider compass.*

*I have been unable to trace the origin of this story. As far as I can ascertain, it was first told by Daniel Spillane in 1890 (*History of the American Pianoforte*, pp. 34–35), who attributed the invention and the object of Haydn's visit to William Southwell of Lad Lane, London. Rosamond Harding, in relating the story (*The Piano-Forte*, p. 60), correctly as-

Experiments with upright pianos had been carried out all the way back in the 1730's and 1740's by, among others, Christian Ernst Friederici of Gera, Saxony. The organist Heinrich Nicholaus Gerber, a pupil of Bach's, seems to have been fascinated with vertical instruments. He built an upright pedal clavichord nine feet high in 1742, and is said to have put a hammer mechanism in a clavicytherium in the same year.[7] Two examples, probably earlier than any of Friederici's, are the earliest Italian pianos known besides Cristofori's. One by Domenico del Mela da Gagliano, dated in 1739, is in the Museo del Conservatorio "Luigi Cherubini" in Florence, and another, attributed to del Mela, is in the museum in Milan.[8] The principle was that the harpsichord-shaped (grand) piano was turned vertically on its head, requiring modification of the action so that the hammers could strike vertical strings horizontally rather than striking horizontal strings from below. Precedent for this disposition of the instrument, if not the model for it, is found in the clavicytherium, which apparently enjoyed something of a revival in the early eighteenth century.[9] The experiments with large vertical shapes for fortepianos seem to have diminished if not died out after 1760 or so. It is anyone's guess whether Stodart or the German and Austrian makers who similarly began in the 1790's to design uprights thought of either the earlier efforts or the clavicytherium. Friederici was a pupil of Gottfried Silbermann's, and the "twelve apostles" may have known of and, in England, passed along reports about his uprights.

In 1810, Stodart was still, consciously or not, following Friederici's lead in bringing the case of his upright down only to keyboard level and setting it on a stand. The instrument is eight feet tall, and if the legs were not very sturdy, one would hesitate to stand in front of it in a stiff breeze. Shelves for storing music or other valuables are fixed in the case toward the top where the

cribed the invention to William Stodart, but in her appendix of patents (p. 345) incorrectly identified the holder of the patent for an upright "in the form of a bookcase" as Southwell (corrected in the 2d ed., p. 347). She further confused the issue by saying that Haydn visited Stodart "in Lad Lane." Lad Lane was Southwell's address, Stodart's being 1 Golden Square. Southwell was granted English patent no. 2017 on Oct. 18, 1794, for a new method of attaching dampers (not a good one, as we saw in discussing the Astor above) and a method of adding "extra keys." Spillane stated (p. 35) that Southwell's invention was for a six-octave piano, FF–f⁴, but the patent drawing shows FF–c⁴ with FF♯ missing. Stodart's patent, no. 2028, granted on Jan. 12, 1795, was for "an upright piano in the form of a bookcase," with an action devised for it.

strings leave space on the right.[10] From this storage capacity, as well as from the external appearance of the instrument, comes the usual designation of the style—cabinet grand. The silking of the front doors of the Stodart has been very beautifully restored and was excellently done in the original. There were, indeed, specialists in such piano silking in London.

The major problem facing the designer of an upright piano like this was the action. How should the mechanism be arranged so that the hammers strike vertical rather that horizontal strings? And how should the dampers (1) be held against the strings, (2) be removed from them at the right time, and (3) be returned to them at the right time? Stodart followed both Friederici and del Mela by simply revolving the grand action 90 degrees, so that the hammers move horizontally instead of vertically. The picture in Figure 4.4 demonstrates the principle.

Notice that in Stodart's design, the hammers strike from the rear, the keys extending under the pin block at the bottom of the case. It is an exact adaptation of the up-striking action used in a grand. If the action had to be taken out for repair and inspection, a panel in the back of the case opened, and the entire keyboard and action slid out the back. The action itself, as we see in the picture, is very lanky. The length of jack and hammer shank, not to say of the rods connected to the damper, issues in a certain leisureliness to its operation. But it is an ingenious solution to a difficult mechanical problem, a problem so difficult that the action of the upright piano cannot be said even today to be entirely satisfactory.

The experiments of Friederici and del Mela were apparently not extended further in their own time. But when Stodart and others took up the problem of the upright piano, their work bore fruit at least to the extent that uprights have been made continu-

By courtesy of Professor and Mrs. G. Norman Eddy

◄ Fɪɢ. 4.3. *Cabinet piano, William Stodart, London, c. 1810.* *Inscription:* "Patent / William Stodart / Maker to Their Majesties & Royal Family / Golden Square, London." *Action:* Stodart upright action, dampers above hammers; leather-covered hammers. *Stops:* 2 pedals: una corda, dampers to e³. *Range:* CC–c⁴. *Stringing:* CC–AA♭ double-strung plain brass, AA–A♭ triple-strung plain brass, A–c⁴ triple-strung plain iron; CC 153.4 cm, c² 27.9 cm, c⁴ 7 cm. Tuning pins at bottom. *Framing:* Wood, with 5 iron gap-stretchers. *Case:* Rosewood with brass inlay, oak, mahogany, front elaborately silked; 245.1 cm high, 113 cm wide. *Location:* Eddy Collection, Cambridge, Mass. Restored by Robert Smith.

ously ever since. The convenience of an instrument that does not occupy so much floor space as either a grand or a square cannot be gainsaid.

Stodart's cabinet grand has the typical English six-octave range, CC–c⁴. This is the same range as in the nearly contemporary Broadwood grand of 1811 that we saw in Chapter Three, the earliest known example of which was the fancy Broadwood of 1796. Though one finds squares with a six-octave range as early as 1810, most English, French, and American squares continued for some years with the smaller FF–c⁴ range. After 1815, however, most German and Austrian squares had their typical six octaves, FF–f⁴. The advances in range were made on the most expensive instruments first; Stodart's cabinet grand is a case in point. In the relatively wealthy home for which this kind of instrument was made, an occasional visitor might well be an accomplished, if not famous, pianist, and to play on a piano like this one would have occasioned no embarrassment in either the pianist or the owner. The instrument was intended to afford the player all the resources—or nearly all—of a concert piano.

The English built most of their large uprights on Stodart's model, like a cabinet on legs, whence came their name. Broadwood in London continued to make them until 1856. Several different forms of large uprights were built. Besides the cabinet grands, the most common were the so-called pyramid grands

By courtesy of Ronald V. Ratcliffe

Fig. 4.4. *Stodart cabinet action.* The key passes under the soundboard, and the hammer strikes the strings from the rear. At the back of the key is the sticker for the damper, which moves the damper by striking the padded block above. Notice the gap-stretcher behind the strings. Model by Ronald V. Ratcliffe.

named from their symmetrically angled cases, sometimes with quite fantastic decorations,[11] and a German-Austrian type that came to be known as the giraffe. The word is used as a technical term for its type even in such usually stodgy publications as museum catalogs. The photograph of the André Stein giraffe in Figure 4.5 shows its propriety.

André Stein is none other than Matthäus Andreas Stein, the son of Johann Andreas Stein and the brother of Nannette Streicher. When the Stein siblings parted company in 1802, and Nannette capitalized on the Stein name by billing herself as "Nannette Streicher, born Stein," Matthäus Andreas called attention to his patrimony by reminding buyers in the nameboard inscription ("d'Aougsbourg à Vienne") that, like his father, he had begun his business in Augsburg. Since the language of all polite and upper-class European society was French, Andreas became on nameboards André.

This is a lovely example of what some may think is an unlovely piano. The cabinetmaker has rather simply embellished an awkward shape to make of it nearly all that could tastefully be made, and the cabinetwork is very good. The giraffe illustrates one significant point that German makers understood sooner than the English did: to reduce the height of the instrument, the case was brought down to the floor. The giraffe could thus be rather massive without its height being overpowering. Another effect of bringing the case to the floor was that the hammers had to be arranged to strike the strings from the front rather than from the rear, as in Stodart's cabinet grand. The alternative would have been to waste large amounts of prospective soundboard area.

Modifying the Viennese action to suit the vertical stringing was easier than modifying the English one. The model pictured in Figure 4.6 illustrates what was done. The designer (we do not know who was the first) simply angled the back end of the key downward and attached the hammer in its fork and the escapement rail to it, as if the whole thing were horizontal. The escapement operates just as in the ordinary Viennese action, and Stein has devised a back check to keep the hammers from bouncing back to the strings. The damper mechanism is likewise a simple one. The damper is pivoted above the action, and a damper jack, which looks remarkably like Zumpe's leather-button old man's head,

FIG. 4.5. *Giraffe, André Stein, Vienna, c. 1810.* *Inscription:* "André Stein / d'Aougsbourg à Vienne." *Action:* "Hanging" Viennese upright action, dampers above hammers; leather-covered hammers. *Stops:* 6 pedals: bassoon (missing), dampers, buff or moderator (third and fourth pedals for same stop; stop missing), Janissary music, una corda (moves keyboard to left). *Range:* FF–f⁴. *Stringing:* FF–D double-strung plain brass, D♯–G triple-strung brass, G♯–f⁴ triple-strung iron; straight vertical stringing; FF 163 cm, c² 26 cm, f⁴ 5.5 cm. Tuning pins along bent side of frame. *Framing:* Wood. *Case:* Mahogany veneered; 214.7 cm high, 114.5 cm wide. *Location:* Smithsonian Institution, Washington, D.C. Catalog no. 299,844.

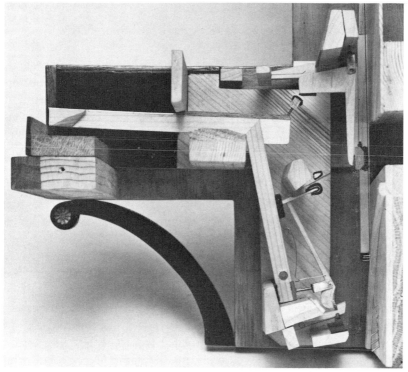

F IG . 4.6. *"Hanging" Viennese upright action*. The motion of the key moves the lower arm forward so that the tail of the hammer, pivoted in its brass fork, bounces from the escapement rail at the bottom. The hook on the spring on the lower arm of the key has a thread attached to the hammer shank, a form of check, which will pull the hammer back from the string. The damper lever above, pivoted in a metal fork at its upper corner, is moved by the small padded head projecting from the top of the key. Model by Ronald V. Ratcliffe.

raises one end of the damper lever, pulling the damper away from the string. When the key is released, the damper jack falls back into place by gravity, and the damper returns to the string.

    With the case extending to the floor, the designer had to decide whether to put the tuning pins below the keyboard, which would entail some interesting gymnastics on the part of a tuner, or up along the bent side, as if in a grand one were to put the tuning pins where the hitch-pins normally are. The solution is obvious: he put them on the bent side. Since the case does not reach as high above the floor as Stodart's does, the tuner would have little difficulty reaching the pins of even the longest strings.

Perhaps because the heyday of the giraffe coincided with some curious musical fads, its designers were more apt to load their instruments with pedals than were the designers of grands. Especially on the Continent, but not exclusively there, the turn of the nineteenth century saw a proliferation of stops, mechanical means to modify the tone or to add other kinds of sounds.[12] One sees pianos from this period with from three to eight pedals (not many of the latter). The Stein has six, though the two middle ones operated the same stop. The photograph of the Stein in plan view in Figure 4.7 shows something of the mechanisms inside the bottom of the case that run from the pedals to their various stops. The interior mechanisms of some of the stops are missing, and we must make informed guesses to identify them.

The left-most pedal, the mechanism of which is missing, was almost certainly a bassoon stop. It brought into contact with the strings of the lowest three octaves or so a wooden rod loosely wrapped in a piece of parchment. When the hammer struck strings so touched, a buzzing quality of the tone reminded its hearers of a bassoon. The next pedal from the left works the dampers. The middle two, working the same levers inside the case, though the rest of the stop has been lost, seem to have been a buff or moderator stop, a kind of mute. What was properly a "buff" stop (an Anglicization of the French term *peau de boeuf*, "cowhide") was usually a set of cloth or leather tongues, each corresponding to a hammer, attached to a rail that the pedal brought down so as to interpose the material between the hammer and the string, as in the Schmidt grand discussed in Chapter Two. The "moderator" was a long, single strip of cloth or leather, graduated in thickness across its short dimension. The farther down one pushed the pedal, the farther the rail was lowered and the thicker the material through which the hammer struck the strings. With thicker material, the sound was softer and more muffled. Such a stop was sometimes called a pianissimo stop.

The fifth pedal from the left is the most interesting, and was the most ephemeral of all the stops devised, though its persistence was remarkable and its occurrence widespread. It was called the Janissary music stop, and it accomplished two things at once. When the

By permission of the Smithsonian Institution, Washington, D.C.

FIG. 4.7. *Plan view of André Stein giraffe.*   In the case below the keyboard can be seen the wooden levers, moved by the pedals, that work the various stops.

pedal was put down, a little mallet struck a bell at the bottom of the case, and at the same time a larger padded mallet struck the soundboard from the rear, giving a fair imitation of a bass drum. The Janissary music stop, then, added percussion and tinkling bells to the piano sound.*

The term Janissary music came from a craze for Turkish band music that swept European royalty during the eighteenth century. It seems to have begun when King Augustus the Strong of

---

*The 1814 Streicher grand discussed in Chapter Three has bell and drum stops, worked by knee-levers. I omitted discussing the matter there in order to take it up here.

Poland received the gift of a Turkish military band at some time after 1710. Other monarchs could not allow themselves to be caught lacking such a marvelous innovation. The distinctive thing about the Turkish band music, in addition to its raucous oboes, was that it had drums, both kettledrums and bass drums, as well as cymbals, triangles, and other jingling and ringing objects. Such instruments had not been used in European military bands before the Turkish fad set in, but their addition has proved lasting. There were even exotic uniforms for the musicians; the leopard skins traditionally worn by drummers in British military bands are a holdover from the finery of Turkish bands. The term Janissary (or Janizary), applied to the entire phenomenon, derives from the name of an elite guard unit of the Turkish army.*

The sixth pedal, finally, is an una corda stop; it moves the keyboard and action to the left instead of to the right, the usual direction.

One last remark about Stein's giraffe: the range is six octaves, FF–f⁴. The Stodart's range is also six octaves, CC–c⁴. These ranges, as we saw in Chapter Three, were typical for the large instruments of their respective countries. The British on the whole extended the FF–c⁴ range downward to CC, whereas the Austrians and Germans on the whole extended it upwards to f⁴, though one occasionally finds FF–f⁴ on English pianos. Like Stodart's cabinet grand, Stein's giraffe would have been destined for a household well able to afford the luxury of a fine piano, a home in which the only question to be answered in deciding between a grand and a giraffe would be the relative amount of floor space to be occupied or the aesthetic balance of the furnishings in the drawing room. Like the family that owned the Stodart, this Viennese family might well have entertained and been entertained by talented amateurs or even professional pianists, or it might have had among its own members one or more enthusiastic players. In any case, Stein's handsome giraffe would have been a step up from a square, both musically and socially.

---

*One of Mozart's most famous piano movements is the "Rondo alla Turca," as he himself titled it, the last movement of the Sonata in A major, K. 331 (1778). Cymbal clashes, triangle ringing, and drum beats, all derived from European perceptions of Turkish band music, are imitated in many piano pieces of this period, and the Janissary music stop on pianos provided the effects in a more realistic way. One also finds Janissary music in orchestral works and operas (e.g., Haydn's *Military* Symphony and Mozart's *The Abduction from the Seraglio*).

The faults in the large cabinet grands were clear, and several English makers set out to make smaller upright pianos, comparable in size and sound to squares rather than to grands and attractive to buyers of much more modest means. Robert Wornum was one of the most successful designers and manufacturers in this en-

FIG. 4.8. *Upright piano, Robert Wornum, London, c. 1814.*   Serial no. 122. *Inscription:* "Robert Wornum (late Wilkinson & Wornum)." *Action:* Upright sticker action with escapement, dampers above hammers; leather-covered hammers. *Stops:* 2 pedals: una corda, dampers. *Range:* FF–c⁴. *Stringing:* Triple-strung plain iron; straight vertical stringing; FF 120.2 cm, c² 29 cm, c⁴ 7.6 cm. *Framing:* Wood. *Case:* Silked front with gold ornament; 148 cm high, 106.5 cm wide. *Location:* Smithsonian Institution, Washington, D.C. Catalog no. 317,023.

deavor, and his little "cottage pianos," of which the upright pictured in Figure 4.8 is a forerunner, were famous for a long time. Our instrument, from about 1814, must be one of Wornum's earlier efforts in miniaturization.

Wornum has figured out how to avoid Stodart's clumsy arrangement of the action, with the keys passing under the pin block to activate hammers striking from the rear. Here the action is in front of the strings. To avoid the great height of the cabinet pianos, Wornum carried his case and stringing to the floor, and the hammers strike the strings quite near the top, where the tuning pins are. The entire arrangement of the stringing has thus simply been reversed from Stodart's design. The picture of the action, Figure 4.9, shows that his upright mechanism has its clumsy aspects, especially with the long "sticker" that moves the hammer. It is not a subtle action, but then, no upright action has ever been really subtle.

It is interesting how compact this piano is, coming as it does near the beginning of a long series of efforts to make a good, small upright that would be serviceable in small homes, would take up very little space, and would allow decent music-making. Wornum had experimented very effectively in the three years since he took out his first patent for such an instrument. The strings are hung vertically, and the height of the case, minus the necessary width of the pin block at the top and the string-plate and framing at the bottom, determines the speaking length of the lowest strings. They are not long, only about three-fourths the length of the bottom string on the same pitch in the Stein giraffe. Little comparison can be made between the tone qualities of the two. One must wonder why Wornum did not string the instrument diagonally, as he did in earlier smaller uprights in accordance with his patent of 1811.[13] Such a thought had already occurred to Thomas Loud of London. In 1802, Loud, thinking of an instrument like this one, had suggested that one could build an upright only five feet high by extending the case and strings to the floor and by "fixing the bass strings from the *left*-hand upper corner to near the *right*-hand lower corner, and the rest of the strings in a parallel direction."[14] This, he pointed out, permits a string length of five feet, two inches in a case only five feet high, which is more than a fourth again the length of the lowest string on Wornum's instrument in a case

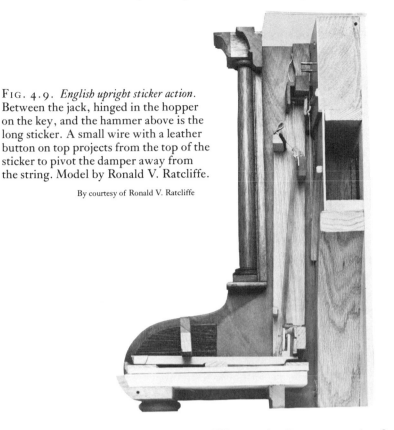

FIG. 4.9. *English upright sticker action.*
Between the jack, hinged in the hopper
on the key, and the hammer above is the
long sticker. A small wire with a leather
button on top projects from the top of the
sticker to pivot the damper away from
the string. Model by Ronald V. Ratcliffe.

By courtesy of Ronald V. Ratcliffe

less than two inches higher than Wornum's. It was not the first
thought of diagonal or oblique stringing. Back in the 1740's,
Friederici of Gera, making pyramid-shaped uprights, had adjusted to the symmetry of the high case by hanging his strings obliquely to follow the line of the left side of the case.[15] But Loud
probably knew nothing of Friederici, nor is it certain that he ever
made an instrument to his own specifications.

The problem to which Loud pointed with his scheme of diagonal stringing was then, and continues to be today, the major
technological problem with the small upright, along with the
problem of the action. The piano's tone, as we saw in Chapter
One, depends significantly on the size of the soundboard and on
the length of the lower strings. The longer and less stiff the strings
are, the more upper partials can be generated, thus enhancing the
richness of tone. A small upright like Wornum's permits only rela-

tively short bass strings, a necessary compromise between the acoustic laws of musical tone and the economic laws governing a small instrument that will overwhelm neither a modest parlor nor a modest purse.

Small squares and uprights allowed a significant spread of musical culture, in Europe and America, however minimal in quality and depth it may have been. The part played by grands and large uprights was confined to large homes, the studios of pianists and teachers, and the concert rooms where the virtuosos played. The work of Wornum and others made the piano the nineteenth-century equivalent to the twentieth century's radio and record player in providing access to musical experience for large numbers of people. And the nineteenth century was a time in which large numbers of people, even of very meager means, aspired to the culture, musical and other, that had previously been the prerogative of the rich, the noble, and the religious. One may justly criticize the workmanship of many of the cheap little pianos that were all some people could afford (Wornum's workmanship, however, was impeccable), but one may not criticize the motives of those who bought them.

The first maker who sought to fill this need was apparently our previous acquaintance William Southwell, who in 1798 turned a square on its side, adjusted the keyboard and action accordingly, and set the whole on the stand. Southwell would return to the idea later, always in search of a viable small vertical design, but it was a dead end. Two men who doubtless knew nothing of each other or of Southwell made small uprights simultaneously in 1800: Matthias Müller in Vienna and John Isaac Hawkins in Philadelphia. Müller made a neat little upright, which he named, with an untranslatable clod of pretentious Greek, the Ditanaklassis. It was slightly over five feet high, with an action modeled on the Viennese action. Hawkins was not an instrument maker but an engineer who knew something about the properties of metals. An ingenious fellow, who later invented the mechanical pencil, he was not hampered by prior training in a piano shop or its attendant conservatism. His instrument, even smaller than Müller's or Wornum's, 54 inches, was portable, with carrying handles on the sides and a keyboard that folded up into the case. Hawkins was well ahead of his time in building metal supports into his piano, bars down the back behind the soundboard and a metal cover on the pin block. He also apparently experimented with using metal springs for the bass notes, an idea that seems not to have worked. Neither of the two surviving Hawkins pianos, one in possession of the Broadwood company in London and the other in the Smithsonian Institution in Washington (catalog no. 313,619), has springs in the bass. Müller and Hawkins seem to have exerted influence on no one. Thomas Jefferson had one of Hawkins's Portable Grand Pianofortes, as he called them—makers of small pianos have often been unable to resist giving them inflated names—but Jefferson wrote to the inventor that he could not keep the thing in tune. Hawkins replied that he knew exactly what was wrong and would be glad to fix it for $40. Jefferson shipped the instrument to Philadelphia, but there is no indication that he ever got it, or any substitute, or his money back.[16]

Nearly simultaneously with Wornum's patent of 1811 for a small upright design were two others in the same year. William Southwell tried his "square-on-its-side" gambit once more. This time he angled his instrument back from the keyboard at about 60 degrees and called his invention, somewhat inelegantly, the "piano sloping backwards." In autumn 1811, Frederick William Collard of London also set a square on its side, much as Southwell had done in 1798. The action had the peculiarity that, though the hammers struck the strings from the front, the dampers operated through a slot in the soundboard from the rear. That must have been a nice tangle for a tuner to remove from the case![17] Both of these efforts stemmed from the desire to aid the self-accompanied singer. Playing a cabinet grand, often with a silked front like that on the Stodart, or even an upright like Wornum's, drawing-room singers complained that they had to sing right into the piano, rudely turning their backs on the rest of the room and having their voices swallowed up by the instrument. Southwell's pianos were small enough that the singer's face could be seen over the top, unless the instrument was turned to the wall.

The three types of pianos for the home that we have seen continued in use for some decades yet. The cabinet grands and giraffes saw little change as the years passed, and they departed earliest from the scene. Some improvements and extensions were made in squares; the major ones will be discussed in later chapters. The small uprights would ultimately carry the field. That outcome no one, looking at Wornum's little instrument and at the other experiments contemporary with it, could have predicted. Even by 1815, the day of the piano as big business was still to come, though it no doubt seemed big enough to those who had been trained in craft shops like Stein's or even Erard's.

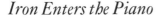

Iron Enters the Piano

The decade of the 1820's saw perhaps the most astonishing outburst of innovation in the history of the piano. In 1820, James Thom and William Allen patented in England a compensation frame for grands that used metal tubes. In 1821, the Broadwood company began putting iron string-plates into squares. In the same year, Sébastien Erard patented his repetition action, anticipating the action of the modern grand. In 1824, Erard made a seven-octave grand that made some public appearances (Otto Clemen alleged that Streicher had made one in 1816).[1] In 1825, Alpheus Babcock patented the full metal frame for squares. In 1826, Henri Pape patented the use of felt for hammer covering, and in the same year he proposed in a French patent to use annealed steel for strings. In that year also, Robert Wornum improved his earlier small upright, the cottage piano. In 1827, James Stewart, formerly of Boston and then working for Clementi and Company in London, patented a method of passing strings around the hitch-pin and back to the adjacent tuning pin, rather than looping each string separately on the hitch-pin. In the same year, the firm of Blanchet et Roller of Paris exhibited a small upright with strings hung obliquely rather than vertically, and Broadwood in London patented a frame for grands with four iron tension bars screwed into the pin block at one end and into a metal string-plate at the other. In 1828, Pape introduced cross-stringing into the upright and produced his first tiny "piano-console" upright, whose case extended only a few inches above the keyboard.

This is a remarkable list of achievements, and at that, it leaves out a goodly number of lesser and finally unsuccessful efforts. But impressive as it is, it does not warrant the remark that "by the time of the romantic upheaval, starting around 1830 in Paris, the piano—with a few later modifications such as Steinway's cross-stringing innovation in the 1850's—was substantially the instrument we know today."[2] This misstatement rests on the false assumption that there is no difference between innovation and adoption, that as soon as something new is done by someone, it is presumably done by everyone. To take only the most significant of the innovations listed above, by 1830 no one but Erard was using the repetition action, Pape's felt hammers were not as good as leather ones and had been adopted by only a few makers, Babcock's frame had not been used by any other maker, and no one had imitated Pape's cross-stringing. We will look at several pianos of the 1830's and 1840's in the next two chapters, and their distance from "the instrument we know today" will be manifest.

In this chapter I will discuss one type of innovation and exemplify it from two of the events listed in the first paragraph. The innovation was the introduction of iron into the piano as a major component (it had of course already entered the instrument in the form of the little gap-stretcher braces). The events are the inventions of the Thom and Allen compensation frame of 1820 and the Babcock square frame of 1825. In both cases, the developments of the 1820's are preserved to us in pianos from the 1830's.

We saw in Chapter Three some of the problems that were posed by the extension of the grand's range, especially noticeable in the 1811 Broadwood grand. The combined tension on the strings in that instrument overcame the resisting power of the framing, causing an alarming-looking warp in the case. The problem had troubled makers for some time, for we can see in a number of pianos from the last decades of the eighteenth century and the first of the nineteenth the results of this imbalance of forces. Musicians wanted a wide range of notes, composers were writing for the wide range, builders wanted to meet the desires. But the widening range put strains on the framing that could not easily be met. Broadwood attempted as early as 1808 to use iron tension bars in grands, running them from the string-plate to the pin block as accessories to the familiar iron arched gap-stretchers. But Broadwood could not figure out a satisfactory way to attach the bars, and they were abandoned.

James Thom and William Allen were employees of William Stodart in London when they took out the patent on the frame used in the instrument pictured in Figure 5.1. Stodart promptly bought the rights to the patent from them, and it is to be found only in pianos from his shop. (Erard patented a copy of the frame in France in 1822, but no Erards with it seem to have survived.) Our Stodart has the CC–f^4 that became more and more common after about 1816, a range that was a major reason why something had to be done to improve the framing. This piano exemplifies the first nearly successful solution to the problem, though it was built about a decade after the actual solution.

It was an idea for using metal in the frame, though interestingly enough, Thom and Allen used metal not to take up the string tension, but to compensate for the tendency of strings to go out of tune by reason of atmospheric changes. The tuning of strings is affected by changes in the humidity rather than by temperature changes. Increased humidity causes the wooden parts around the strings, the framing, the pin block, and the soundboard to swell. The swelling of the soundboard increases its upward pressure on the bridge, thus stretching the strings tighter and making them go sharp. Dryness, on the other hand, causes a soundboard to contract, lessening the upward pressure against the bridge and slackening the tension on the strings, thus sending the pitch flat.

The Thom and Allen compensation frame consisted of nine metal tubes placed lengthwise above the strings, bolted by crosswise plates into the pin block at the front and the string-plate at the back, and held in place by cross strips of wood at intervals down their lengths.* The tubes were of the same metal as the strings below them, brass in the bass and iron in the treble. The purpose of the matching metals was that the tubes were supposed to expand and contract at the same rates as the strings, which would keep the tension the same at all times, thus "compensating" for temperature changes. This principle shows, by the way, that Thom and Allen were actually on the wrong track in supposing that what caused strings to go out of tune was temperature change, not humidity. The expansion and contraction was based on the

---

*Rosamond Harding's reproduction of the patent drawing (*The Piano-Forte*, p. 207) shows 13 tubes, whereas Alfred Dolge (*Pianos and Their Makers*, p. 70) shows the nine that occur in our example. Perhaps 10 years or so of experience with the frame showed that more than nine tubes were not necessary.

FIG. 5.1. *Grand piano, William Stodart & Son, London, c. 1830.* Serial no. 9024. *Action:* English grand action, under-dampers; leather-covered hammers. *Stops:* 2 pedals: una corda, dampers to c♯³. *Range:* CC–f⁴. *Stringing:* CC–EE double-strung plain brass, FF–BB triple-strung plain brass, C–f⁴ triple-strung iron; straight-strung; CC 164.4 cm; c² 29.3 cm, f⁴ 5.5 cm. *Framing:* Thom and Allen compensation frame. *Case:* Mahogany veneered with string-of-pearl stringing, open at bottom; 220.5 cm long, 123 cm wide. *Location:* Kunsthistorisches Museum, Vienna. Catalog no. 647.

observation that large metal objects expand with heat and contract with cold. But it seems that strings do not react noticeably to temperature change alone. Nevertheless, the Thom and Allen frame worked. The string-plate in the Stodart is not bolted to the case and to the underframing, but sits loosely on the soundboard, and the strain of the strings is taken up entirely by the metal tubes and the wooden plates at either end of them. The tubes are acting, therefore, not merely as a compensation against the strings' going out of tune, but also as a tension frame. It would not have worked, I suspect, if Thom and Allen had bolted the string-plate down, but with it unattached, the swelling and contracting of the sound-board and bridge would not affect the bearing of the strings on the bridge.

The breakthrough had been made. A virtual flood of other ways to put metal framing pieces, mostly of iron, into the piano followed in England, France, and America in the next years. Broad-wood claimed to have introduced metal string-plates into squares in 1821 and tension bars, solid iron bars unlike the compensation tubes, into grands in 1822. The Erard firm in Paris and London copied the Thom and Allen frame for grands in 1822; Pleyel in Paris followed in 1825. Jonas Chickering in Boston was already using metal string-plates in squares in 1823 or 1824, and a square by Clementi and Company of London, probably from 1825–30, in the Eddy Collection, Cambridge, Massachusetts, has a cast-iron string-plate.

Piano makers were then, as they have always been, conservative. What worked for the old man in his little two-apprentice shop was good enough for the old man's son and grandson, even when the shop employed 30 workers. Many piano makers were recruited from the ranks of cabinetmakers, John Broadwood, Conrad Graf, and Jonas Chickering being but three of the most famous. Cabinetmakers live and die by wood, and they resisted the introduction of iron. It may have been the great new fact of their time, as they watched the railroad tracks and steam locomotives go through town, saw the factories go up with cast-iron pillars supporting their upper stories, listened to their wives exclaim over the new, cheap fabrics woven with iron-framed automatic looms. But to a worker wedded lifelong to wood, iron is just wrong in a musical instrument. Wood is alive, has, one might say, "soul," but iron is dead and cold. The predictions were dire: put iron in the piano, and the tone would go all hard and metallic.

For all that, there were some enthusiastic reports. An unnamed writer in an unnamed French paper quoted in the *Franklin Journal* in 1827 was positive but not very specific:

Here, in Paris, we have lately got pianos, the frame-work of which is formed of cast iron. These instruments have been brought to such perfection, by MM. Pleyel and Company, that not only do they rival, but, in many particulars, surpass the best English instruments. The solidity of the frame-work is so great, that they seldom get out of tune, and the soundboard, relieved from those enormous pieces of wood with which it was formerly cumbered, in order to resist the strain, possesses much more elasticity, and seconds the vibration of the strings, much better. The tone of these instruments is wonderful, both in power and mellowness; and the mechanism is so perfect, that it admits of the most delicate, as well as of the strongest touch.[3]

The Pleyel company used tension bars and a cast-iron string-plate. The account of the soundboard's improved elasticity is somewhat unclear. Whether by "those enormous pieces of wood" the author meant the rather massive wooden string-plates that had come to be used, or whether he was speaking of the underbracing, is not certain. Some tension on the sides of the soundboard is necessary for its elasticity, though it does not have to be so much as to give the soundboard the crown we discussed in Chapter One. At any rate, this author believed that the tone in a metal-framed piano was superior. A year later, the editor of the *Franklin Journal* admitted that his own opinion of iron in the piano had been changed by seeing an Erard with the tension bars: the bars did not injure the tone as he had thought they would.[4]

A breakthrough—but not everyone instantly jumped to mimic. Even Stodart built grands after 1820 without the compensation frame; the Victoria and Albert Museum in London has one from about 1825 (catalog no. W.5-1952) with gap-stretchers but no metal tubes. The French followed suit after their fashion, but by no means all the English did. And the Germans and Austrians on the whole did not; they had for some time been building grands in what has been called the Empire style, which called for curves and rounded shapes. The photograph of the André Stein grand in Figure 5.2 shows that style.

Notice the rounded cheek of this piano. That thick slab of wood forms a kind of S-curve with the curve of the bent side, and thus the rounded corner avoids a weak joint just at the corner where grands tended to warp. The strength of case at that crucial place of intersecting stresses did for the German and Austrian pianos in this style what metal bracing did for the English and French ones. The German and Austrian cases, moreover, were deeper and

FIG. 5.2. *Grand piano, André Stein, Vienna, c. 1825.* The "Empire" style of case is constructed so that the curved cheek is strong enough to withstand the string tension without metal framing. Collection of the Smithsonian Institution, Washington, D.C. Catalog no. 316,467.

more massive, and had carefully contrived wooden bracing underneath the soundboard. The English and French cases were slimmer and more graceful (and often, as we saw in Fig. 3.5, p. 88, above, had rather haphazard bracing), and what they gave up in tension-bearing strength they had to give back with metal in the frame. The earliest German grand I have found with metal bracing is one made in about 1830 by Heinrich Kisting in Berlin, specifically for export to the United States (Smithsonian Institution catalog no. 94,888). It has three iron tension bars screwed to the pin block and the string-plate, one bar in the high treble, one in the middle, and one in the bass. The bracing may have been introduced to meet the rigors of the American climate, for another Kisting of about the same date, owned in Berlin for many years and now in the collection of the Schubert Club, Saint Paul, Minnesota, does not have the iron bars. Earlier German grands sometimes had a different kind of gap-stretcher from the arched ones in English grands, small iron rods under the strings between the pin block and the belly rail. An Anton Walter grand in the Kunsthistorisches Museum in Vienna, made about 1785 (inventory no. 454), is the earliest example I know of. But for a long time these pianos had only one such brace, where the English pianos usually had four or five of their characteristic, arched braces.

One further critical step in the introduction of iron into the piano was made during the 1820's, and it occurred in the United States. It is exemplified in the lovely Babcock square shown in Figure 5.3. This is the first American-made piano to enter centrally into the story. As I have noted, a German immigrant named Johann Behrendt apparently made the first piano on the North American continent in Philadelphia in 1775. The place is consistent with Philadelphia's preeminence in the crafts before the American Revolution.[5] The piano was present in North America before 1775, of course; its earliest public appearance seems to have been on March 21, 1771, when David Propert played the "fortepiano" in a Boston concert.[6] Until about 1790, the growth of local piano manufacturing was slow, and then it began to pick up in Philadelphia, New York, and, perhaps a little later, Boston. In Philadelphia and New York, many of the early makers' names were German, whereas English names predominated in Boston. The Germans frequently put Viennese actions in their pianos, whereas the English more generally used the familiar grasshopper action that we saw in the Astor square (Fig. 4.2). The trade in Boston apparently began with Benjamin Crehore, who was making instruments in nearby Milton by about 1790, though when he began to make pianos is uncertain. Crehore had three apprentices who have a place in the story: John Osborn and the Babcock brothers, Lewis and Alpheus. Osborn later trained Jonas Chickering, which would be enough to assure his right to be remembered. Alpheus Babcock made his own remarkable contribution.

Babcock had diverse fortunes as a businessman and maker of

FIG. 5.3. *Square piano, Alpheus Babcock, Philadelphia, 1833–37.* Serial no. 1517. *Inscription:* "Made by A. Babcock at / William Swift's / Piano Forte Manufactory / Philadelphia." *Action:* Babcock patent action, over-dampers; felt-covered hammers (not original). *Stops:* 2 pedals: buff, dampers. *Range:* FF–f⁴. *Stringing:* Double-strung; FF–Bb wound, B–f⁴ plain; FF 147.6 cm, c² 28 cm, f⁴ 7.2 cm. Tuning pins at back of case. *Framing:* Cast-iron tubular rim with string plate, held down with 4 iron straps bolted into wood underframing. *Case:* Crotch mahogany veneered; 177 cm wide, 73.1 cm deep. *Location:* Smithsonian Institution, Washington, D.C. Catalog no. 315,690.

FIG. 5.4. *Plan view of Babcock square.* The tubular iron rim and string plate take up the string tension.

pianos. The instrument pictured in Figure 5.3 represents his product toward the end of his career. He and his brother Lewis, having learned the craft with Crehore, began business together in Boston in 1810, and Alpheus remained there until 1829. Various partnerships were formed and dissolved along the way, and after Lewis's death in 1814,[7] Alpheus built pianos for others, especially for a whole series of Mackays, one of whom, John Mackay, will turn up later as Jonas Chickering's partner. In 1829, Babcock moved to Philadelphia, where he joined John G. Klemm; and later, from 1832 to 1837, he was foreman in the establishment of William Swift. Swift evidently appreciated Babcock's good reputation, allowing him to label pianos in his own name. Babcock was a very fine workman indeed. A good number of his instruments survive, and all of those that I have seen are impressive testimony to his craft.

Babcock's name would endure in the history of the piano if he had made only one instrument. For it was he who demonstrated the feasibility of a one-piece metal frame. He took out the patent in Boston on Dec. 17, 1825, and the instrument pictured, made in Philadelphia after 1832, is the only known exemplar of the frame. The plan view (Fig. 5.4) shows the disposition of the frame. Babcock certainly made pianos after 1825 without the metal frame. Unhappily, we know very little specific about the technology that went into this innovation. His own patent text is not very helpful, and indeed, is much more general than some later descriptions of it indicate: "My invention and improvement consists in manufacturing the frame, to which the strings of the piano forte are attached, of cast iron, wrought-iron, brass composition metal, or some other metal, or compound of metals, suitable to this purpose."[8]

It has always been said that Babcock's frame was cast iron. Though he mentions cast iron first in the patent, he is evidently willing to use any "suitable" metal, though he does not specify what makes a metal suitable. In fact, the Babcock frame shown in Figure 5.4 is somewhat different from the one he patented.

Figure 5.5 shows Babcock's patent drawing.* In it, the outside

*The U.S. Patent Office and its contents were destroyed by fire on Dec. 15, 1836. The patents recorded there had to be reconstructed, new drawings made, and new documents of specification submitted by the patentees. It is that restored patent document of Babcock's metal frame that we have.

ring of the frame has the form of a flange, rectangular in cross-section. If the frame was to be of cast iron, the outer ring, string-plate, and what looks like an iron nut bridge (a bridge next to the tuning pins) would presumably be cast in one piece. But the outer ring of the frame in the piano shown in Figure 5.4 is a cast-iron tube, open at the bottom, and there is no metal nut bridge. The string-plate in Figure 5.4 is also cast iron in a single piece with the tubular frame. The frame was doubtless cast upside down in one piece in sand, the usual molding material. Some sort of insert in

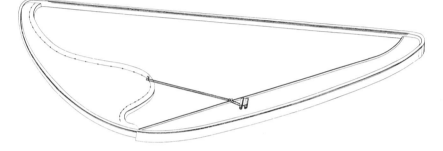

FIG. 5.5. *Patent drawing of Alpheus Babcock's metal frame.* Designed for a square piano, the frame was patented by Babcock on Dec. 17, 1825.

the ring portion must have been used to bring about the open tubular form. The frame is attached by wrought iron straps to wooden blocks underneath the soundboard. Other Babcock pianos with metal frames might show both different materials and different forms, but if any are to be found, I do not know where they are.

Babcock and three other makers exhibited their products at the Franklin Institute exhibition in Philadelphia in 1827. Thomas Loud took a medal for an "organized piano," a combination piano and organ, and Charles Pommer of Philadelphia won a special prize for two cabinet pianos, one with mother-of-pearl keys. Babcock's iron-framed square got an "honorary mention," as did Joseph J. Mickley's example of a "plain and cheap instrument." The fact that the official report of the exhibit mentioned Mickley's name first may mean, in fact, that Babcock was last. The *Franklin Journal*, which published the report, said of Babcock's "honorary mention": "Also, a horizontal piano by Mr. A. Babcock, Boston, of an improved construction; the frame which supports the wires being of iron, and sufficiently strong to sustain their enormous tension."[9]

It is curious that Daniel Spillane, the historian most clearly responsible for establishing the claim for Babcock's priority in the metal frame, falsified this report. He quoted from "records" of the Franklin Institute of Philadelphia about pianos exhibited there in October 1827: "Especially mention is made of a horizontal piano by A. Babcock of Boston, of an *improved construction*, the frame which supports the strings being of *solid cast-iron*, and strong enough to resist their enormous tension" (italics Spillane's).[10] The differences between Spillane's quotation and the report itself show that Spillane copied the quotation inaccurately and tendentiously. By inserting "Especially mention is made," he implied a higher reward than Babcock actually received. The italicized phrase "*solid cast-iron*" bespeaks his wish to find unimpeachable early evidence that Babcock had originated the one-piece, cast-iron frame.*

We do not know whether Babcock himself did the foundry work for the frame. Nor do we know what led him to use metal. No special excellence of New England or American iron technology seems to be at issue; indeed, the meager testimony I have been able to find suggests that American foundry technology was then somewhat backward as compared with English methods. Babcock certainly did not know of the English and French experiments with metal string-plates and tension bars, such as the Thom and Allen frame of 1820. In a controversy carried on in the Philadelphia *Daily Chronicle* in 1833, between Thomas Loud and Babcock,[11] Babcock admitted ignorance of any similarity between his metal frame and the ones of European makers mentioned by Loud, but showed that he knew John Isaac Hawkins's experimental use of metal in uprights, which he deemed "a complete failure." Neither Loud nor Babcock noted that Chickering in Boston was using iron string-plates in squares as early as 1823 or 1824, though it would be surprising if Babcock, who was working in

---

*Spillane was irked by the claims of Conrad Meyer, a Philadelphian, to the invention of the one-piece cast-iron frame. Meyer claimed that he had patented a frame in 1832, which he had not, and he exhibited what he asserted was the original iron-framed piano, a square that he had made in 1833, at the 1876 Centennial Exhibition in Philadelphia. For a time, Meyer's claims were accepted by many writers, but after Spillane took up the cudgels for Babcock's priority, Meyer's name dropped from view.

Boston at that time, had not known of Chickering's experiments and been influenced by them. Babcock was surely troubled, as other makers were, by the tendency of pianos to warp under the strain of the strings.

The function of resistance was Spillane's major talking point in his arguments on behalf of Babcock. He took Alfred J. Hipkins, the authority on instruments, severely to task for thinking that Babcock's frame was a device for compensation and was a failure.[12] Spillane said that, having procured a copy of Babcock's patent drawing, he was in a position to deny categorically that it was a compensation frame. "It contains no suggestion of compensating rods, tubes, or other contrivances . . . arranged so as to 'give and take' with the process of tuning and atmospheric changes."[13] Spillane looked at the drawing, but perhaps Hipkins had read the language of the patent specifications. The second paragraph reads as follows:

The advantages resulting from said invention and improvement are as follows, to wit,—The frame being made of iron or other metal, is stronger and more durable than a wooden frame or case, it is not liable to be affected by the dampness of the atmosphere which, in common Piano Fortes, by causing the wood to swell, affects the strings, likewise Piano Fortes constructed on this principle will not be put out of tune by any alteration in the temperature of the air, as is the case with those which are constructed according to the common method; as the strings and the frame being alike made of metal will expand or contract equally, and simultaneously, and such expansion and contraction will not therefore, affect the tone or tension of the strings of the instrument; and they are therefore less liable to get out of tune than in Piano Fortes of the common construction.[14]

That is a fascinating paragraph. Keith Grafing, from whom I quote this material, is most impressed with the fact that Babcock refers first to resistance to tension and second to compensation, "inasmuch as the former is adjudged the more important of the two in the development of the metal frame."[15] Spillane denied that Babcock had any interest in compensation at all. But the paragraph quoted above is quite clear to the contrary: though Babcock mentions resistance, he spends most of his space and energy on compensation in arguing the advantages of his invention. Moreover, he adds to the dubious point that temperature changes cause strings to go out of tune, thus calling for equal expansion and contraction of frame and strings, the correct perception that humidity changes affecting wooden parts cause the strings to go out of tune. Indeed, Babcock is much more detailed in noting the effect of temperature and the necessity of compensating for it than in referring to humidity as the culprit. The paragraph in the patent specifications suggests that Babcock's prime motivation was to compensate for temperature changes, his second to compensate for humidity changes, and his third to provide resistance. But anyone could see, as Spillane did, that the frame as drawn would not in fact compensate for temperature changes, and Hipkins was doubtless right in thinking that, for compensation purposes, Babcock's frame was a failure. The writer in the *Franklin Journal* correctly saw in 1827 that its main usefulness was in resisting tension.

Piano strings at that time were made of wrought iron, which is malleable and ductile, and possesses great tensile strength (i.e., resistance to forces tending to pull material apart). Most of the iron gap-stretchers and, when the time came, tension bars in English pianos were of wrought iron. It was cheap and easily worked, and it was a familiar product. Cast iron, which has a relatively high carbon content, has some characteristics opposite to wrought iron. For a start, it is brittle, and once cast into shape it can be changed only by punching holes in it, filing it down, or melting it and starting over. Moreover, it is relatively low in tensile strength but is very high in compressive strength (i.e. resistance to forces pushing in on the material). The frame of the piano wants compressive strength against the enormous inward pressure of the strings. Though wrought iron was used successfully for framing and bracing, having sufficient compressive strength, cast iron is superior to it in that regard, and almost all modern frames are of cast iron. Did Babcock know these characteristics of cast iron? We do not know. But whether or not his mentioning it first among the suitable metals for his frame meant that he knew its properties to be best fitted for the purpose, he was right to name it first.

Not everyone thought so. Babcock took out an advertisement in the Philadelphia *Daily Chronicle* for July 26, 1833, to object to Thomas Loud's advertised offer to make iron-framed pianos to order. Babcock sternly noted that he held the patent. Loud replied three days later, arguing that pianos with iron frames had been made in England and France for a long time, and Babcock had no claims to originality. But, Loud went on, he himself made the frames only on special order, since he thought the iron frame "*a decided injury to tone*" (italics Loud's).* A further exchange of letters in the paper ended in Loud's disavowing any wish to infringe on Babcock's rights. Now another Philadelphia maker, Emilius N. Scherr, chimed in, first accusing Loud of making quite inconclusive claims about the priority of the iron frame, and then turning on Babcock, to ask just what he meant by the superiority of tone that he claimed for the iron frame, and what he saw as the "principles of natural philosophy which operate in the case." Scherr himself thought the iron frame was not a good idea.[16] Interestingly, Loud changed his mind. In July 1835, he patented a metal compensation frame with tubes, like that of Thom and Allen in London. A piano like the one pictured in Figures 5.3 and 5.4 must be taken as the occasion for all of this argument, for Babcock's letters in the controversy carried the address of William Swift's Piano Forte Manufactory.

Alpheus Babcock worked on more aspects of the piano than the frame. He was an exemplar of stubborn Yankee ingenuity—he had to be, to survive through many partnerships and subordinate positions with other makers. In addition to the 1825 patent for the frame, he patented a scheme of stringing that he called cross-stringing in 1830, in which he rang a change on Stewart's idea of running the string around the hitch-pin instead of looping each one individually. Babcock crossed the two strings of a double-strung note between the bridge pins and the hitch-pins, thus producing a loop around the latter.† In 1833, he patented a new action, used in our example, and a new method of hammer covering. The hammers of our piano are covered with felt, which almost

---

*It is interesting that the report on Babcock's iron-framed piano exhibited at the Franklin Institute in 1827 refers to its tone, though not with excessive enthusiasm: "The tone of this piano is not powerful or brilliant, but remarkable for its uniformity from the lowest to the highest note" (*Franklin Journal*, O.S. 4: 406; 1827). The Thomas Loud of this controversy was Thomas Loud Jr., who began to make pianos in Philadelphia in 1816. His father, Thomas Loud Sr., who came to New York from London to make pianos after 1816, first suggested oblique stringing in uprights.

† The fact that Babcock used this term for his arrangement has misled some historians to suppose that he meant what was later called cross-stringing (or over-stringing), i.e., running the long bass strings at an angle over the shorter upper strings to a separate bridge. Grafing ("Alpheus Babcock: Pianoforte Maker," pp. 50–58) has adequately laid this myth to rest.

certainly means that they are not original. Babcock's patent called for tightly rolled cylinders of cloth, felt, or leather, set into a notch in the hammer head and covered on top with strips of leather. One is reminded of Cristofori's parchment-cylinder hammer head tipped with leather, but Babcock could not have known of that predecessor. The cloth roll could be made of uniform hardness and would not, so Babcock claimed, harden with repeated use, as leather does. It has occasionally been claimed that Babcock originated felt coverings for hammers,[17] but this patent followed Henri Pape's French one by several years and did not involve a felt covering for the hammer.

It could almost have been predicted that Babcock would design his own action; many other makers of his time did so. His is an ingenious arrangement in which the jack on the key engages the shoulder of a corresponding jack that is suspended from a pivot on the hammer shank. The blow of the key-jack on the suspended jack sends both hammer and jack flying upward, but a spring attached from the hammer rail to the suspended jack holds it forward, serving as a check on the hammer to keep it from bouncing back to the string. (Grafing has a nice drawing of the action.)[18] No one but Babcock used this action, which is to be found in our example, but that was typical. No one wished to pay royalties to a patent holder, and there was always the old grasshopper action, which builders could use with impunity.

Perhaps the best measure of Babcock's quality as a builder is that his pianos are still to be found. Grafing, in doing the research for his dissertation, found 13, and notes that they do not constitute the entire corpus of extant Babcocks.[19] I myself have seen five others, four of them in or near Boston. It is not possible to be sure of his total output, because such serial or inventory numbers as he used are sporadic and eccentric. Another Babcock in the Smithsonian Institution (catalog no. 291,106) carries the same serial number as our example, 1517. But Babcock was a keen, conscientious builder, thoughtful and original. Too much may have been claimed for him by enthusiasts like Spillane, but he deserves a place of high honor in the annals of piano technology.

In 1837, Babcock severed his connection with William Swift and went back to Boston, where he worked for Chickering until his death on April 3, 1842. It seems hardly coincidental that in

1837 Chickering attempted to patent a full iron frame for squares, which was refused on a technicality. The patent was finally granted in 1840, the same year in which Chickering began to put iron frames in grands. A patent for the grand frame was granted Chickering in 1843, after Babcock's death. I have no proof that Babcock galvanized Jonas Chickering into developing the metal frame, but the conjunction of his employment with Chickering and that company's sudden development of patents, after some 14 years of piano making in Boston, seems more than fortuitous. Jonas Chickering could scarcely have been ignorant of Babcock's 1825 patent, taken out in Boston. Babcock, after all, had worked for that very John Mackay who was Jonas Chickering's partner from 1830 until Mackay's disappearance at sea in 1841. In fact, Mackay signed Babcock's patent specification of 1825 as witness. He may have helped Babcock to obtain his position at Chickering in 1837. At the least, it is worth notice that, before Babcock came into the company, Chickering used only iron string-plates, and when Babcock joined him, Chickering started working on full iron frames.

The conservatism of the piano industry is shown by the reluctance of other makers to follow Babcock's lead. This reluctance must have involved more than the fact that he held a patent. Any shrewd tinkerer could figure out ways of making a frame different enough from the one patented to avoid paying royalties. It is clear that Thomas Loud and Emilius Scherr represented the real opinion of most piano makers: the iron frame was a poor idea because it would injure the tone. The argument had been made for a long time that metal in the frame would render the sound metallic. Whatever else the opinion demonstrates, it shows that piano makers were technologists and artisans and not acoustical scientists. They knew what worked and what did not out of long trial and error, but they did not have what Scherr asked Babcock for—and what Babcock probably could not have told him—the "principles of natural philosophy [meaning science] which operate in the case."

That Jonas Chickering, the doyen of American piano makers for so long, waited 12 years after Babcock's patent, taken out in the same city where Chickering worked, to come around to using an iron frame is perhaps the best index of caution in the trade. Chickering was no timid soul. Only a couple of years after Broadwood began to use iron string-plates in squares, Chickering was doing so. A square in the Smithsonian Institution (catalog no. 315,718), made in 1823 or 1824, has one. Perhaps Chickering felt that the string-plate did enough. Or perhaps only as the ranges of pianos were extended past six octaves did he find an iron frame necessary. It is also possible that for the time being metal frames, whether wrought iron or cast iron, were more expensive than wooden ones, and only later, as iron came to be used more generally, proved to be more economical. I have not found any figures to support the theory, or to deny it.

The rejection of the iron frame was not an American peculiarity. Shortly after Babcock's patent, we find Henri Pape and the Pleyel company in Paris both taking out patents for iron frames in squares. Yet hardly anyone took them up. In the 1840's, when the square was already beginning its decline in Europe, most squares of which I have knowledge had iron string-plates, but very few had complete iron frames. The acceptance of the iron frame required a dramatic breakthrough of a magnitude equal to that entailed in the successful invention. That had still some years to wait.

The French Take the Lead

It is an index of the piano's acceptance in the homes and concert halls of the European world that the title of this chapter can imply a competitive market. Of course, the French firms, whose names and products dominate the pages of this chapter, did not produce the most instruments. The numerical lead remained in England for years yet.

Technological developments are not necessarily signs of progress in any absolute sense of the term. But the objective observer of the history of the piano must acknowledge that from 1820 or so until the 1850's the French piano artisans and designers contributed more, and more lasting, innovations to the instrument than those of other nations, save only with respect to the subject of Chapter Five, the introduction of iron. Even there, the French, if not themselves the innovators, were in the front ranks of the eager followers.

Even from the standpoint of the social history of music, this is the French epoch. The names of the great Parisian houses, Erard, Pleyel, Pape, Kriegelstein, Herz, came to have high status in homes and in concert rooms. The status was, to be sure, only partly related to technological advance; it had as much to do with the sense, in Paris and in other cities, that the culture of Europe revolved around Paris, so that anything that could claim Parisian origin could command cultural respect.* And the musical, and more especially pianistic, culture of Europe certainly did revolve

---

*It is a comment on the history of the time, and on Paris's place in it, that all five of the names of the major Parisian piano makers were originally German, and the founders of all five firms had come to Paris from Germany, Austria, or German-speaking Alsace.

around Paris. Was not the great poet of the piano, Frédéric Chopin, in residence there? Few heard him play, to be sure, because
he played seldom and usually privately—but he was in Paris. The
purveyors of the glittering tradition of the virtuoso were all
located in Paris: Sigismond Thalberg, Friedrich Kalkbrenner,
Johann Peter Pixis, Henri Herz, Franz Hünten (again a plethora
of German names). And above all, Franz Liszt, who reigned over
Paris in person as he reigned in spirit over all of Europe. Musical
culture paid obeisance in the throne room of Liszt, and Liszt presided over his domain in the *salons* of the great in Paris and in the
Salle Erard, the concert room built and managed by the house of
Erard.

The beautiful grand pictured in Figure 6.1 first belonged to
Those who defined musical culture by whatever Liszt might be
doing at any moment cared but little about the technological innovations that French makers were introducing. That makes the innovations no less significant. And because the house of Erard was
the leader of the French piano firms, in point of production, of
reputation ("ce Stradivarius du piano," as one writer put it),[1] and
of lasting innovation, it is well to begin discussing the French
epoch with an Erard.

The beautiful grand pictured in Figure 6.1 first belonged to
Moritz Schlesinger, a well-known music publisher in Paris,
whose home—and piano—were a gathering place for the musical
elite of the city during the 1840's. Chopin, though he preferred
Pleyels, consented to play Schlesinger's Erard more than once.
After the publisher's death, the Erard came into the collection of
the Stuttgart piano maker Walter Klinckerfuss, and from there
went to the Rück Collection, which is now held by the Germanisches Nationalmuseum in Nuremberg.

I am discussing this Erard out of strict chronological order. At
least two, and perhaps three, of the pianos illustrated later in this
chapter were made earlier. But this instrument, made in 1840 (the
date is stamped on the cheek), is typical of those made by the
largest of the Parisian builders during the two decades or so before
it, and it contains an innovative action that belongs here in the
story. It also has at least two other Erard innovations. In 1808,
Sébastien Erard had invented the agraffe, the metal stud at the
tuning-pin end of the strings, with holes through which the
strings pass; see Figure 1.4 above, p. 11. As I explained there, the

FIG. 6.1. *Grand piano, Erard, Paris, 1840.* Serial no. 14832. *Action:* Erard double-escapement repetition action; felt-covered hammers. *Stops:* 2 pedals: una corda, dampers to b². *Range:* CC–f⁴. *Stringing:* CC–EE double-strung wound, FF–C♯ triple-strung wound, D–f⁴ triple-strung plain; straight-strung; CC 152 cm, c² 29 cm, f⁴ 5 cm. *Framing:* Cast-iron tension bars between pin block and wooden string-plate. *Case:* Mahogany veneered; 203 cm long, 121 cm wide. *Location:* Rück Collection, Germanisches Nationalmuseum, Nuremberg. Inventory no. MIR 1125.

agraffe exactly and efficiently forms one end of the speaking length of the string and also causes the string to bear upward against it, preventing the possibility of its being knocked from its seating and out of tune by an especially hard blow of the hammer. In 1838, Pierre Erard, Sébastien's nephew, patented the harmonic bar, a larger metal bar with holes that did for the treble strings what the agraffes did for the lower ones. This harmonic bar was further improved by Antoine Bord of Paris, who in 1843 patented the capo tasto bar, a more easily manufactured equivalent of the harmonic bar.

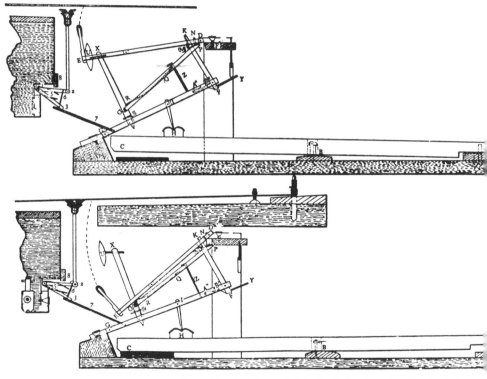

By permission of Gresham Books Ltd., The Gresham Press, Old Woking, England

F I G . 6 . 2 . *Erard repetition action, 1821.*   The patent drawing, from which this diagram was drawn, shows a somewhat different damper mechanism from later forms of the action. The action is very slender in construction, showing why some pianists complained that it went too quickly out of adjustment. Diagram from Rosamond E. M. Harding, *The Piano-Forte: Its History Traced to the Great Exhibition of 1851*, 2d ed. (Old Woking, Eng., 1978).

I traced the earlier career of Sébastien Erard in Chapter Three. As an inventive genius, Erard has few peers in the history of the piano, and none at all in the history of the harp, for which he devised, in 1810, the definitive pedal mechanism, still in use today. One of Erard's main obsessions was with the action of the piano. He designed several varieties, for both squares and grands, modeled mostly on English prototypes. In 1808, he made his first attempt at an action that would afford quick repetitions of notes. It was not very satisfactory, this *mécanisme à étrier* ("stirrup action," so called because the piece that caught the hammer butt was stirrup-shaped),² and Erard kept after the problem. In 1821, he had it in a usable form, and the patent in that year of the double-escapement "repetition" action is a landmark in the development of the grand. Figure 6.2 diagrams it.

Several features of this complex-appearing action are worth careful notice. When the key goes down, the end of the jack strikes the staple beneath the hammer shank to send the hammer to the string. As the jack rises, the tail at the back of the intermediate lever forces it to pivot toward the front of the instrument, disengaging it from the staple. When the jack ascends, the upper horizontal lever, the "repetition" lever, is forced upward, coming to rest immediately under the hammer shank forward of the jack, thus holding the hammer up at one end while the check holds the hammer head at the other. The jack, meanwhile, has slipped into a slot in the hammer shank. But the jack is still very close to the staple, and a slight partial release of the key permits it to slip back under the staple. The jack is then ready to deliver another blow to the hammer shank while the hammer is still held only part of the way down by the check and the repetition lever. This quick responsiveness of the action gave it the name repetition action.

It was a significant step in the development of Cristofori's original action. The complaint before this had been that the English direct-blow jack action was stiff and heavy, though to one familiar with the modern piano's touch, it seems exceedingly light.* With this ingenious escapement, where the jack not only easily escaped

---

*Alfred J. Hipkins found in 1901–2 that the weight of touch required to produce the faintest sound on an 1817 Broadwood grand ranged from 2½ ounces in the bass to 1⅝ ounces in the high treble, compared with a range of from 3½ to 2 ounces on a modern Broadwood grand with repetition action (*Description and History*, p. 29). Technicians tell me that 3 to 2 ounces from bass to treble is an average weight of touch for contemporary pianos.

from its contact point with the hammer shank but could quickly slide back to it, the jack action could be more readily adjusted for touch and was capable of very rapid repetitions of notes.

One may well ask why rapid repetitions were important. There are several schools of thought about that question, all with something to recommend them. Around 1821 was the heyday of the piano virtuosos, pianists who toured the great cities of Europe, astounding audiences with the technical marvels of their playing. One school of thought holds that Erard improved the action under the influence of such virtuosos as Carl Czerny, Friedrich Kalkbrenner, and Johann Nepomuk Hummel, to name the least ephemeral of the species (Hummel had studied with Mozart, Czerny with Beethoven). These performers needed an action, so the argument goes, that would allow their techniques full play with the most rapid trills and note repetitions. Well, perhaps, though repeated notes are not the most evident characteristic of the works of such pianist-composers, who, by the way, seldom played anything but their own works (Czerny was an important exception). After all, they were the only composers who wrote works that demonstrated the full ranges of their own powers (and omitted to make demands on their weaknesses).

Franz Liszt was another matter, in this as in other respects. He used repeated notes, and he liked to play Erards. But it must be noted that the repetition action was patented before Liszt came before the public. Indeed, he made his Paris and London debuts at the age of thirteen in 1824 on the new seven-octave grand (CC–c⁵) that Erard was making to go along with this new repetition action. The Paris performance is said to have been something of a disaster. Playing Hummel's Concerto in B minor, Liszt knocked some strings out of tune and broke some; everything had to stop until the strings could be replaced and the piano retuned.[3] Later Liszt always insisted, evidently with good reason, that a second piano be ready in reserve during his performances. He had a reputation for being notoriously hard on pianos. Heinrich Heine, the German poet and sometime music critic, wrote from Paris of Liszt in 1844: "He is here, the Attila, the scourge of God, for all Erard's pianos, which trembled at the news of his coming and now writhe, bleed and wail under his hands."[4]

Another school of thought about the repetition action is that the amateur market had more to do with it than the virtuoso, concert-hall market, always a negligible economic, though not public relations, factor. In those days, any music people heard outside of church, opera house, or concert hall was in their own or their friends' homes, and was made by themselves or their friends. They became acquainted with operas, oratorios, symphonies, and string quartets through arrangements for piano, either for two hands or for four, often made by the composers themselves or by their designated pupils. The last work Beethoven wrote for the piano was the four-hand transcription of his Grosse Fuge, op. 134, for string quartet, made only a few months before his death. The newly emerging Romantic style, especially in the operatic works of Carl Maria von Weber, was making more and more use in the orchestra of the affective device of string tremolo, in which the string players move their bows very quickly back and forth on the strings. To imitate that effect on the piano by very quick alternations of two notes called for an action that could repeat notes very rapidly. It may seem an out-of-the-way explanation, but the enormous popularity of opera, especially in France, cannot be gainsaid. Nor can one doubt that the piano makers wished to make instruments that they could sell in large quantities. To be sure, the repetition action was developed for the concert instrument, but later in the 1820's Erard modified it specifically for the squares that were the staple of the household market.

A third possibility must be mentioned. Most of those arguing both of the above points have assumed that most pianists by preference played English-type pianos, an assumption that is unexamined and almost surely false. The standard Viennese action of the time was light, responsive, and capable of very rapid and secure note repetition. Pianists who have tried it tell me that even the accompaniment to Franz Schubert's song "Der Erlkönig," a marathon exercise in repeated notes that every modern accompanist shudders to see placed on the music desk, is not terribly difficult to play on a Viennese piano of the sort Schubert, who was no virtuoso, used. Perhaps Erard wanted an action that combined the power of the more sluggish English type with the repetitive ease of the light Viennese action.

I do not wish to choose among these schools of thought. When several good explanations of a phenomenon are available, they should not be reduced to one out of a false principle of parsimony. And we ought not to overlook the tendency of a mechanically minded man like Sébastien Erard to improve something simply for improvement's sake or to tinker for tinkering's sake. Erard had worked on a repetition action since before 1808, and his nephew Pierre continued to work on it, patenting an improved version in 1833. It is that form of the repetition action that is contained in the Rück Collection's instrument. In about 1840, Henri Herz, who had made a wide but not deep reputation as a virtuoso pianist before entering the manufacture of pianos, put out a simplified version of Erard's action that, with a few minor changes in format, some in materials, and the addition of weight to the leverage, is the basis of the grand piano action of today.[5]

The point I have emphasized before holds good here too: invention is not tantamount to adoption. Many other makers, especially in France, set furiously to work on their own repetition actions, but very few makers took up Erard's design for many years. In the 1880's, Pleyel was still using its own types, and the Germans and Austrians were still making Viennese actions, though they frequently offered the Herz-Erard action as an option.* Broadwood remained faithful to Robert Stodart's English action throughout the century. Chickering in Boston used an American action devised by Edwin Brown, and Steinway used variants of the English action for some time, though, we will see in Chapter Seven, Erard-type repetition actions are to be seen in Steinway grands as early as the late 1850's. As time went along, several companies, the best-known of which was the Herrburger-Schwander firm in Paris, came to specialize in the manufacture of actions, and though they also put out their own designs, their influence brought Herz's modification of the Erard action to be the standard in the late nineteenth century.

------◆------

French influence spread far beyond the bounds of France. In Germany, as the next instrument shows, we find a combination

---

*An interesting evaluation of the Erard action was made by the unidentified German author of the article "Pianoforte" in Hermann Mendel's *Musikalisches Conversations-Lexicon* in 1877: "The repetition action invented by Erhard in Paris has several advantages, but it is still too complicated to find wider dissemination" (vol. 8, p. 87; Erhard was the original family name in Alsace). The author goes on to praise the simplicity, durability, and ease of repair of the German action. It is true that the mechanical complexity of the Erard action was otherwise criticized, but the mechanism persisted despite the doubts.

FIG. 6.3. *Square piano, Adolph Ibach Söhne, Barmen and Düsseldorf, after 1839.* *Action:* Adjustable jack action; felt-covered hammers. *Stops:* 1 pedal (missing): dampers to b². *Range:* CC–g⁴. *Stringing:* CC–GG♯ single-strung wound, AA–E double-strung wound, F–g⁴ double-strung plain; CC 149.2 cm, c² 29.4 cm, g⁴ 5.2 cm. Tuning pins in front of case. *Framing:* Cast-iron string plate with 1 iron tension bar. *Case:* Mahogany veneered; 178.5 cm wide, 86.5 cm deep. *Location:* Händel-Haus, Halle, GDR. Catalog no. MS-23.

of German or Austrian, French, and English aspects, the last perhaps mediated through French channels. The Ibach square pictured in Figure 6.3 is eclectic and international in design.

The firm of Ibach, now located in Schwelm, in the Ruhr Valley, has the distinction of being the oldest existing German piano company. Johann Adolph Ibach began making pianos in Barmen, just a few miles from Schwelm, in 1794. He himself had apparently all but bowed out of the business by 1834, when his son Carl Rudolf took over its direction, and the company became Adolph Ibach und Sohn. In 1839, with the addition of another son, Richard, to the management, the name changed again, to Adolph Ibach Söhne. In 1869, Carl's son Rudolf took over and renamed the firm for the last time, Rudolf Ibach Sohn. The name Adolph Ibach Söhne on the square in Figure 6.3 thus shows that it was made in or after 1839 and before 1869, but without a serial number its date cannot be pinpointed.

We have not examined a Continental square, and it is time to do so, partly because it was soon to disappear from the trade. The latest German square I have found listed in any collection is dated 1863, and indeed only a few from the 1840's have survived. The Ibach is interesting on a number of counts. The square piano has grown. This one is nearly six feet wide and 34 inches deep, with a correspondingly massive case. Earlier squares were considerably smaller: one of Anton Walter's square pianos of the early 1820's is only about five feet, five inches by 30 inches.[6] This growth in size, necessitated by the wider ranges pianos were reaching, was running precisely counter to a trend already discernible in European cities toward apartment living. Floor space in city apartments was precious. Thus the square was even then losing to the small upright its advantage of taking less space than the grand. The square footage covered by the Ibach would be nearly the same as that of a smallish grand about 75 inches long.

The Ibach has one arrangement common to many German and Austrian squares. Back in about 1780, John Broadwood had moved the tuning pins from the right side of the case, where they had been in clavichords, to the back of the case, an arrangement that most British, French, and American makers adopted and retained. German and Austrian makers, however, did not imitate Broadwood, but had kept the tuning pins at the right until perhaps 1815 or so—the exact date and the identity of the originator are unknown—when someone thought of moving them to the front, next to the keyboard. The earliest existing square I know of with the tuning pins in front is one by Matthäus Andreas Stein in 1816.[7] (In London, George Garcka, one of "the 12 apostles," patented an arrangement with tuning pins in front in 1792. The German and Austrian makers who later did the same probably knew nothing of Garcka's experiment, a now familiar story.)

The direction of the strings in the Ibach, then, is from front left to back right, just the reverse of the back-left-to-front-right arrangement in Broadwood-type squares. This new arrangement freed the makers to extend the soundboard to the left, since the keys did not reach to the back of the case, and the resulting larger soundboard area mitigated one of the problems of the square design, that the resonated sound was so small for so large a case. The Broadwood arrangement of tuning pins prevented British and American builders from enlarging soundboards to the left until new methods of bracing below the soundboard were conceived. Squares like the Ibach, with a larger soundboard, could put out a volume comparable to that of a small grand.

Nevertheless, the Ibach's sound could not have been very large. Its lowest notes are single-strung, and from AA to the top it is only double-strung. There is a necessary trade-off. The range has grown to six octaves and a fifth $(CC-g^4)$, only two notes more than the 1830 William Stodart grand with the Thom and Allen frame discussed in Chapter Five. But an interesting result appears when we compare string lengths in the Ibach with those of a nearly contemporary grand having the same $CC-g^4$ range—an 1835 grand made by the Streichers' son Johann Baptist Streicher in the Händel-Haus collection.[8] In the Ibach, CC is 149.2 cm (vs. 196.8 in the Streicher), c^2 is 29.4 cm (vs. 21.0), and g^4 is 5.2 cm (vs. 4.9). I have no information on the relative thicknesses of the wires. The higher strings in the Ibach, being longer than those in the Streicher, must either have more tension or be thinner to reach the pitches. If the former, the greater tension will likely bring out more stiffness, if the latter, they will give a smaller tone. The Streicher's lowest string is nearly one-third longer than the lowest in the Ibach; hence the Ibach must have much thicker strings to reach the low pitches. Any way you look at it, the design of the Ibach demands that it have a poorer tone quality than the Streicher. The Streicher grand, moreover, has no iron in its frame, only an iron gap-stretcher under the strings in the octave above middle C. To take up the strain required by the longer treble and thicker bass strings, Ibach had to use an iron string-plate and a tension bar bolted to the pin block, and he had to be content with double-stringing, where Streicher used triple-stringing. Large as the square was becoming, it had design shortcomings to eliminate before it could claim to be as much piano as any grand.

The international influence on the Ibach had been a long time in coming. We find here, for example, the English grasshopper action that John Geib patented way back in 1786. It was a very simple, durable action for squares, but most German makers still used the Viennese action. In another respect, the Ibach shows a distinctly French influence: the hammers are covered with felt instead of with leather. This piano, which cannot have been made before 1839, is the earliest German-made piano I know of with original felt hammers, which Henri Pape had begun using in the late 1820's.

Pape was a remarkable inventor over whom we may profitably pause. He spawned new ideas for the piano by the dozen, though he seemed unable to distinguish really good ideas from mere gimcracks. Pape tried using springs as vibrators, an idea whose theoretical merit he was not the first to see, but it never worked practically. He built pianos with large, bowl-shaped copper resonators, for all the world like a piano mounted on a kettledrum. But he was also very early in the successful effort to make a small upright that sounded like a piano, and in the process he was the first to employ cross-stringing, and both ideas are with us yet. Pape expended years and untold thousands of francs to perfect a down-striking horizontal action, an undertaking in which he had some success but not enough to make the down-striker a permanent part of the piano world.* He took out a total of 137 patents, and Arthur Loesser has expounded many of them in three closely written pages.[9] Pape's career is worth an entire book. In some ways he was the quintessential piano maker of 1820–50. Never satisfied with an old machine if a new one could be devised, a man of restless mind and artful inventiveness, he spewed out novelties at a rate that would be the envy of any inventor. Several besides his down-striking action were dead ends. One such design was a piano of

---

*The down-striking action is an interesting footnote to the story as one of the most persistent dead ends. Pape was by no means the only maker to pursue the problem. Thomas Loud, Robert Wornum, and Johann Baptist Streicher, Nannette Streicher's son, were among those who worked at it. Down-strikers in fact turned up very early in the piano's history—both Jean Marius in France and Christoph Gottlieb Schröter in Saxony proposed models of them, doubtless in imitation of Pantaleon Hebenstreit's mallets—and they continued to attract the wistful attention of piano designers far into the nineteenth century. Besides the seeming naturalness of the downward motion, another factor made the down-striker theoretically attractive. In the standard action, a heavy blow from the hammer could unseat the string from the bridge, with dramatic consequences for the tuning. The down-striker solved this problem, but Sébastien Erard's agraffes and the down-bearing bars invented by Pierre Erard and Antoine Bord also solved it for the up-striker. What finally kept the down-striker from success was its inability to get the hammer securely *away* from the string, a more difficult mechanical problem than that of getting it to the string from below. Most designers of down-strikers used spring-loading, a quick-acting catch, or a counterweight to keep the hammer from falling back to the string. By 1880 or so, down-striking actions had become practically extinct. A grand by Robert Wornum of about 1875 in the Victoria and Albert Museum in London has been recorded on Oryx no. 1811.

eight octaves, which was played in public a couple of times between 1844 and 1849 and retired into discreet silence (we will see a modern eight-octave grand in Chapter Ten). Another was for a piano of eight and a half octaves, a design that he patented in 1845 (English patent no. 10,668) but probably never built.

One of Pape's really lasting innovations was his hammer covering. The search for the perfect hammer covering had gone on since the first leather hammer was split by a string or cracked from old age. It would have to be cheap, hard enough to give volume but soft enough to give mellow tone, and resistant to being cut and compacted by thousands of blows on hard metal. Rosamond Harding describes experiments with cloth (including molton, a coarse woollen cloth, and combinations of leather and cloth), cork, gutta-percha, india rubber, sponge, and tinder, in addition to various kinds of leather and felt.[10] Pape had the idea of using felt in 1826 and immediately began to cut up beaver hats to cover hammers. He soon found that the felt that made for good beaver hats did not make for good piano hammers, and finally he commissioned a felt maker to put up felt to his own specifications, a combination of lamb's wool and rabbit hair, made in sheets that tapered in thickness from the bass to the treble end. Pape could thus obtain several complete sets of hammer covers from a single sheet of felt.

It is perhaps not so surprising that this international influence should be exerted on the Ibach firm but not on Austrian or more eastern and southern German makers. With the Rhine River in close proximity, the Ruhr district where it was located was exposed to French commercial and political influence. Indeed, this may also help to explain Ibach's use of the English action, since it had been widely adopted by French makers. Interchanges among countries were not so frequent as they later became. English pianos were better known in France than in Germany or Austria, better known in northern than in southern Germany. But the great piano-exporting wars were yet to come.

◄━◆━►

That the innovations introduced by French and other makers did not achieve universal acceptance is well demonstrated by the instrument pictured in Figure 6.4. Made in Vienna in 1839, one of

FIG. 6.4. *Grand piano, Conrad Graf, Vienna, 1839.* Serial no. 2616. *Action:* Viennese action; felt-covered hammers, replacing original leather. *Stops:* 4 pedals: una corda, two buffs or moderators, dampers to a³. *Range:* CC–g⁴. *Stringing:* CC–FF♯ double-strung wound, GG–g⁴ triple-strung plain; CC 181 cm, c² 28.5 cm, g⁴ 5 cm. *Framing:* Wood, with 1 iron gap-stretcher. *Case:* Rosewood; 237 cm long, 126 cm wide. *Location:* Kunsthistorisches Museum, Vienna. On permanent loan from Gesellschaft der Musikfreunde, catalog no. 16.

the latest by Conrad Graf, it clearly illustrates the relative isolation from foreign influence of the Viennese makers.

This beautiful piano has a lovely history. It was presented by the Graf firm to Clara Wieck in 1840 when she married Robert Schumann. At twenty-one, Clara Schumann was already one of

Europe's foremost pianists, and any maker would have been proud to claim her as the owner of one of his instruments. Robert also gave Clara a piano on their marriage, and he may well have used the Graf more than she did, for she later referred to it as "Robert's piano." To be sure, his crippled hand had for some years prevented his being a performing pianist, but he continued to use the piano for composing. The Graf remained in the Schumann household until Robert's death in July 1856. Then Clara gave it to the young Johannes Brahms, who had been her support and stay while Robert lived out his last three years in an insane asylum.

Either just before or just after the Graf was given to Brahms, it was repaired by J. B. Klems in Düsseldorf, where Clara then lived, for he signed his name and the date, Sept. 30, 1856, in the piano. Doubtless at that time the original leather hammers were replaced by the present felt ones. Brahms kept the old Graf for some years, though he consulted Clara about what ought to be done with it. For a time it was apparently stored by a friend in a suburb of Hamburg, Brahms's native city. In 1871, Brahms moved permanently to Vienna (he had lived there since 1862 but had considered it temporary), and about then the Streicher firm presented him with one of their latest-model grands. He had to decide what to do with the Schumann Graf. In 1873, he had it exhibited at the Vienna Exposition, and from there it went as a gift to the Gesellschaft der Musikfreunde in Vienna. When the instrument collection of the Gesellschaft went on permanent loan to the Kunsthistorisches Museum in Vienna, the old Graf went along.*

No particular technological advance is to be noted in the Graf. Indeed, that is part of the reason for discussing it. Not every piano used by a leading musician was the latest word in design and development. The range of the Graf is less than could have been had. Grands with a CC–a^4 range and even of the nearly modern AAA–a^4 were available then. But Schumann's music very seldom ranges past g^4 and never past a^4, nor did anyone else's at the time. Even in the late 1830's, composers who wrote for pianos with the compass of this one, or for those with seven octaves, often pro-

---

*Jörg Demus has recorded this instrument in a Romance by Clara Schumann and several works by Robert Schumann—Papillons, op. 2; Kinderszenen, op. 15; Arabeske, op. 18; eight pieces from the *Bunte Blätter*, op. 99; and two from the *Albumblätter*, op. 124—on Deutsch Harmonia Mundi 1C 151-99773.

vided alternative versions of high or low passages for players who owned six-octave pianos. And there were many. A superficial sense of the variety of ranges available can be gleaned from the following tabulation, showing all the pianos I know of from the years 1835–40, culled mostly from catalogs and checklists of collections:

Type and range	*No.*	*Origin*
GRANDS		
CC–a⁴	1	German
CC–g⁴	12	8 Viennese, 2 French, 1 English, 1 German
CC–f⁴	4	2 French, 1 German, 1 Viennese
FF–g⁴	1	Viennese
FF–f⁴	4	3 Viennese, 1 English
UPRIGHTS		
CC–c⁵	1	German (giraffe)
CC–a⁴	4	German
CC–g⁴	3	2 English, 1 German
CC–f⁴	4	2 English, 2 French
EE–f⁴	1	German
FF–f⁴	8	2 French, 1 German, 1 Swiss, 1 English, 1 Belgian, 1 Austrian, 1 American
SQUARES		
CC–a⁴	1	German
CC–g⁴	3	1 French, 1 German, 1 Swedish
CC–f⁴	1	French
DD–g⁴	1	American
EE–g⁴	1	German
FF–g⁴	1	German
FF–f⁴	11	5 American, 3 German, 1 English, 1 Swiss, 1 Viennese
FF–c⁴	1	American

The variety is typical of the entire period from about 1820 to 1850, and it does not exhaust the actual variety that was available.

Take the Graf's pedals. There are four, but none operates the exotic stops that graced the earlier pianos of even the finest builders, no bassoons, no Janissary drums and bells. Graf has installed two moderators (one of which moves the thicker part of the felt between hammer and strings), an una corda (probably already moving the action only far enough for the hammers to strike two strings of the triple-strung notes), and a damper. This is more pedals than most pianos had, but no novelty is there.

Or take the frame. No iron is to be found, not even an iron string-plate or tension bar. The string-plate is a wider and thicker wooden plank than the one on, say, Beethoven's Broadwood of 1817 (which has a very slender board). But the Graf, for all that it has seven higher notes than the Broadwood, has only one iron gap-stretcher, not five. Nor does the Graf have the Broadwood's closed bottom. Instead, it has thick wooden braces from the belly rail to other cross-braces to support the string-plate against the tension of the strings. That tension, at a guess, is somewhere in the vicinity of 10 to 12 tons, well under half that of a modern concert grand. But it is held, and held well, by the wooden bracing and that one skinny little gap-stretcher.

This piano may have had one technological advance, the origin of which still eludes me. I shall tell below what I have found, and perhaps the full story can someday be told. The plain strings in the Graf *may* have been steel rather than wrought iron. Since steel has greater tensile strength than iron, the wires would have been thinner and perforce more flexible. I do not know that these strings were steel. When J. B. Klems repaired the piano for Brahms in 1856, it seems a fair guess that he replaced some or all of the strings, and by that time steel wire was becoming fairly common.

Steel piano wire was almost surely being used by 1840, but I have been unable to discover with certainty when it was first used. L.-A. de Pontécoulant says that it was first tried by Count von Bruhl, the Saxon ambassador to England, in 1786, and that in 1830 Erard began to substitute strings "wound in steel" (*filées en acier*) for the hitherto usual brass bass strings.[11] Rosamond Harding suggests, from Broadwood's account books, that steel was being used in about 1815.[12] Other scholars say variously, 1826, 1838, and 1850.[13] The 1826 date seems to me plausible, for that was the year of Henri Pape's patent on the use of annealed steel for strings. But we cannot be certain that Pape actually used steel strings. The piano historian has the difficulty of never being sure that the strings in an old instrument are the original ones. Replacing strings was an easy job that seldom left traces, and in the early days it had to be done rather often. Another difficulty is that some early piano historians did not know the difference between iron and steel and used the terms interchangeably. One piece of hard evidence about steel strings is two patents of 1840, granted to John Hawley in London and Sanguinède and Company in Paris, that give formulas for tempering steel piano wire.[14] Since wrought iron cannot be tempered, we may be sure that the patentees really meant steel. There is also the fact, as Samuel Wolfenden has pointed out, that good steel wire could not be made until 1819, when Brockedon hit on the idea of drawing wire through dies made of diamonds and rubies.[15] Before that, wire was drawn through holes in steel plates, which wore out rapidly and could handle only softer metal than their own. Steel wires so drawn tended to be uneven in thickness and musically unacceptable.

Steel, which has a higher carbon content than wrought iron, had been known and manufactured for a long time. Aristotle himself mentions it, and there are written directions for making steel dating back to the sixteenth century. But not until the rise of analytic chemistry in the eighteenth century did anyone know what gave steel its properties.[16] Before the Bessemer process, announced in 1856 but not commercially successful until 1864, steel was made very slowly and in small batches, mostly by the "cementation" process. It took six days of cooking iron bars with charcoal to give perhaps 25 pounds of mild steel. Little steel was made, because it was so expensive, and carriage springs, clock springs, and hard-edged tools accounted for most of the trade. But sooner or later (I can say only between 1825 and 1840) its qualities for piano wire came to be appreciated. Though the invention of telegraphy may have spurred advances in techniques of wire drawing,[17] steel wire must have continued to be dreadfully expensive until the Bessemer converter inaugurated the possibility of large-scale steel manufacture.*

To return to the Graf, this piano was the property of three extremely fine pianists and leading musicians in Germany and

---

*Rosamond Harding, *The Piano-Forte*, Appendix D, pp. 359–69, gives a great deal of data on English and German wire gauges, stringing patterns of various pianos, the composition and weight of certain strings, and the prices of wire. Her date of 1815 for steel wire is here on p. 368. Regrettably, all of this material is so haphazardly gathered and presented as to render conclusions from it all but impossible. For example, she presents prices of piano wire from the Broadwood books for the years 1815, 1816, 1817, 1819, 1828, and 1831. In the first four years, the prices are for various kinds of wire by the pound. In the last two they are for sets of wound strings for various models of piano, but not for the entire stringing except for one model. The prices are not related to gauges or to useful weight or mass. The final impression of the figures given in those several pages is of miscellaneous information partially digested—a kind of table of random numbers and, for historical purposes, nearly as useful.

Vienna for a period of over 30 years. Schumann probably wrote his Piano Concerto, op. 54, his chamber music for piano and strings, and many other works on it. Those works sounded very different on the Graf from the way they sound on a modern Steinway or Bösendorfer. The volume was less, the timbre thinner, the sound very much more open and less rich and sonorous than the sound we are accustomed to. But it was quite enough to move Schumann to flights of romantic rhetoric when, in 1853, the twenty-year-old Brahms came and played his own works for the Schumanns, doubtless on this very instrument.

Sitting at the piano, he began to reveal wonderful regions. We were drawn into ever more magical circles. There came playing of utter genius, which made of the piano an orchestra of lamenting and loudly jubilant voices. There were sonatas, rather veiled symphonies—songs whose poetry one would understand even without knowing the words, though a profoundly songful melody pervades them all—single piano pieces, some of them of a demonic character with the most graceful forms, then sonatas for violin and piano—string quartets—and each differing so from the others that each seemed to flow from a different spring. And then it seemed, like a roaring stream, that he united them all as into a single waterfall, over whose rushing waves soared the peaceful rainbow, while butterflies played upon its banks, accompanied by nightingale voices.[18]

It seems fitting that Clara Schumann gave Brahms the piano with which he had inspired that last published essay of the already failing composer.

———————◄◆►———————

But our subject, after all, is French leadership, so let us return to the developments in France. Though it was Robert Wornum of London who pioneered in building a successful small upright, the idea was quickly taken up by French makers. About 1815, when Henri Pape was still working for Pleyel, he was set to copying Wornum uprights for the French market.[19] After he struck out on his own, Pape continued to have a lively interest in small uprights, making some very important contributions to their design. He was not alone in this interest. As early as 1824, Pierre Erard, then working with his uncle Sébastien, foresaw that as square pianos grew and apartment rooms shrank, a small upright would sell better than a square as the home instrument.[20] The French makers, shedding the traditional conservatism of their craft for the time being, surpassed the English in their attraction to small uprights, of which the Mehl pictured in Figure 6.5 is an example. (I have been unable to unearth any information about Mehl, the maker of this attractive piano, not even his first name. The date, c. 1840, is a guess, but it seems a comfortable fit.)*

Because the French were so active in producing small uprights, the action of the sort used in this instrument, though it had been devised by Wornum in England, came to be known as the French action. Design trade-offs must be made in any instrument, of course, but as someone has said, the blood and sweat of the designers show on every part of the upright action. The French action in the Mehl, as diagrammed in Figure 6.6, illustrates this nicely.

The problem with the upright action is exactly the same as with the down-striking horizontal action, and it finally spelled failure for the down-striker. Indeed, if an upright piano with its action in front of the strings were laid out horizontally, it would *be* a down-striker. The problem is to make certain that the hammer rebounds from the string and does not bounce back to it. Wornum's tape check solved the first half of this problem but was not proof against the second, though the tape pulled the hammer back if the key remained down. This is a rather neat, economical little action, and it forms the basis of modern upright actions, as a comparison of Figure 6.6 with Figure 1.9 will show. One design element of the tape-check action led American technicians to nickname it the birdcage action. The dampers are above the hammers, and the damper lifters extend up from the rocker levers at the bottom to the damper levers at the top. In looking at Figure 6.7, the inside of the Mehl with its front panel taken off, the aptness of the nickname is plain: the first thing that meets your eye is the row of long damper-wires, looking for all the world like a birdcage.

Neat as this little action is, the upright action is always chancy.

*At about the time Mehl made this handsome little upright, Henri Pape was building his "piano console," the top of which was no more than eight inches higher than the keyboard. Such instruments, and even uprights the size of the Mehl, were widely known in Europe as pianinos. Robert Schumann himself, in the mid-1840's, came to prefer a pianino to his Graf. At the time he was having some symptoms of depression and nervous disorder that may have made him wish a smaller tone than the Graf gave. However that may be, he is quoted as enjoying the small, intimate sound and feel of the little upright. (See Kurt Hahn, "Schumanns Klavierstil," p. 125.)

FIG. 6.5. *Small upright, Mehl, Paris, c. 1840.* *Action:* Tape-check upright action, over-dampers; felt-covered hammers. *Stops:* 1 pedal: dampers to c^3. *Range:* CC–f^4. *Stringing:* CC–C single-strung wound, C#–c double-strung wound, c#–c#^{3} double-strung plain, d^3–f^4 triple-strung plain; straight vertical stringing; CC 94 cm, c^2 29.8 cm, f^4 6.4 cm. Tuning pins at top of case. *Framing:* Iron string-plate; 3 iron strap braces down back of frame from top of pin block; 4 brass pieces set into soundboard and pin block (function not clear). *Case:* Mahogany veneered, openwork front with green silk backing, brass candle sconces on each side; 113.7 cm high, 120.7 cm wide. *Location:* Eddy Collection, Cambridge, Mass.

The balance and regulation of the parts goes too easily out of adjustment. It is not a wholly satisfactory machine, however satisfactory a piece of furniture it may be. The one advantage of the upright is that it can have a large soundboard area relative to the length of the strings, with all the resonance that this implies. But the soundboard, being vertical like the rest of the works, must be framed so as to keep it tightly joined to the bridge, for if anything

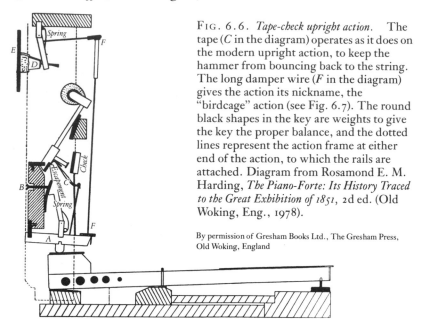

FIG. 6.6. *Tape-check upright action.* The tape (*C* in the diagram) operates as it does on the modern upright action, to keep the hammer from bouncing back to the string. The long damper wire (*F* in the diagram) gives the action its nickname, the "birdcage" action (see Fig. 6.7). The round black shapes in the key are weights to give the key the proper balance, and the dotted lines represent the action frame at either end of the action, to which the rails are attached. Diagram from Rosamond E. M. Harding, *The Piano-Forte: Its History Traced to the Great Exhibition of 1851,* 2d ed. (Old Woking, Eng., 1978).

By permission of Gresham Books Ltd., The Gresham Press, Old Woking, England

happens to separate them, the resonance is gone. And since the natural thing to do with an upright is to set it against a wall, the sound may be rather muffled no matter how large the soundboard.

Beyond the soundboard, which is a plus in the upright, the quality of sound depends on the strings, and they, together with the action, have always been a difficulty in vertical instruments. If the case is to be small enough for convenience, the strings must be correspondingly short. The longest string in the Mehl is 94 cm (37 inches). Compare that with the length of the string for the same pitch on a roughly contemporary grand, 178.7 cm (70.4 inches). So short a string as the Mehl's cannot have the elasticity to produce the partials of a good tone. Some makers, as we have seen, attempted to solve the problem by stringing their instruments obliquely. Others set out on a different tack, which turned out to be extremely important.

The indefatigably innovative Henri Pape seems to have been the first to think of cross-stringing, whereby the lower bass strings are strung above and across the line of the shorter higher strings (see Fig. 1.2, for the pattern in a modern upright). This arrangement, which he devised in 1828, requires two separate bridges, and Pape saw no way around a second, smaller soundboard beneath the bridge for the lower strings. Some other makers sporadically followed suit in England, France, Bavaria, and Austria during the 1830's, and some experiments were to be found in America. The New York firm of Bridgeland and Jardine made a few cross-strung squares in 1833. But our old story holds true: most makers did not take up the new idea until it had become quite an old one.

So Mehl's piano stands in the middle of the road. He used the relatively new Wornum-type action, the relatively new felt hammers of Pape, and framing of both iron and wood, which we have not seen on earlier uprights. But the stringing is straight and vertical, involving both wound and plain strings and single-, double-, and triple-stringing. Only the top octave and a third are triple-strung, however, suggesting Mehl was not entirely confident that his iron-braced frame would hold the tension of more triple-stringing.

This is, of course, a piano designed for amateurs to play at home. Its usage is shown by the two swinging candle sconces at either side of the music rack. The family could sit around the parlor of an evening while one of the daughters played and sang the latest gems from the music publishers. (Arthur Loesser has vividly depicted the way daughters were the principal carriers of the

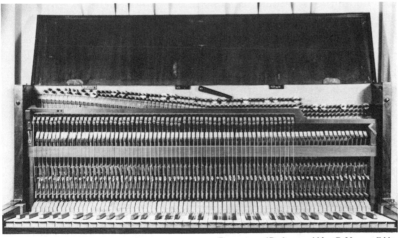

By courtesy of Professor and Mrs. G. Norman Eddy

FIG. 6.7. *Plan view of Mehl upright.* The row of long damper wires gave the type of action in this piano the nickname "birdcage" action.

piano's social functions and status in the nineteenth century.)[21] Perhaps these works were simplified transcriptions of airs from the current hit operas, transposed down to where the amateur soprano could handle the tune if not the coloratura, or perhaps they were more lowly popular songs. If she was a diligent student of the keyboard, she might finger one of John Field's nocturnes, or a valse or "feuillet" by Stephen Heller. But that is beginning to verge on the dizzy heights of serious music for most French maidens of the 1840's, and we must not be too ambitious for our fictional family entertainer.

———————◆◆———————

With the Pleyel grand pictured in Figure 6.8 we return to the grand form. Certain makes of pianos bring certain pianists and composers to mind: Stein and Walter make one think of Mozart; Streicher, Graf, and Broadwood bring up Beethoven, and Graf also suggests the Schumanns; and Erard recalls Liszt and Moscheles. Pleyel makes us think immediately of Frédéric Chopin. Chopin preferred Pleyels, finding the Erard a bit "ready-made" in tone, as he said.[22] The Pleyel had a silvery tone that allowed him, as Liszt said, "to draw therefrom sounds that might recall one of those harmonicas of which romantic Germany held the monopoly" (Liszt meant glass harmonicas).[23] Legend has it that Chopin played on the Schubert Club's Pleyel, which is our exemplar, but legend cannot now be turned into fact.

The Pleyel firm was the second of the great French makers to come into existence. Like the Alsatian Sébastien Erard, Ignaz Pleyel, an Austrian, grew up speaking German.* One of Haydn's best pupils, Pleyel began his career as a practical musician and composer, whose rather facile late-classic style can still be heard in concerts and on recordings. Pleyel began to manufacture pianos in 1807, at the age of fifty. He was joined in this business by his son Camille in 1821 and then, a few years later, by the famous pianist Friedrich Kalkbrenner, another German transplanted to Paris.†

Like Clara Schumann's Graf, our Pleyel, built in 1838–39, is

---

*One of the more interesting coincidences in the piano's history is that Ignaz Pleyel and Sébastien Erard both died in 1831, and their successors, Camille Pleyel and Pierre Erard, also died in the same year, 1855. No moral seems to attach to the fact.

†It is interesting to note that a fair number of pianists of the early nineteenth century turned to piano manufacture. Besides Pleyel and Kalkbrenner, there was Muzio Clementi,

notable mainly because it is fairly typical of its day, not because it exhibits anything new. In fact, in one respect it is conservative. Pleyel did not adopt the repetition action that made Erard a household name. Of course, the firm would hardly have relished paying royalties to its chief local competitor, and it is not suprising to find it sticking close to what had worked before. During the 1830's and 1840's, several makers were designing repetition actions to compete with Erard's. Pleyel was content for the time being to use the old English grand action that we saw in the 1790 Stodart and the 1811 Broadwood, made heavier for thicker strings and now equipped with Pape's felt hammers. That one of Pape's inventions is to be found in a Pleyel is not surprising, since he worked for Pleyel until 1818.

Pleyel had rather quickly taken up the composite frame with iron string-plate and tension bars during the 1820's. Since then, the only change in the design had been the addition of one or more tension bars. A Pleyel of the mid-1820's in the Royal Ontario Museum, Toronto (serial no. 2499), has only three tension bars, whereas the Schubert Club's grand has five. Possibly the three were found inadequate, for a thick wrought-iron bar is bolted into the wooden bracing under the soundboard in the Toronto Pleyel. But it is not clear whether this additional bar was original or was added later. Pleyel may have been the first maker to combine the tension bars with a metal string-plate, though Broadwood also claimed priority. In the early 1820's one may find one or the other but usually not both. As we will see, both Pleyel and Erard hung back for a long time from the complete iron frame on the American model; Pleyel came over around 1880, but Erard stood clear of it until into the twentieth century.

---

who took over the bankrupt Longman and Broderip shop in London in 1802 (he may have taken it over as early as 1798, but it had the Clementi name in 1802). After his death, the company became Collard and Collard, still one of England's leading piano manufacturers. There was Henri Herz, mentioned earlier, who improved the Erard action around 1840. And John Baptist Cramer, "Glorious John," as the British affectionately called him, was briefly in the piano business in England. With the advent of the age of the public concert, the musician who sought a concert career often found it necessary to find some related work to supplement a precarious living on the concert rounds. In Clementi's case, commercial success entirely usurped the energies from his performing career. The personal participation of artists and composers in the manufacture of pianos died almost entirely away in the second half of the century. As the Industrial Revolution took hold in this as in other trades, the demands of what were coming to be factories required full-time commitment to business, so that one could no longer live successfully in both worlds.

F IG . 6.8. *Grand piano, Pleyel, Paris, 1838–39.*   Serial no. 7025. *Action:* English grand action, over-dampers; felt-covered hammers. *Stops:* 2 pedals: una corda, dampers to d^3. *Range:* CC–g^4. *Stringing:* CC–EE single-strung wound, FF–D double-strung wound, E–g^4 triple-strung plain; straight-strung; CC 173 cm, c^2 27.5 cm, g^4 4.6 cm. *Framing:* Composite frame: iron string-plate, 5 iron tension bars bolted to string-plate and pin block, with cross bars. *Case:* Rosewood veneered with brass inlay; 227 cm long, 127 cm wide. *Location:* The Schubert Club, St. Paul, Minn.

By the time Camille Pleyel joined his father, theirs was one of the larger firms. In 1827, the company employed about 30 workers to make about 100 pianos a year.[24] However small that output seems, it ranks Pleyel alongside a maker like Conrad Graf and considerably above the Streicher firm in Vienna, which was probably making no more than half that number at the time. The two biggest houses were Erard, which made about 600 pianos a year in

Paris, fewer in its London factory, and Broadwood in London, which in the 1820's produced about 1,650 pianos yearly, of which about 1,400 were squares.*

A 30-man shop was a relatively big one. But we should not think of it as a factory on the model of a modern one. Each of the 30 workers, save such apprentices as are doubtless included in the number, was probably capable of making a piano from the ground up all alone, and there may have been little division of labor. The tools were strictly hand tools—saws, hammers, gougers, chisels, adzes, and the like, though the company from which Pleyel bought its wire may have used a steam donkey rather than the time-honored water-wheel in its wire-drawing operations. So the craft tradition was still the rule in the piano industry. On the other hand, several firms may well have begun to contract out certain parts to pieceworkers: tuning pins or bridge pins, hammer coverings, damper cloth, for example. It is known that Broadwood used such cottage-industry contracts earlier in the century, and it is highly likely that it was not the only house to do so.

———◆———

The last two chapters have emphasized a series of significant innovations in piano design, most of them made during the 1820's and extended and improved in the 1830's and 1840's. It is fair and accurate to say that insofar as these innovations were adopted, they found their ways into English, French, and American pianos. With the Germans and Austrians, the pianos of the 1830's and 1840's were for the most part not unlike those of the first three decades of the century, though ranges were widening, strings were thickening, and actions were putting on weight. To be sure, more and more German and Austrian grands came in the 1840's to have metal string-plates and sometimes tension bars, some even to have the new capo tasto bar that Bord had patented in 1843. But there were no innovations in action design, and the German and Austrian builders saw no reason to abandon Stein's action except

*Production figures in this or any book on the subject cannot be taken as exact. Even a modern company like Steinway & Sons refuses to give them out. Serial numbers must be used with great care, and chronological lists of serial numbers, such as those in the *Pierce Piano Atlas* and Herzog's *Europe Piano Atlas*, differ from each other and are not to be accepted implicitly. Nevertheless, the relative numbers are probably close to reality and can be used for relative purposes.

when, like Johann Baptist Streicher, they tried down-strikers. Critical voices were heard about this backwardness. In 1844, Carl Kützing, a German-born Swiss theoretician and piano maker, proclaimed that "Vienna [had] long ceased to be the school of the art of fortepiano building," and felt that Germany should "endeavor to forget the old Viennese ways."[25] It was in England and America that iron framing was first tried, and in France that it was quickly adopted. France saw the proliferation of repetition actions once Erard's model had broken away from the direct-blow English action, and it saw the extension of the cottage piano style into the tiny consoles of Pape and the pianinos of other makers.

That England, France, and America were in the forefront of industrial development, where Germany lagged behind for the time being, may be one reason for the relative readiness for change. New developments were in the air, with the steam locomotive and the building of railroad lines in England, the use of iron in building construction in France and England, the development of wood-working machinery in the United States. There was a climate of what was widely assumed to be technological progress, which could not but influence every manufacturing and commercial group. A growing assumption that a problem was a challenge to be solved, not a difficulty to be avoided or to be met in the same way Grandfather met it, the assumption that human beings had both the will and the intelligence to solve new problems in new ways, was part of the social and cultural air that mid-nineteenth-century people breathed, especially in the rapidly industrializing countries. To be sure, there were bizarre solutions in the piano industry no less and no more than in others, some of them proposed by as fine an intelligence as that of Henri Pape. But the odd, unworkable experiment is as good testimony to the supposition that the new is there to be tried and the challenge there to be surmounted as is the brilliant breakthrough.

The breakthrough that had not yet happened with respect to the piano was the combination of previously discrete innovations into a single instrument. When that came about, the modern piano came into being. From 1820 on, the experiments and innovations were, as we can see from hindsight, aiming toward the modern piano. But for all the pretensions of the London Exhibition of 1851 (boastfully called The Great Exhibition) to exhibit the definitive state of the modern world, among the pianos displayed were several that had some parts of the modern piano but none that had them all. It remained for the Americans to bring the separate innovations together.

7

The Radical Americans

I suggested at the end of Chapter Six that the period from about 1820 to 1850 brought the piano to a point short of the modern instrument. The point would perhaps not have been short of that step if anyone had thought to incorporate all of the significant innovations of those years into a single instrument, or, even better, if everyone had incorporated them all. But no one did. We have seen that most of the instruments in the 1830's and 1840's have some of the innovations, but none has very many until the 1850's.

The achievement of the American makers, especially of Steinway & Sons of New York, was, first, to combine the innovations and, second, to persuade masses of buyers to purchase the result. The first was a design breakthrough. The second exploited the new means of distribution that resulted from advances in the technology of transportation, especially of railroads and ships, and of communication technology, especially of telegraphy and the use of railroads to carry mail. The Americans of the Victorian era can be accused of many things, but technological and economic timidity is not one of them.

Before we move on to what the Americans did with the piano, let us look at the situation of the piano industry in about 1850. At that time, the total annual English production of pianos was about 23,000, the French 10,000, the American 9,000.[1] In each case, one leading manufacturer accounted for about 10 percent of the national production, Broadwood in England, Erard in France, and Chickering in the United States. Few figures are available for Austria or Germany, which was so politically split up that no one conceived it as a unit. The Kingdom of Saxony produced 3,150 pianos in 1850, and Vienna produced about 2,700 in 1856.[2] In Vienna, 116 instrument makers, employing some 900 workers, produced those 2,700 pianos, for an average of 23 per firm, 3 per man, a year. It was an inefficient industry in German-speaking Europe, and for the time being, as Carl Kützing had pointed out in 1844, it was in the doldrums. A few large producers across the piano-making world used the beginnings of a factory technique, and a great many small producers made the majority of the instruments, using the same kinds of artisans' shops and apprentice systems that Johann Andreas Stein and Americus Backers had used in the 1770's.

Broadwood is perhaps the best example of the large producer, being the largest of them all, indeed, one of the dozen largest establishments in London manufacturing anything. The firm had begun near the start of the century to use a certain rudimentary division of labor in its manufacture, together with an exploitation of the techniques of the cottage industry. By 1851, it was stated, each Broadwood piano passed through the hands of 42 different specialists, from the brass stud maker to the tone regulator, from the sawyer to the polisher.* Whether power tools were to be found in the Broadwood factory is, in the information I have found, quite unclear. But though Broadwood used a specialization of function and a division of labor, and manufactured more pianos in 1851 than any other maker in the world, seven pianos per worker year (Broadwood's figure) was not yet mass production.

Probably excepting the wire, Broadwood made everything that went into its pianos. The boast that the entire instrument was actually made, not merely assembled, on the premises of the firm whose name decorated the fallboard was a proud assurance of quality for a long time. But already in the 1840's specializing supply companies had begun to appear. Some of the larger makers, like Broadwood, apparently supplied actions to other makers before then. In 1842, J. C. L. Isermann of Hamburg established the first action-making firm, and two years later Jean Schwander followed him in Paris. A London directory of 1851 lists about 200

*The year 1851 was the great year for such information, being the year of the Great Exhibition in London. Piano makers, like other exhibitors at the fair, saturated the advertisement-reading public with information about themselves.

firms in the piano trade. Some of those in the trade were only shopkeepers and tuners. Among the rest—perhaps a remnant of cottage industry—were ten key makers, five fret makers, five producers of hammer rails, five "pianoforte silkers," who did the kinds of silk fronts we saw on the Stodart and Wornum uprights, two suppliers of pins and one of cloth for hammers and dampers, and 21 string makers (some of whom may have dealt in violin strings and the like). The supply industry was not exactly booming. In 1855, T. & H. Brooks began to make actions in London.[3]

As the century wore on, the separate manufacture of parts for pianos took on larger dimensions. The growth of a supply industry meant two things to the piano trade. First, the standardization of parts suggested a standardization of design and the interchangeability of parts. The economies of scale that interchangeability implied was an important consideration for the trade. It is an interesting fact that though the development of mass production by the use of interchangeable parts manufactured by specialists was in general an American technological innovation,[4] the European piano makers were quicker to adopt the system than the Americans. Until after the Civil War, the piano trade in the United States was not large enough to support an economically sound supply industry.

Second, even small firms with small capitalization could profit from the economies of a parts industry. An action from Schwander or Isermann did not cost the small assembler much (if any) more than it cost the larger one, nor did those companies particularly care whether they sold their actions in lots of 1,000 or 25, so long as they sold all they made. The parts industry was one means by which the small producer could stay in business. What militated against small business was not technology but marketing, not manufacture but distribution. Consideration of that matter lies beyond our scope here.[5]

It must be emphasized that specialization in the trade was barely beginning in 1850 or so. But with it, and with various developments in design and materials that occurred over the next decades, the start of a modern manufacturing technology in piano making can be discerned, coming to something like maturity by the end of the century. Perhaps the Industrial Revolution caught up with the piano somewhat later than it did with some other

FIG. 7.1. *Square piano, Nunns & Clark, New York, 1853.*   Serial no. 8054. *Action:* "Rocker" action (Nunns patent), dampers on overhead arms; hammers AAA–f felt-covered, f♯–a⁴ leather over felt. *Stops:* 2 pedals: buff, dampers. *Range:* AAA–a⁴. *Stringing:* AAA–GG single-strung wound, GG♯–F double-strung wound; F♯–a⁴ double-strung plain; cross-strung; AAA 173.3 cm, c² 28.8 cm, a⁴ 4.3 cm. *Framing:* Composite cast iron frame: iron string-plate with metal strut and tubular brace to pin block. *Case:* Rosewood and rosewood veneered, deep-relief carved, with carved legs and pedal lyre, ornate strapwork music rack, painted frame and tension bars; 223.3 cm wide, 118 cm deep. *Location:* Metropolitan Museum of Art, New York. Accession no. 06.1312. Gift of George Lowther, 1906.

manufactures. But catch up it did, and the growth of the American industry in the second half of the nineteenth century is one of its prime success stories.

To study it, we come to a piano from the early 1850's. The remarkable piece of furniture pictured in Figure 7.1 is the next-to-last stage in the evolution of the square piano before it became as extinct as the dinosaur. Indeed, looking at the photograph, one is tempted to call it a dinosaur. More than seven feet wide, decorated in a manner that no piano maker today would dream of emulating, the instrument evokes an antebellum appreciation of size, solidity, and ornateness that suited mid-nineteenth-century America and its headlong rush toward national maturity. For our tastes, beautiful as it is as representing its kind, it is just too much.

To be fair to the taste-makers of the time, such embellishments did not meet unanimous approval. The jury for musical instruments at the 1853 Crystal Palace Exhibition in New York objected strenuously to the "vulgar, tawdry decorations of American pianos, which show a great deal of taste, and that very bad. Not only do we find the very heroics of gingerbread radiating in hideous splendors, fit for the drawing-room of a fashionable hotel, adorned with spit-boxes among other savageries; but even the plain artistic black-and-white, of the keys—that classic simplicity and harmonious distinction—is superseded for pearl and tortoise-shell and eye-grating vermilion abominations."[6] One might nearly believe that the jury had seen this very instrument.

It is a big piano, opulent and resonant, the kind to furnish the sumptuous parlor of a rich or nearly rich whaling captain (his portrait and his wife's, over a pair of dolphins and a trident, are in a medallion on the back of the front panel, but who they were is unknown). Mother-of-pearl and tortoise-shell keys add a luster of luxury, unnecessary by definition, and the carvings on legs and case bespeak a lack of concern for cost. Seen with the eyes of a businessman of 1853—and a whaling captain of that era was surely a businessman, however much the seaman he may have been—it is a splendid symbolic accompaniment to what he would never have called his life-style. Indeed, he would probably have cared little about the piano's musical quality. It may have been played but seldom, being intended mainly to take a prominent place in the parlor. The entire style is an evocation of the heavy, the immovable, the occupier of space that, when occupied, shows how much space is left. It is a fascinating example of the ways in which American society, similar as it was in general atmosphere to the British and European societies of the Victorian age, at least on the social levels represented by this instrument, had a totally different sense from them of space and of object. For as we have seen, the European and English piano makers were moving, or had already moved, away from the increasingly bulky square toward the upright, especially the small upright or pianino, as space on the floors of town-houses and city apartments became more and more at a premium.* If a European wanted a big instrument in the house, it would be a grand like the ones that Liszt or Clara Schumann played in the concert hall.

For all its excess of decoration, this is a very fine instrument. It has nearly the full modern range, $AAA-a^4$ having become increasingly standard beginning in the 1840's and continuing until the 1880's, when the additional third to c^5 became more common. A partial iron frame, with an iron string-plate and both a strut and a tubular brace (not, it seems, a compensating tube) to the pin block, takes up the tension. No one but Chickering seems to have used full iron frames in squares at this time. The partial metal frame may account for the use of only double-stringing. Thus there is a compromise in the probable tone quality. The double-stringing, typical in squares at the time, suggests that the string tension may not have been as high as it could have been. At the same time, we now have a soundboard whose area is considerably increased by its being extended to the left over the keys. The larger soundboard could compensate to some extent for the double-stringing, and means of bracing the soundboard when the keys passed under it had been found.

The very width of case with the Nunns & Clark allowed the longest strings consonant with the square design. We have here, moreover, our first example of cross-stringing, where the longer bass strings cross over the line of shorter higher ones. Henri Pape, it will be recalled, first experimented with this arrangement in his small uprights. Several experiments and patents had been known in the United States during the 1830's, and in 1851 Frederick Mathushek, newly arrived in New York from Germany, patented a design for squares with cross-stringing (U.S. Patent no. 8470), pictured in Figure 7.2. Nunns & Clark's design coheres with that in Mathushek's patent.

The action of this piano has two peculiarities. A somewhat developed form of one patented by John Nunns in 1831, when the

---

*The shift from squares to uprights in Europe, and the American independence from the shift, are shown by some figures from the Great Exhibition of 1851 in London. On exhibit were 56 grands, 19 squares, and 116 small uprights. All 116 uprights were European products, as were 54 of the grands; only 10 squares were exhibited by the 99 European makers who participated. (Edward Rimbault, *The Pianoforte*, pp. 217-20.) If American makers read the message in those figures, they must have assumed it did not apply to them.

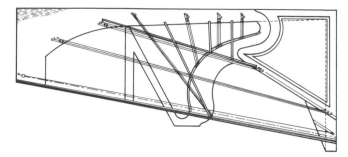

FIG. 7.2. *Patent drawing of Frederick Mathushek design for cross-stringing square pianos, 1851*

Nunns brothers, Robert, William, and John, were still working together in New York, it is a form of what was known as the French square action, in which the jack is mounted on a "rocker" flange on the key. This flange pivots back and forth, allowing the jack to achieve its escapement. The rocker action came in with a repetition action that Erard designed for squares in 1827. Its drawback was the difficulty of keeping it in regulation. The other peculiarity is in the hammers, which are felt in the lower notes and leather-covered felt in the upper ones. What makes these hammers especially interesting is that they were almost certainly covered, at least with the felt, by machine. In 1850, both Rudolf Kreter of New York and Mathushek patented machines for putting felt on hammers. Nunns & Clark purchased Kreter's patent rights and his hammer-covering machine ("for a trifle," according to Daniel Spillane),[7] and became the first company to mechanize the covering of hammers.

Nunns & Clark had the reputation for being among the best builders in New York, both for musical quality and for cabinetry. Perhaps that is why, according to family lore, one of the sons of Heinrich Engelhardt Steinweg sought out employment with Nunns & Clark when the men of that family fanned out to the best shops in New York on their arrival from Germany on June 29, 1850.[8] Wilhelm Steinweg worked at Nunns & Clark for about three years,* and it is at least conceivable that he had a hand in

*Daniel Spillane says that William went to work for William Nunns, who was not then in partnership with his brother Robert and with Clark (*History of the American Pianoforte*, p. 216). Spillane was a careful assembler of facts, and he sometimes turns out to be right when later writers have gone wrong. But in this case, I am inclined to trust the family's tradition.

building this square. But in March 1853, the year that this piano was made, the Steinweg family took the two momentous steps of beginning their own piano-manufacturing business and of Anglicizing the name of their company to Steinway.

Just as the Nunns & Clark square was the next-to-last stage in the development of its kind, the Steinway grand pictured in Figure 7.3 is the next-to-last stage before the modern grand. But the square piano was already on its way to oblivion, whereas the modern grand has continued a long, happy life.

This is the first American grand we have examined. The form

By permission of the Smithsonian Institution, Washington, D.C.

FIG. 7.3. *Grand piano, Steinway & Sons, New York, 1857.* Serial no. 1199. *Action:* Repetition action (probably not original); felt-covered hammers. *Stops:* 2 pedals: una corda, dampers to c♯³. *Range:* AAA–a⁴. *Stringing:* AA–FF single-strung wound, FF♯–E♭ double-strung wound, E–a⁴ triple-strung plain; straight-strung; AAA 187.1 cm, c²?, a⁴ 4.8 cm. *Framing:* One piece, cast-iron frame, bolted into pin block and underframe. *Case:* Rosewood veneered; 242 cm long, 136.4 cm wide. *Location:* Smithsonian Institution, Washington, D.C. Catalog no. 74.6.

was not one that American makers built very often, though a few grands were apparently made in this country before 1840. When European virtuosos came to these shores, they brought their own Erards, Pleyels, or Broadwoods with them. Of native American pianists, after all, there were hardly any, and none of international reputation until Louis Moreau Gottschalk of New Orleans set the Parisian musical world abuzz after his debut in 1845 at the age of sixteen. Not until 1853 did he return to conquer his native land, and then he brought two Pleyels along.

Jonas Chickering was among the first American manufacturers to design and market grands on a continuing basis, his first one having been made in 1840. The earliest American grand to which I have found certain reference was exhibited by Bridgeland & Jardine at the Mechanics' Institute in New York in 1833.* Chickering was the first, not only in America, to experiment with adapting Babcock's iron frame to the grand, perhaps under Babcock's personal influence, and he patented that innovation in 1843. As American musical culture matured, and pianists and orchestras began to be spawned by it, the demand for grands grew.

When, therefore, Henry Engelhardt Steinway and his sons cut loose from Nunns & Clark and the other builders with whom they had been gaining a shrewd sense of the American trade, and began their own business in 1853 (Steinway had made pianos since about 1825 in his native Harz area in Germany),† their high ambitions made it natural that they would soon begin to build grands, which they did in 1856.⁹ Steinway squares were soon in wide demand, and uprights followed in the next decade. The Steinway story is a remarkable one, which will unfold in more detail as this chapter proceeds. It is not unfair to anyone to say that the modern piano was of the Steinways' devising—not of course full-blown, but

---

*Daniel Spillane, *History of the American Pianoforte*, p. 158. An advertisement in a New York newspaper of 1791 stated that a pianist named Kullin would perform a concert "on a Grand Concert Pianoforte" made by Dodds & Claus of New York. It might have been what we call a grand, but it could equally have been called "grand" in the parlance of the day to make ticket buyers expect a large instrument, for concert purposes most likely square. John Isaac Hawkins, who called his tiny upright a Portable Grand Pianoforte (another indication that the meaning of "grand" is not unambiguous), advertised in 1800 that his little instrument took up only a quarter of the space occupied by a "grand," again perhaps meaning a large square. (See Arthur Loesser, *Men, Women and Pianos*, pp. 460–61.)

†Steinway & Sons has a square and a grand made by Heinrich Engelhardt Steinweg in Germany during the 1830's. (See Figs. 3 and 4 in Cynthia Hoover, "The Steinways and Their Pianos.")

building on the decades of experiment and development that I have sketched in the preceding chapters.

The grand in Figure 7.3, built in the fourth year of the company's existence, the second year in which it made grands, is not yet the modern Steinway. But nearly all that separates no. 1199 from the modern instrument is that it is straight-strung and has only two pedals. The range is a full seven octaves, the hammers are felt covered, the strings are close-wound copper on iron and cast steel, and the frame is a single-cast piece of iron. The piano now has what looks very much like Erard's repetition action, though Henry Steinway Jr. also designed some variations of the English jack action for grands.*

We have come a long way from Cristofori's little four-octave gem, nearly as far from Zumpe's square or Schmidt's grand. No longer could Beethoven have complained, as he did around 1795 in a letter to Johann Andreas Streicher, that the piano sounded too much like a harp.[10] That small, quickly decaying tone was a thing of the past, except on the most shoddy of instruments made for the most modest parlors.

In another respect, too, we have come a long distance from the piano's beginnings. By the time the 1857 Steinway was made, and certainly by the time our next example had come from the factory, the Industrial Revolution had ceased to be revolution and had become a settled fact of European life. Both the shape of labor as an occupation and the shape of the family were in flux. The most obvious demand of industrialization was a constant market for manufactured products, and the industrial tendency was to stimulate a market by changing the products marketed. The era of obsolescence, planned or not, was under way, and the piano trade was by no means unaffected by its impact. In order to be sure of selling their products, the piano makers had to engage in advertising and to show the other symptoms of a newly competitive system.

In the second half of the nineteenth century, that competitive system gave birth to the international expositions. These were grand fairs, designed to show the world the technological advances being made in all fields and to identify the leaders in the

---

*The action in the piano may not be the original one. It is unlike actions that Henry Steinway Jr. patented in 1857 and 1858. Hoover (*ibid.*, p. 54) suggests that the present action may have been installed as a replacement in 1863, when the instrument was back at Steinway.

various industries by means of prizes. To be sure, there had been local exhibitions in England, the United States, and Europe since the 1820's at least, but the great series of international exhibitions began in London in 1851 with the Great Exhibition. Others followed in Europe and the United States (the Philadelphia Centennial Exposition of 1876 and the Chicago World's Fair of 1893 were the great ones in this country) and as far distant as Australia. They were the predecessors of the twentieth century's World's Fairs at New York, San Francisco, Brussels, and Montreal.

These nineteenth-century expositions were increasingly truly international in their exhibits, presenting the opportunity for technologists to profit from the advances made in all parts of the world. The fairs were the nineteenth-century equivalent of mass media, an important means by which technological development was communicated throughout the world; and that communication formed Europe and North America into essentially one technological culture. That is not to say that differences were erased. In the piano industry, the French and British makers continued to produce what had made them dominant in the first half of the century. The Americans and, as the century progressed, the Germans provided most of the innovations. A certain national pride turned up in response to these technologies, conservatives devaluing the new technology as unnecessary, and progressives eagerly exploiting it. The chauvinism was an element in the continuing story of technological developments that were not universally adopted.

It is accurate to say, I think, that the Paris Exposition of 1867 was a major factor in making the best American pianos international in influence and acceptance and in giving the radical Americans the feeling that they had assumed the leadership of the entire industry. The mere gold medals were not by themselves sufficient to that end, though no American maker concealed the prizes awarded. The makers had to be willing to establish and maintain an export trade to follow up their successes. They were willing.

The grand pictured in Figure 7.4 is probably the kind of piano with which Steinway & Sons won the first prize for grand pianos at Paris in 1867. I will return to some details of that exposition after discussing the instrument itself.

Though this piano does not contain all of the improvements that Steinway would later introduce, it can be called our first modern

FIG. 7.4. *Grand piano, Steinway & Sons, New York, 1864.* Serial no. 13547. *Action:* Repetition action, over-dampers; felt-covered hammers. *Stops:* 2 pedals: una corda, dampers to c^3. *Range:* AAA–c^5. *Stringing:* AAA–DD♯ single-strung wound, EE–GG double-strung wound, GG♯–C♯ triple-strung wound, D–c^5 triple-strung plain; cross-strung; AAA 197.5 cm, c^2 33 cm, c^5 4.4 cm. *Framing:* One-piece cast-iron frame with agraffes. *Case:* Rosewood veneered; 257.2 cm long, 143.5 cm wide. *Location:* Yale University Collection of Musical Instruments, New Haven, Conn. Acquisition no. 334. Bequest of Susan Dwight Bliss. Photograph by Thomas A. Brown.

grand. It incorporates the full modern range of seven octaves and a third, Pape's felt hammers, Babcock's one-piece cast-iron frame, and Erard's agraffes. Its strings are of steel—and it has what Steinway was the first to use successfully in the design of grands, cross-stringing.

Steinway & Sons began to use cross-stringing very early in its career. A square made perhaps in 1853, the first year of the company's existence, is cross-strung.* Steinway's first appearance in

*The piano, serial no. 483, is in the company's possession in New York. It is about six and a half feet wide and has a one-piece cast iron frame and a seven-octave range, CC–c^5. (See Cynthia Hoover, "The Steinways and Their Pianos," Fig. 5 and p. 52.)

the public eye was at the Crystal Palace Exhibition in New York in 1855, where it won a gold medal for a cross-strung square. Pape, as we know, made cross-strung uprights beginning in 1828, and the American makers Bridgeland & Jardine and perhaps a few others had tried cross-stringing squares in the 1830's. In 1836 Isaac Clark of Cincinnati patented cross-stringing just six days before John Godwin took out a patent in London. Cincinnati seems to have been a hotbed of American experiments in cross-stringing: Henry Klepfer patented a method of cross-stringing for uprights there in 1851 (U.S. patent no. 6002). Frederick Mathushek of New York took out his patent for cross-stringing squares in the same year, which perhaps prevented the Steinways from patenting their scheme of doing the same. We saw cross-stringing on Mathushek's design in the Nunns & Clark square at the beginning of this chapter, and perhaps that company had some influence on the Steinways. At any rate, it remained for Steinway to succeed with grands where others, if they had tried (I have found no certain evidence that anyone did), had failed. In 1859, Henry Steinway Jr. obtained a patent for cross-stringing grands on the design reproduced in Figure 7.5.

Steinway ran the strings in a fan-like disposition out from the tuning pins. Since cross-stringing allows for longer strings in a smaller space, the designer can obtain a richer pattern of partials, which depends in part on the increased flexibility of the long strings. Even with the added length, especially of strings in the middle range, the bridges could now be positioned closer to the center of the soundboard. The board is more responsive at the center because of the elasticity of the "crown," thus giving a better resonance to the vibrations it receives through the bridge. Cross-stringing thus appears as the principal means by which the tone was enhanced in richness and volume. In this sense our 1864 Steinway is in all essentials a modern piano and sounds like one.

In some respects, moreover, it was made like a modern piano. In 1860 Steinway moved to an expanded factory that occupied the entire block between Fifty-second and Fifty-third streets and Fourth (now Park) and Lexington avenues in New York. It was to some extent a mechanized factory as well, for in line with a number of developments in American manufacturing technology, Steinway used wood-working machinery driven by a Corliss steam

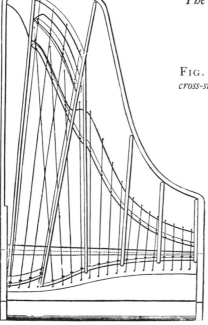

FIG. 7.5. *Patent drawing of Steinway cross-stringing design for grand pianos*

engine, with rows of line-shaft-driven planing and sawing machines. Such acceptance of the latest available manufacturing technology marked Steinway off from most of its competitors, very few of which apparently felt the need to do anything differently from the way it was done in the 1830's. The Steinways, as newcomers, had nothing to gain from emulating someone else's Grandpa. And they had nothing to lose from striking out in the new ways provided by their new country. For wood-working machinery, though by no means confined to the United States, was more widely and efficiently used there than anywhere else.

There may be good reason for that development. Wood was incredibly abundant in North America, and Americans had depended heavily on wood from the very beginning. Even as early as 1799, America's per-capita wood consumption was 5.8 times as high as Great Britain's.[11] As society developed and the population grew, the dependence became little short of prodigious. American labor, moreover, had been scarce from the beginning. Given a plentiful supply of wood and a short supply of labor, the motivation to use machinery for the more efficient use of the material is quite clear.[12] Thus at the same time that wood was becoming scarcer in Europe, leading to the development of iron and other materials for construction, American technology was discovering ways to make better use of its own seemingly inexhaustible supply of wood. Machine-driven saws, planing machines, and steam-powered lathes were invented and improved at a remarkable rate in the first half of the nineteenth century, to the point that a British parliamentary committee, looking into the "American system of manufactures" in 1854, was especially impressed with the speed and efficacy of the wood-working machinery for the building trades: "In one of these manufactories twenty men were making panelled doors at the rate of 100 per day."[13]

It is unlikely that Steinway was the first piano maker to profit from the American advance in wood-working machinery, though the company had adopted it within ten years of the family's arrival in New York. There is some indication that Chickering had equipped its new factory, begun in 1853, with steam-powered machinery (a matter difficult to establish, because the Chickering records were destroyed some years ago by fire).[14] Europe had seen the first automation of parts of piano manufacture. Henri Pape (who else?) invented an automatic saw for cutting veneer, with which he even managed to cut sheets of ivory 10 to 12 feet long. Rosamond Harding reports that he exhibited an ivory-veneered piano in 1827.[15] Arthur Loesser believes that Broadwood used steam-driven machinery relatively early in the nineteenth century, but he has found no more specific information about it than I have found.[16] And as we saw above, Nunns & Clark was using a hammer-covering machine after 1851. But even the official Steinway history, written for the company's centennial in 1953, in the same breath extols Steinway's forward-looking role in the adoption of machinery and emphasizes the craft of piano making. The Steinway plant, it claims, is "one-third modern factory and two-thirds a craftsman's shop."[17] The proportion on the "modern factory" side would doubtless have been less in 1864 but was still higher than in perhaps any other piano-manufacturing establishment.

Such was the background of the grand that was the centerpiece of Steinway & Sons' exhibits at the expositions in the 1860's. The firm won one of the eight gold medals awarded for pianos with a cross-strung grand in London in 1862. No one seems to have realized the magnitude of what the Steinway represented save perhaps Johann Baptist Streicher, the heir to the Stein-Streicher tradition in Vienna. After seeing the Steinway grand at the London Exposition, he went home and began making copies of it. He was the only one to do so, as far as I can determine. The London jury was impressed with the qualities of the instrument but assumed that the technology was no different from that used in some Russian cross-strung pianos that had been shown at the Great Exhibition of 1851. The Russians, like Henri Pape, had used a second soundboard under the bridge of the cross-strung strings. Acoustics experts argued in 1862 that the Steinway was theoretically defective, but they could not blink the fact that its sound was extremely good.[18]

With the Paris Exposition of 1867 the battle lines were drawn. A serious crisis had arisen for Steinway since 1862. Two of the Steinway sons, Charles and Henry Jr., died suddenly in 1865. Charles had been in charge of sales, and Henry had been responsible for the technological innovations, having worked out the company's first seven patents, including the iron frame and the cross-stringing. The one son who had remained in Germany, Theodore, had been making pianos there since the rest of the family had emigrated to New York. On the deaths of his brothers, he sold out his business in Braunschweig and came to New York. Scientifically trained and technologically curious, Theodore took over the manufacturing end of the business; he would later bring the Steinway to its apogee, develop the upright to the point of respectability, and lead the way in the decline of the square in America. But there was not time before the Paris Exposition for Theodore to put his mark on anything, except perhaps for some sign of his passion for meticulous construction, a trait not lacking in other members of the family. The ardors of Paris were anyway borne by William, who turned out to be the family's business and marketing genius.

The two leading American firms, Steinway and Chickering (recall that the 1867 exposition took place when the Steinway company was only 14 years old), prepared well for the contest, spending, it is alleged, some $80,000 each in promotion, advertising, the engagement of pianists, and other sorts of puffery. We will see Chickering's contribution to the competition below. In the event,

FIG. 7.6. *Cartoon by "Cham" (Amédée de Noé) from 'Le Charivari,' Paris, 1867.* The success of Steinway at the Paris Exposition, 1867, is caricatured in this cartoon, the caption of which reads, "The public at the Exposition is suddenly seized with the rage to become pianists on hearing the admirable American Steinway pianos." The lithograph was presented to Steinway & Sons by the pianist Vladimir Horowitz.

the Americans simply walked away with the honors, galvanizing a great deal of comment in the process. Steinway received what the chairman of the jury said was the first prize, Chickering the second. Broadwood was given a prize mostly, it seems, in acknowledgment of past achievements, and Streicher of Vienna received one for a piano that was, in effect, a copy of Steinway's.

The combination of the technologies, then, brought the Americans their victory in Paris. And Steinway had more of those technologies, since its piano had the cross-stringing that Chickering's lacked. It is interesting and indicative of the jury's objectivity that not a single French piano figured in the gold medal list (Erard did not compete). A number of French observers took this episode as a defeat for France. L.-A. de Pontécoulant wrote a series of articles, later brought together in a book, severely castigating his compatriots' failure to make any sort of innovation for 20 years. "Oh, Pierre Erard, where are you?" he declaimed.[19]

Defeated or not, the piano-buying French public recognized something desirable in the Steinway, as witness the amusing cartoon in Figure 7.6 published in *Le Charivari* in 1867. Cartoons, to be sure, make their points by exaggeration. But it is no exaggeration to say that the musical world was impressed with what Steinway had wrought.

The year 1867 was a watershed, then, as most historians of the piano have agreed. From then on, the German and Austrian makers, leaping for the most part to the Steinway bandwagon, joined the world of the modern piano. The French and British makers, having led the way up to the 1850's, now stayed mostly with what they had been making for 20 years or more, as the Germans and Austrians had done while the French were leading the way.

As the nineteenth century wore on, the total production of pianos rose astronomically, and the Americans and Germans between them took the greatest share of it. The phenomenon can be seen in the following tabulation, showing the approximate annual output of pianos in the four major producing countries (the figures are in thousands):[20]

Year	England	France	Germany	U.S.
1850	23	10	—	9
1870	25	21	15	24
1890	50	20	70	72

The figures for 1890 are particularly striking. Production in France had fallen slightly since 1870, and though England's output had doubled in that 20-year period, America's had tripled—

and Germany's had nearly quadrupled. A similar story comes out in export figures. By 1890, Germany was exporting about £35,000 worth of pianos annually *to England*, had completely captured the Australian market from English makers, and was running away from English competition in South America. We must suppose that the political unification of Germany, completed in 1871, with its removal of remaining commercial barriers, had some effect on this expansion of the piano trade.

In Britain, the two long-dominant firms of Broadwood and Collard and Collard (formerly Clementi and Company) lost their market share: where Broadwood had made 2,800 pianos annually in 1870, its output fell to 2,600 in 1880 and to only 1,000 in 1890; and Collard and Collard went from 2,500 in 1870 to 1,950 in 1880 and 1,840 in 1890. Meanwhile, the comparable German firms, Bechstein and Blüthner, increased their market position: Bechstein's output grew from 600 in 1870 and 900 in 1880 to 2,500 in 1890; and Blüthner's went from 800 in 1870 to 1,000 in 1880 and 1890.

In France, the fall in the total output of pianos between 1870 and 1890 was insignificant next to the drastic decline in the country's share of world manufacture. In the 1860's, France had made about 40 percent of the 50,000 pianos produced each year around the world. The expansion of the market in the next half century brought total production to about 650,000 in 1910, an increase of 1,200 percent; over that period, though France's production had risen about 25 percent, its share of the market had dropped to just under 4 percent.[21] In the meantime, the American share of the market rose from about 20 percent to 54 percent. Production figures for individual firms in France remained almost level over most of this period of enormous expansion in production and distribution. Erard went from 1,500 instruments annually in 1870 to 2,000 in 1890 (the earlier figure incorporates an estimated 500 made in Erard's London factory, which was closed in 1890). Pleyel showed no advance at all, producing 2,500 annually in both 1870 and 1890.[22] Steinway in New York grew less than one might expect, expanding from about 2,000 in 1870 to 2,500 in 1890, but another American firm, Knabe of Baltimore, went from about 500 in 1870 to 2,000 in 1890.

Whatever else these numbers may demonstrate, they certainly

show that the British and French lost market leadership to the Germans and Americans. To be sure, popularity is no guarantee of excellence. But the German and American makers seem to have been able to persuade buyers, not only in their own territories but also in foreign ones, that their instruments were superior in quality and competitive in price. In this connection, we must not underestimate the impact of advertising, which the Americans and Germans pursued with real ardor. As a persuasive art, advertising has never felt constrained by regard for the strictest accuracy, let alone for the virtue of modesty. But one cannot criticize Steinway, Chickering, and the others for calling attention to plain facts of the past, such as the gold medals in Paris in 1867, whatever other claims may have been made in addition. And it is to be noted that the Steinway "system," which was the word both that company and its imitators used to describe the technological combination in what Steinway had achieved, entailed what was at the time perceived very widely as the durability of first-rate construction methods and the rich fullness of tone that the music of later Romanticism required. The Steinway was, without question, an extremely fine piano.

We are getting in years a bit ahead of the story. The Paris Exposition of 1867 was, however, so distinctly a turning-point that it has been worthwhile to pursue its ramifications. Before turning elsewhere, we will look at Steinway's American competitor in 1867.

The lovely grand pictured in Figure 7.7 is the model that earned Chickering a gold medal in Paris. Indeed, Chickering claimed to have won the first prize above Steinway, since C. Frank Chickering, who handled the company's exhibit, was decorated by the French government as a Chevalier of the Legion of Honor. Someone got the idea that the decoration was really the top prize of the exposition, and before the official report was written, the intelligence was transmitted to Boston by the new transatlantic cable that the Legion of Honor was "officially" proclaimed higher than any gold medals. The Chickering factory had an instant holiday, and the workers paraded in the streets of Boston. William Steinway lost no time in objecting to Chickering's interpretation of the award, and a small tempest ensued. Charges and countercharges were spewed about, and since the official documents of the exposition were in French, interpretations of them by various partisans demonstrated that, on the whole, Americans had a less than perfect command of the French language.

The bad blood between Steinway and Chickering did not abate

By courtesy of The Schubert Club, St. Paul, Minn.

FIG. 7.7. *Grand piano, Chickering, Boston, 1868.*   Serial no. 32685. *Action:* Edwin Brown repetition action, over-dampers; felt-covered hammers. *Stops:* 2 pedals: una corda, dampers to d³. *Range:* AAA–c⁵. *Stringing:* AAA–FF single-strung wound, FF♯–C♯ double-strung wound, D–c⁵ triple-strung plain; straight-strung; AAA 194.7 cm, c² 33.1 cm, c⁵ 4.9 cm. *Framing:* One-piece cast-iron frame with agraffes. *Case:* Rosewood veneered with spirit varnish finish; 254 cm long, 145 cm wide. *Location:* The Schubert Club, St. Paul, Minn.

for some time. Both companies agreed not to exhibit at the Vienna Exposition of 1873, but William Steinway did some private showing and entertaining. When the official report of the exposition's piano selection made specific reference to Steinway's absence, regretting that "the famous, path-breaking firm of Steinway & Sons, New York, to which the whole art of piano making owes so much, was not represented," Chickering responded quite furiously, as might have been expected.[23]

Our example, now owned by the Schubert Club, was made in 1868. It differs from the Steinway in two major respects: the Chickering's action is unlike the one used in the Steinway, and its one-piece frame incorporates straight-stringing rather than Steinway's patented cross-stringing. Some observers in Paris preferred Chickering to Steinway, perhaps because its straight-stringing seemed a bit more conservative.

Chickering was not always conservative, though the company focused more on the quality of its instruments than on innovation as such. Its founder, Jonas Chickering, had left his apprenticeship with John Osborn to join in partnership with James Stewart, whom we have met before. It was apparently during this fruitful partnership, from 1823 to 1826, that Stewart originated the idea of running the strings around the hitch-pins and carrying them back to the adjacent tuning pins. But Chickering pianos made after 1827, the year Stewart patented this idea in England, show the old method of attaching strings singly to the hitch-pins, as does this 1868 grand, suggesting that Jonas Chickering was never convinced that Stewart's idea was a good one.

In 1830, Chickering teamed up with a businessman named John Mackay, and the company was soon on its feet. Chickering was the artisan, with perhaps not much of a head for commerce, and Mackay, who had been associated earlier with Alpheus Babcock, was the entrepreneur and organizer. It was a happy partnership until 1841, when Mackay, on a voyage to South America to sell Chickering pianos and to buy fine woods for the factory, was lost at sea. By then, Jonas Chickering was the acknowledged leader in a rather scattered American piano industry, and the 1840's saw him extend that leadership. We have seen that a patent for an iron frame for squares was granted in 1840 (Alpheus Babcock had gone to work for Chickering in 1837), and that another, for an iron frame for grands, followed in 1843.* Chickering was one of the very few American makers who built grands in those years. When the firm exhibited its iron-framed grand at the Great Exhibition in London in 1851, the instrument impressed the jury enough to win a medal, but it did not inspire emulation. It is sometimes claimed that Chickering was using cross-stringing in the 1840's, but I have seen no evidence of it.

Like most makers of the time, Chickering used an action that was peculiar to that company's pianos. There was no established specialist company making actions in the United States at that time, and besides, the leading manufacturers felt it important to be able to claim complete control over both manufacture and assembly of their instruments. Chickering's action was one patented in 1843 by Edwin Brown, who vacillated between working for Chickering and trying vainly for independent success. Brown's action was a staple on Chickering grands for about sixty years, it seems; I have seen it in a grand from about 1902 and have been unable to find out when Chickering switched over to the developed Herz-Erard action. As the diagram of the Brown action, Figure 7.8, shows, it was a modification of the English grand action. I have seen a Brown action on only one piano other than Chickerings: a monstrous pedal grand (a grand piano with a pedal board, like that on an organ, for playing bass notes) made by J. W. Brackett in Boston in the 1870's.†

The year after the success at the Great Exhibition, the Chick-

---

*Unfortunately, what was said to be Chickering's first grand, made in 1840 and containing the experimental frame that was patented in 1843, was destroyed in a fire at the Henry Ford Museum in Dearborn, Michigan, in 1970. A photograph of the instrument is in Helen Rice Hollis, *The Piano*, Plate 91, p. 105.

† The instrument is in the collection of William E. Garlick of Boston. Pianos with pedal boards were made for a long time, beginning in the eighteenth century. Mozart owned a Walter grand with one; the piano is in the Mozarteum in Salzburg, but the pedal board has disappeared. The Metropolitan Museum of Art in New York has a pedal grand made by Johann Schmidt. An 1815 instrument made by Josef Brodmann of Vienna with pedals is in the Kunsthistorisches Museum. In about the 1840's, pedal boards were sometimes attached to pianinos. Robert Schumann came into possession of one, was enraptured by it, wrote two works for it (the "Studies for Pedal-Piano," op. 56, and "Sketches for Pedal-Piano," op. 58), and persuaded Felix Mendelssohn to institute classes in pedal piano at the Leipzig Conservatory. By the late nineteenth century, when William Garlick's Brackett was made, they were quite rare, and that instrument may have been made to special order for an organist who wanted to practice at home. The pedal action for pianos is difficult to design and hard for the player to control. I doubt whether a pedal piano has been made for 100 years or so now.

ering factory at 334 Washington Street, Boston, was totally destroyed by fire. The manufacturing and showrooms occupied temporary space while a new, larger factory was built on Tremont Street. The building still stands, and when it was completed, it was the largest building in the United States except for the Capitol Building in Washington, D.C. The new factory was still going up

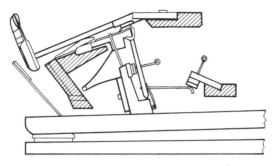

FIG. 7.8. *Edwin Brown repetition action.* The patent drawing represents the action for a square piano, but only the shape of the hammers differentiates it from the action for a grand.

when Jonas Chickering died, Dec. 9, 1853, and his three sons, who in the fashion of the day had been trained in their father's vocation, took over the management. C. Frank, the middle son, became head of the company, his older brother, Thomas, handled the business end, and George, the youngest, worked at various positions in the factory.

Chickering pianos were being sold all over the United States by this time, and the company had a deserved reputation as the front-ranking maker, in both quality and quantity, in the country. Steinway would soon enough bring its challenge. No American-born piano virtuosos had yet emerged to enlarge the demand for grands. Still, surprisingly large numbers of now unknown but accomplished pianists were performing in the United States, judging by the reports in *Dwight's Journal of Music*, a weekly published in Boston from 1851 to 1881. European pianists who came to the United States on tour usually brought their own instruments with them, but they sometimes consented to play on domestic pianos. A concert in Boston in 1856, when Sigismond Thalberg played both his own Erard and a Chickering, gave John Sullivan Dwight

the opportunity to comment interestingly on the comparison between them:

It is quite evident that he regards the Chickering instruments as the most
formidable rivals [to Erard], and pays them practically the highest com-
pliment. To our ears there is still a purely musical quality in the Erard
tone, which has not quite been reached by others. Forced to loudest effects, they sound a little antique and metallic, particularly in the middle
treble octaves; yet is the quality still musical, the *altissimo* tones exquis-
itely so, the bass magnificently rich. The Chickering tones are rounder,
mellower throughout the whole compass, but they come to the ear less
distinct, as if the tone were not yet refined to its purely musical element.
. . . It is said the Chickering instruments stand in tune the best.[24]

Dwight, a personal friend of the Chickerings, father and sons,
and a great booster of things Bostonian, was a sober and scrupu-
lously neutral observer and reporter. In his diffident last sentence,
he put his finger on an aspect of piano manufacture in which
the Americans could rightly claim superiority over Europeans.
Americans typically liked temperatures higher in their buildings
and homes than the Europeans, and devised heating systems to
match the preference. European pianos in American buildings did
not enjoy those warm and dry atmospheres, and many a fine piano
from England or France simply collapsed and died because the
wooden parts dried too quickly. American cabinetmakers, accustomed to making furniture that would survive the rigors of American heating systems, passed on their knowledge to the piano makers, and in competition after competition in the United States,
French pianos especially were judged inferior to American ones in
their capacity to stay in tune. It is possible, but not demonstrable,
that the American leadership in the development of the iron frame
stemmed from Yankee know-how in building things to withstand
the heating of American homes. Certainly the American superiority in construction that would survive both the subarctic climate
of Alberta and the Dakotas and the subtropical climate of Florida
and the Gulf States aided the Americans to lead in developing
worldwide markets in the late nineteenth century.

It was in the very year of Jonas Chickering's death, 1853, that
the first real American virtuoso returned to his native country
after dazzling the musical capitals of Europe. Louis Moreau Gottschalk brought a pair of Pleyels when he came, and concertized

extensively with them. Two years later, he sold them at one of his financial low points, and the Chickering company, sensing that so popular a pianist could do some good even for the leading piano manufacturer, gave him two concert grands, probably very similar to the one pictured in Figure 7.7.* Together with a tuner, they accompanied Gottschalk wherever he went in his fantastically busy concert career, even to South America, where he died. Gottschalk's memoirs give proof of his affection for the Chickerings and of his sensitivity to the hard times they went through in his service.[25]

Eventually piano virtuosos became the mainstay of the concert stage in America, as they had been for some time in Europe. This led piano companies to contract with pianists for concert tours, providing the instruments and making sure that everyone knew the piano's brand name. Steinway sponsored such a tour by Anton Rubinstein in 1872–73, and Chickering retaliated by contracting with Hans von Bülow in 1875–76. Doubtless this practice paid off in sales to those who thought that if von Bülow sounded so good on a Chickering, they might sound good on one too. Certainly the motivation of such sales played a large part in the subsidies piano companies paid to have their instruments played by well-known pianists.

In some instances, more value accrued to the manufacturer than might have been predicted. Hans von Bülow, the great German pianist, was a lifelong user, critic, and commentator on the qualities of Bechstein pianos, and his shrewd criticisms influenced the Bechstein firm's design and manufacturing policies. To be sure, one should probably add seasoning to such testimonials as those attributed to Liszt. To the firm of Bösendorfer in Vienna, Liszt wrote, "The perfection of your grand piano surpasses my most idealistic expectations."[26] To Steinway, he wrote, "Your grand piano is a glorious masterpiece in power, sonority, singing quality and perfect harmonic effects."[27] And when C. Frank Chickering presented one of the 1867 prize-winning grands to Liszt in Rome, the pianist is said to have stopped after a few bars and said, "It is imperial! I never thought a piano could possess such qualities."[28] Can one believe anything of such testimonials? Well, perhaps one can. After all, Bösendorfers, Steinways, and Chickerings were

*The portrait next to the piano in Figure 7.7 is of Gottschalk.

among the finest pianos made in the 1870's. Liszt may have been fulsome, but he was probably not hypocritical.

In 1896, the last of Jonas Chickering's sons died, and the company had to go on as best it could. Along with a sizable number of other companies, it was absorbed into the American Piano Company in 1908. In 1932 the American Piano Company in its turn merged with the Aeolian Company to form the Aeolian-American Corporation, later the Aeolian Corporation. Chickering pianos are still made by the Aeolian Corporation, though the manufacturing plant was removed from Boston to East Rochester, New York, some years ago. Still, it is not quite the same thing, at least to the sentimentalist who has played a Chickering made by or under the supervision of people named Chickering. The Schubert Club's fine grand is a splendid exemplar of one of the glories of the American piano trade.

———————◆▶———————

It is time to complete the story of the square piano. The massive Steinway in Figure 7.9 may stand as the ultimate stage in the model. From the tiny Zumpe, indistinguishable externally from a clavichord, to this housekeeper's nightmare is a long distance. I referred before to dinosaurs. The Steinway square is unquestionably a dinosaur among pianos. Ironically, well before no. 37600 was made, Theodore Steinway had decided to concentrate on improving the grand and the upright and to let the square die out. The decoration may strike us as over-ornate, but it is almost simple compared with the carving on the Nunns & Clark we saw at the beginning of this chapter.

Steinway had been making squares ever since the company had started business in New York. Indeed, the application of the cast-iron frame and cross-stringing to the square had brought domestic fame to the Steinways in 1855. But for all the massiveness of such an instrument, nearly seven feet from end to end, it did not produce as much pianistic racket as a grand of roughly the same length. And as the nineteenth century was drawing to a close, housing patterns in the United States were changing, and tastes were beginning to turn toward a simpler style and a smaller floor space. The shortcomings—perhaps we should say longcomings— of the square doomed it to extinction.

FIG. 7.9. *Square piano, Steinway & Sons, New York, 1877–78.* Serial no. 37600. *Action:* Steinway square action, dampers in frame; felt-covered hammers. *Stops:* 2 pedals: moderator (felt strip between hammers and strings), dampers to bb^3. *Range:* AAA–c^5. *Stringing:* AAA–GG single-strung wound, GG#–G double-strung wound, G#–c#^{2} double-strung plain, d^2–c^5 triple-strung plain; cross-strung; AAA 177.8 cm, c^2 30.5 cm, c^5 5.1 cm. *Framing:* One-piece cast-iron frame. *Case:* Dark rosewood veneered, ornately carved legs; 210.8 cm wide, 106.7 cm deep. *Location:* Smithsonian Institution, Washington, D.C. Catalog no. 381,444.

I may be allowed the speculation that it did not have to be so. Had piano makers not felt it necessary to make squares ever larger as technological changes allowed, the square might have survived, just as the small upright survived to return to favor in the mid–twentieth century. But in the twentieth century, small uprights were but modifications of current models, whereas the square had been extinct in Europe since about 1860.* I have heard piano people say that the square was an intrinsically poor design. I am not quite convinced. The horizontal action is potentially much more effective than the action of any upright. With a metal frame, the square could equal a small grand in volume and tone, and could withstand the torque that warped earlier squares. If the tun-

---

*To be sure, in a sense the square is making a comeback in the twentieth century, as we will see when we get to the electric piano. But the instrument involved is technically not a piano in our definition.

ing pins were placed at the front of the case instead of at the rear, following Matthäus Andreas Stein's lead rather than John Broadwood's, the tuner would not get a sore back from leaning over the instrument to tune it. To be sure, an una corda stop is not possible on a square because the hammers do not sit parallel to the strings' direction, but Steinway and most other makers had reinstated the old moderator stop, which we saw in the eighteenth and early nineteenth centuries, a strip of felt brought between hammers and strings to produce a muted sound (a stop that is reappearing on contemporary small uprights). The damper system that most makers used, with the dampers mounted in a rack above the strings and pushed up by damper-lifters attached to the keys, is ineffective on all the squares I have played. But it is not the only conceivable damper system. The problem of getting long enough strings for good tone into a small enough case always remains a difficulty in a small piano, but I believe that one could put longer strings in a smallish square than in an upright console or spinet model.

No, the square did not die because it was intrinsically a poor design. It died because the manufacturers persisted in making it as big as possible when the consuming public needed a more efficient use of floor space. In the United States, to be sure, people went on buying big squares for a time, as they would later go on buying big automobiles, and probably for many of the same reasons. Steinway made its last square in 1889, not long after our example was made. Other manufacturers came more slowly to realize that only a decisive action would prevent the square's lingering in a slow decline and death. In 1904, at a meeting of the manufacturers' association in Atlantic City, New Jersey, the makers gathered together all of the squares they could find, piled them 50 feet high, and burned them. So ended the square piano.

Steinway's square may be taken, however, to demonstrate a manufacturing advance in two respects. For one thing, the hammers were almost certainly machine-felted. A hammer-covering machine is recorded from Germany in about 1835, but it was ahead of its time. I mentioned earlier two American models patented in 1850. Rudolf Kreter's machine, which Nunns & Clark bought, was the more complex of the two; Frederick Mathushek's was a bit too light, especially as strings increased in weight and hammers had to match them.[29] Such machines depended on the availability of good quality felt, made specifically for piano hammers. The felt was made in sheets, tapered from a thick end to a thin one. The sheets were first passed into the machine along a plane and cut off at the requisite width; the set of wooden hammer cores, already treated with glue, was then pressed down on the center of the prepared sheet, and the machine forced the felt up around the hammer cores and held it there until the glue set.

In 1887, Alfred Dolge patented the improved machine shown in Figure 7.10. With the earlier models, the hammers had to be left in the machine until the glue dried. Dolge designed removable elements, and the whole set of newly covered and glued hammers could be taken out to dry elsewhere, a new set inserted, and the process continued without interruption. The glue was usually sufficient to attach the felt firmly to the hammer cores, but now and again one sees that a manufacturer supplemented the glue with staples through the sides of the hammers.

The second manufacturing advance in our 1877 Steinway is reflected in the quality of the machine-wound strings. Very sim-

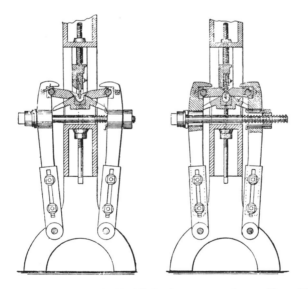

FIG. 7.10. *Patent drawing of Alfred Dolge hammer-covering machine, 1887.* The drawing on the left shows the felt before it is forced up around the hammer core. The drawing on the right shows how the outside arms of the machine are brought inward, forcing the levers inside to move the glued felt up around the hammer core.

ple winding machines had been known for a long time, consisting of a wheel turned by a hand crank, the speed of the turning regulating the closeness of the winding. More efficient winding machines were introduced in the second half of the nineteenth century, and they allowed very close, even winding. The more even and close the winding, the better tone quality the string produces, and the less the likelihood that the winding will come loose to rattle horribly. By the time this piano was made, Steinway was using these newer machines to wind the bass strings.

Such considerations as these do not exhaust the contributions of the Steinways to the late-nineteenth-century piano. Responsibility for several of them rests with Theodore Steinway, a shrewd, foresighted designer of instruments and a perfectionist in matters mechanical.* Even the official Steinway centennial history calls him "irascible," which suggests that he was downright difficult to live with.[30] It was Theodore who recognized that the square piano was doomed to obsolescence and turned the company's efforts toward improving the upright. It is reported that even the workers in the Steinway plant objected to this trend, but they failed to move Theodore Steinway.[31]

Another of his innovations was the perfection of an idea that had been tried in the 1840's by the French firm of Blanchet et Roller: the sostenuto pedal, the middle pedal in modern American-style grands, which holds up the dampers of those notes that are being held down at the time the pedal is depressed, but no others. Steinway patented a sostenuto pedal for squares in 1874 and for grands and uprights in 1875.[32] Still another improvement, especially for grands, helped to keep Steinway & Sons in the lead among the more radical piano makers of the late nineteenth century. This was the so-called cupola iron frame, in which the frame proper is curved up from the rim where its fastenings are, and a series of rosette-shaped holes in the casting protrude from the plane of the string-plate. It was supposed to improve the dissemination of resonance from the soundboard. In concert grands, the frame sloped slightly upward from keyboard to tail, thus allowing the bridge to run continuously around from the main portion to

---

*There is a long panegyric on Theodore Steinway's career and achievements in Fanny Morris Smith, *A Noble Art* (pp. 110–58). Some of it is surely the fictionalized imagination of "what it must have been" that was so characteristic of admiring Victorian biographers. But Smith gives an accurate, albeit uncritical, account of Steinway's work.

the cross-strung portion. The longer bridge brought into contact with the soundboard was intended to transmit more vibrating energy to the soundboard.

Theodore Steinway was a friend of Hermann Helmholtz's, the German physicist whose book *On the Sensations of Tone*, first published in 1862, laid the foundations of the science of physiological acoustics. Helmholtz was one of those wide-ranging German scholars of the last century, the despair of ordinary scholars, who found time and energy to make fundamental contributions to a number of related fields. Besides his interest in acoustical science, he collected old musical instruments. (The pianos he collected eventually found their way to the Neupert Collection and are now, with the rest of that collection, housed in the Germanisches Nationalmuseum in Nuremberg.)

Theodore Steinway studied Helmholtz's book, corresponded with him, provided him on occasion with pianos to use in his experiments, and sought to apply his findings to the advantage of the piano. One of those findings was that the pattern of overtones or partials is what establishes the quality of tone in a vibrating string. In response to that discovery, Steinway designed the "duplex" scale (scale is the technical term for the design of the stringing in a piano). The idea here had occasionally been tried before, unscientifically. In the duplex scale, the length of the string between the tuning pin and the capo tasto bar or agraffe was made proportionate to the string's speaking length, so that this supposedly nonvibrating part of the string would vibrate at the frequency of a partial of the string's fundamental tone.* Theoretically, the additional vibration of a partial ought to enhance and enrich the tone. Helmholtz himself remarked to Steinway that his innovation had improved the tone, and optimistically supposed that the design, "being based upon scientific principles, [was] capable of still greater development."[33]

The immediate contribution of science to piano design has been very slight.[34] Apart from Helmholtz's work, the only instance I know of is some experiments carried out in 1788 at the behest of John Broadwood by two scientists from the British Museum,

---

*Most descriptions of the duplex scale presume that the proportioning of length was done at the other end of the string, between the bridge and the hitch-pin. But the diagrams in Fanny Morris Smith's *A Noble Art* (pp. 59, 61), taken from Steinway catalogs of the time, demonstrate that it was as I have described it.

Tiberio Cavallo and Dr. Edward Gray. They resulted in Broadwood's use of a separate bridge for the lowest strings, bringing the
bridges closer to the center of the soundboard. No one to my
knowledge has tracked down the details of those experiments,
which might be very interesting clues to the scientific method in
the late eighteenth century.

————————◆▶▬————————

In a significant sense, the story of this chapter is not complete
until that of the next is told. This has been the radical side of the
story. The rest of it was a conflict of ideals, one side finding in the
achievements of Steinway the path to the future, the other hearing
the preferable music in other sounds.

As for the Americans themselves, they had little doubt that the
future belonged with them. Even the amazement with which they
greeted the musical prodigies of Europe gave rise to an almost
equal amazement about themselves. William H. Fry, composer
and music critic of the New York *Tribune* in the 1850's, was moved
by a concert of Sigismond Thalberg's to remark that "the manufacture of pianos in this country is a prodigious branch of artis-
tico-mechanical industry." And as Fry went on to comment on
Thalberg's performance, he reflected something of the American
imagination about America in a rhetorical flight that no music critic of today could sneak past an editor. It was a peculiarly American vision, in which the music reminded the writer of the great
new achievements of American technology:

There is certainly something mightily akin to the whole vast looming of
the age—to the new telescopic dragnet used for the skyey depths bringing out the "gems of purest ray serene" which have slept there for billions
of years—to the locomotive engine, burning to ashes all old journey mea-
surements and crushing miles in moments—to the electric telegraph,
which turns into dazzling, immortal fact the wildest poetry or prophecy
of the Arabian Nights—there is something mightily akin to all these in
this wide world of new octaves, those fresh continents of sounds, and the
master grasp which can hurl them together in genial contrast.[35]

The brash assurance in such a vision was the kind of motivation
that propelled the radical Americans to revolutionize, among
other things, the piano industry.

——————◀─◆─▶——————

The Europeans Imitate— or Do Not

The American challenge in 1867 was clear and vigorous. In hind-sight one can easily say that the die was cast, the only question being whether the Europeans would join the parade or decline. At the time the question was not so evident. It remained to be seen whether the new technology would be a temporary challenge, whether the big sound entailed in it would be the coming sound.

In some realms of technology, the only question to be asked is the question of improvement. If an airplane can be made that will safely transport more people greater distances at a higher speed and without damage to the environment, then it is likely that people will ask only whether anyone can afford to buy it when it is made. That the new design is an improvement no one doubts. In such a case, we can speak quite unambiguously of technological progress. The case is different with the technology of the arts. Not, to be sure, with every facet of them. The invention of the screw top for oil-pigment tubes was an indubitable improvement. It had no effect on the quality of the paint as such, nor did it cause any change in the way people painted. But an artist could keep paints usable for a much longer time, wastage was diminished, and the expense of an artistic career was to that extent reduced.

With piano technology, the innovations cut right to the center of aesthetic considerations. Music is sound, and technology provides the means of sound production. Changes in piano technol-ogy affected the objective qualities of the tone. On some grounds, one could argue that the changes were improvements, for exam-ple, in the increased tensile strength of steel strings. But there is no arguing with the person who listens to music played on a piano made with the new technology and says, "I prefer the sound of the older one." Aesthetics involves taste, and though taste is not a purely individual matter, being formed in and by social contexts, it is an attitude of mind that goes deeply into the subjective.

Preferences, then, had a great deal to do with the fact that some European makers shifted over to the kinds of technology involved in Steinway's innovations, and some did not. Preferences in taste must also account for the marketing successes of the American makers and their German adherents. They advertised shrewdly and insistently, and the time came when the sound that the new technology produced was viewed as the norm. That is the social context of taste. The new technologists set out to modify taste and, with time enough, succeeded. But the success was not inevitable. The public and the artists who preferred the sound of the older-style instuments were many. The year 1878 saw another exposition in Paris, and this time the French makers were awarded all the high prizes in sight in a kind of backlash against the new technology. The proponents of the more radical makers were furious, cried foul, and accused the jury of shutting its eyes to the facts of the matter. To agree uncritically with them is too simple and too dependent on hindsight.[1] Preference cannot be ascribed simply to hedgehog, conservative mentality, an unwillingness to enter the modern world.

As we look in this chapter at European pianos from the last 30 years of the nineteenth century, we will see some that reflect wholehearted acceptance of the Steinway system with only minor modifications or none at all, some that exhibit basic acceptance of it with a fair degree of independence, and some that contain little of its technology. We begin with one of the last.

The Streicher grand in Figure 8.1, from 1870, is not representative of the more progressive tendency among German and Austrian firms. We might have expected it to be, considering that Streicher had taken a gold medal in Paris in 1867 for a piano that he had frankly copied from the Steinway exhibited in London in 1862. Our example, no. 7011, is not a copy of a Steinway. Though some of the makers in Vienna saw advantages in the Steinway system, they continued to make more conservative pianos like this one alongside more progressive ones. They had, after all, to think of selling them to Viennese burghers whose mentality did not run avidly to innovation.

FIG. 8.1. *Grand piano, J. B. Streicher, Vienna, 1870.* Serial no. 7011. *Inscription:* "J. B. Streicher / k. k. Hof & Kammer-Pianoforte-Fabrikant / & Sogn in Wien." *Action:* Viennese action; leather-covered hammers. *Stops:* 2 pedals: una corda, dampers to g^3. *Range:* AAA–a^4. *Stringing:* AAA–BBB single-strung wound brass, CC–D♯ double-strung wound iron, E–a^4 triple-strung plain steel; straight-strung; AAA 175.5 cm, c^2 34 cm, a^4 7.8 cm. *Framing:* Bronzed cast-iron string-plate, 2 bronzed cast-iron tension bars, capo tasto. *Case:* Walnut; 240 cm long, 137 cm wide. *Location:* Kunsthistorisches Museum, Vienna. Inventory no. 541.

Streicher's no. 7011 is straight-strung rather than cross-strung and has the old Viennese action, unchanged except for the weight of the parts from the action Nannette Streicher had made for Beethoven's contemporaries in 1816. It has leather hammers instead of the modern felt and a partial, composite iron frame with only two tension bars. The result is a piano with a lighter sound than the Steinways and Chickerings that won prizes in 1867, a much lighter action than either Chickering's Brown action or the modified Erard repetition action. The tone, especially in the bass, is open, has relatively stronger higher partials than a Steinway would have, and gives a somewhat more distinct, though not hard, sound. The range is the seven octaves that had been relatively standard since the 1840's, without the additional third that was on both the 1864 Steinway and the 1868 Chickering. The iron frame, partial and composite though it is—the tension bars are bolted into the iron string-plate rather than being cast with it—is stouter than many frames that had appeared up to this time on Austrian and German pianos.

One of the most interesting facts about no. 7011 is that it is almost identical to Streicher's grand no. 6713, made in 1868; and no. 6713, which so far as anyone knows, no longer exists, stood in the music room of an apartment at no. 4 Karlsgasse in Vienna, the home of Johannes Brahms. We have already seen an earlier piano that Brahms owned, the 1839 Graf that Clara Schumann gave him in 1856, and that he in turn gave to the Gesellschaft der Musikfreunde in Vienna in 1873. That was about the time the Streicher firm presented no. 6713 to Brahms, and until his death in 1897, the Streicher was his piano. On it were written his works from about opus 56 on, including the Second Piano Concerto, his late piano pieces, and the mature chamber music with piano, beginning with the completion of the C-minor Piano Quartet, op. 60, which he had begun some years earlier.

When we ponder the two pianos we know Brahms owned during his productive career, we find that one was a typical Viennese grand of the late 1830's, the other a conservative one of the late 1860's. Neither was a truly modern piano, if the cross-strung, iron-framed Steinway is the touchstone of the modern piano. To hear Brahms's music on an instrument like the Streicher is to realize that the thick textures we associate with his work, the sometimes muddy chords in the bass and the occasionally woolly sonorities, come cleaner and clearer on a lighter, straight-strung piano. Those textures, then, are not a fault of Brahms's piano composition. To be sure, any sensitive pianist can avoid making Brahms sound murky on a modern piano. The point is that the modern pianist must strive to avoid that effect, must work at lightening the dark colors, where Brahms himself, playing his Streicher, did not have to work at it.

J. B. Streicher was, of course, Johann Baptist Streicher, the son of Johann Andreas and Nannette Stein Streicher. Johann Baptist wanted no one to forget that fact; on the soundboard of this instrument is the inscription "Nro. 7011 / J. B. Streicher / & Sohn / vormals N. Streicher geb. Stein und Sohn / Wien / 7.0."[2] Streicher was still in 1870 referring to his parents as the heirs of the Stein tradition ("previously N. Streicher born Stein"). By the time the company gave Brahms his piano, but not by the time no. 7011 was made, Johann Baptist was dead, having passed nearly 50 years in making pianos. He came actively into his parents' firm in 1823 and was effectively in charge of it for several years before 1833, when both Johann Andreas and Nannette Streicher died. Toward the end of his life, Streicher more and more brought his son Emil into the business. Whether Emil or his father was mainly responsible for taking up the Steinway developments after 1862 is not certain. The gold medal in 1867, however, was the last gasp of a company that was descended from Johann Andreas Stein, the bellwether of German piano making in the late eighteenth century, and that had been one of the leading Viennese makers in the first three decades of the nineteenth century. Business did not significantly improve after the Paris gold medal, it seems. Vienna was an almost invincibly conservative city by then, at least in the social reaches where fine pianos were bought and housed. In 1896, Emil Streicher had to liquidate the firm.

Though the Streicher company had an important name, its business was never of high volume. Brahms's no. 6713 was made two years before no. 7011. In two years, then, the company had made only about 300 instruments, 150 or so annually, compared with Broadwood's 2,800, Pleyel's 2,500, Steinway's 2,000, and Chickering's 1,500. It was a time when the craft was being seriously modified, though not completely displaced, by the methods of the factory, and international marketing was becoming the formula for continued success. Streicher's small-shop craft was finally the victim of advancing manufacturing technology and, perhaps, of unyielding pride. Johann Baptist Streicher had probably repaired pianos for Beethoven; his father and mother had done so, and his uncle Matthäus Andreas Stein too. That would be enough to give anyone pride.

———————◆▶———————

Though the Viennese grand, modified and enlarged as it was, continued to have a place in the catalogs of Austrian makers, the enlarged upright of the type Steinway had pioneered in the 1860's

FIG. 8.2. *Upright piano, Chr. Schmidt, Halle, late 19th century.* Action: Upright repetition action, dampers above hammers; felt-covered hammers. Stops: 2 pedals: soft (shortens hammer blow), dampers to c^3. Range: AAA–c^5. Stringing: AAA–GG$\sharp$ single-strung wound, AA–c double-strung wound, c$\sharp$–c^5 triple-strung plain; cross-strung; AAA 129 cm, c^2 35.2 cm, c^5 6.3 cm. Framing: Cast-iron frame (does not cover pin block). Case: Walnut veneered with inlays of root walnut and decorated with cutwork; 147.5 cm high, 150.5 cm wide. Location: Händel-Haus, Halle, GDR. Catalog no. MS-529.

was increasingly occupying the drawing rooms and parlors of European homes. Such an instrument, copied in Europe from the Steinway model, is pictured in Figure 8.2.

There is a mild mystery about this piano. It has no serial number or date that allows us to pinpoint its manufacture more closely than the late nineteenth century. Furthermore, nothing is known of a piano maker in Halle named Chr[istian?] Schmidt. There was a furniture manufacturer and seller of that name in Halle in the latter part of the century,[3] and it is a fair guess that he and the piano maker are one and the same. The identification is in any case not on the order of the stencils found on the nameboards of inexpensive pianos of the nineteenth and early twentieth centuries, where a manufacturer would gladly put anything the purchaser, buying at wholesale to sell at retail, wished to have there. Stenciling was very common, though most of the front-rank makers frowned on the practice and fixed their names to the products so that they could be removed only with great difficulty.* Chr. Schmidt's name is cast into the iron frame of this piano.

The mystery of its origin apart, this is a typical late-nineteenth-century upright of the sort that progressive German makers increasingly produced. It has the full modern range, a one-piece cast-iron frame (this one does not cover the pin block), and cross-stringing. (It is the stringing that dates this instrument to the last three decades or so of the century.) Schmidt's upright is a relatively large instrument, standing nearly five feet high. An enlargement of the upright was not especially problematic, as it was for the square, because a larger upright took only more wall space, not more floor space.

Not until Steinway succeeded in 1863 in designing an upright with cross-stringing on a single soundboard did the truly modern upright come into being. During the 1870's, Theodore Steinway worked to perfect the upright at the expense of the square, having seen that the square, which had died out in Europe, was doomed. The vertical piano was a greater challenge anyway, and, working on the basis established by Henry Steinway Jr., Theodore succeeded in putting Steinway in the forefront of the development of the upright. Chr. Schmidt's instrument gives eloquent testimony to the success.

The cross-strung upright posed an interesting problem. The old vertically strung uprights were often equipped with a keyboard shift or una corda pedal, as grands were, which moved the

---

*See Alfred Dolge, *Pianos and Their Makers*, pp. 179–83, for some disapproving "tut-tuts" about the stenciling business. Often, the aim of the stenciling manufacturer and the retailer was to make people think they were getting pianos from the leading makers. Thus one finds stencils with such barely legal changes on the name of Steinway as Steinbay, Steinbeck, Steindell, Steinman & Son, Steinmetz, Steinvey, and Steinwebb (all picked from the *Pierce Piano Atlas*, pp. 261–63). In Europe, there were Bradwoods and Erarts. The names of other makers were distorted in the same ways. Some stencilers used the name of the retailer, or some brand name (e.g. Parlor Gem or Phalharmonic), or a composer's name (Mozart or Haydn). The great proponent of stenciling in the United States was a somewhat shadowy figure named Joseph P. Hale, a Massachusetts Yankee, who turned it into a fine and profitable art. Arthur Loesser's discussion of stenciling (*Men, Women and Pianos*, pp. 526–31) is rather less moralistic than Dolge's but still disapproving.

action sideways so that the hammers struck only two strings of the triple-strung notes. With cross-stringing, the strings hung at an angle to the hammers. A shift of the action to either side would likely bring hammers into contact with strings of adjacent notes. To mount the hammer heads at an angle to the shanks so that they would more nearly follow the angle of the strings was a conceivable solution, which Chickering used in its so-called cocked hat grands. These instruments, made rather briefly around the 1860's, were horizontal pianos in which the spine (the side of the case beside the bass strings) ran at an acute angle from the keyboard, with a correspondingly deep curve in the bent side. The piano, seen from directly above, resembled the shape of a cocked hat. Here the strings ran at an angle to the keys, and Chickering mounted the hammers at a similar angle so that an una corda stop could be used.*

It was not a usable solution for uprights, for the angled hammer-head would unbalance the upright action much more than it would a horizontal action. Something different had to be done with the cross-strung upright to give the player a means of consistently softer playing. The solution adopted by Steinway was a mechanism worked by the left pedal that moved the entire hammer rail forward a short distance toward the strings. Since the hammer has a shorter distance to travel to the string, the same weight of finger blow now produces a softer sound. The volume of sound is determined by the speed of the hammer blow to the string. With the hammer starting from a position closer to the string, it cannot get up as much speed as it can from the usual position.

This method of a "soft" stop may have been invented independently at several different times. We find something like it in the extremely early pyramid upright attributed to Domenico del Mela in the Museo degli Strumenti Musicali in Milan. An English pat-

---

*Cocked hat grands are relatively rare. I myself have seen only one, a Chickering in the collection of William E. Garlick in Boston, and some photographs of a few others. Chickering was the principal exponent of the form; its chief advantage was that the instrument could be put close to a corner, conserving floor space. It was a descendant, whether or not the nineteenth-century makers realized it, of the old "spinet" form of harpsichord and of a type of horizontal piano used infrequently in the late eighteenth and very early nineteenth centuries that the Germans called a Querflügel (diagonal or transverse grand). Among the few surviving examples of the Querflügel is a late-eighteenth-century instrument made by Johann Jakesch of Vienna in the Händel-Haus collection in Halle (catalog no. MS-32).

ent was granted to Joseph Lidel in 1836 for a mechanism that, in Rosamond Harding's description, sounds like a "soft" stop but is not unmistakably the same: "Pedal to work a mechanism for the purpose of obtaining 'piano' and 'crescendo' without alteration to the character of the tone."[4] In the next year, Georges-Frédéric Greiner obtained an addition to a French patent for a "pedal to work a mechanism to lessen the course of the hammers for the purpose of producing loud or soft effects without changing the nature of the sound."[5] It is interesting that both Lidel and Greiner wished to achieve a dynamic change without an alteration of the timbre. One of the charms of the true una corda is precisely that it does change the tone quality. The stop that shortens the hammer blow is a crutch for the pianist who cannot control muscles sufficiently to produce a consistent dynamic range.

Since Steinway took it up, this use of the left pedal has become the nearly universal means of a "soft" stop for the upright piano. It almost seems that designers have assumed that any object called a piano had to have at least two pedals, even if one of them can be reasonably deemed useless. Recently some makers have installed in addition a moderator or mute stop, worked by a third pedal in the middle, which moves a strip of felt or leather between hammers and strings. I have seen that stop on contemporary small uprights (e.g., from Rippen in The Hague and Yamaha in Hamamatsu, Japan).

For all the upright's problems of design, including the action, it was the piano that finally conquered the nineteenth century and continued its dominance into the twentieth. The reason is easy enough to see. Chr. Schmidt's upright occupies only a little more than 11 square feet of floor space, whereas the big Steinway square of 1877–78 (Fig. 7.9, p. 193) occupies about 25. Though the Schmidt is not as much piano as a good square, it was acceptable for the musical purposes of those who purchased it. Perfection was seldom one of those purposes, and large uprights like this one, still to be encountered where used pianos are sold, were frequently well enough made that they are a better buy, musically, than many a smaller but higher-priced contemporary upright. And a great many people in Europe and North America, myself included, can recall learning to play in the first instance on an instrument technologically not at all unlike the Schmidt.

Not all of the imitations were so complete. Piano makers may have been conservative on the whole, but they were not often slavish. The point of a good idea was not simply to take it over, but to adapt and modify it to suit one's own predilections. The Blüthner grand pictured in Figure 8.3 profited from the new technology but was by no means a copy of a Steinway.

With Blüthner we come to the third in rank of the Big Three makers of the late nineteenth century, "big," to be sure, not so much in terms of numbers of instruments manufactured as in terms of international reputation. Many American readers will not have heard of Blüthner, though the company, founded by Julius Blüthner, dates back to 1853 and is still producing pianos in Leipzig, where it began. Not many Blüthner pianos are to be found in the United States. I vividly remember my own first introduction to one. About to accompany a rehearsal, I was shown to a very seedy-looking black grand. It looked as though it had been through a battle, with great gouges out of the case, scratches and stains on the finish, and dirty keys, some of which were missing their ivories. I thought to myself that it would be a long afternoon. A tentative chord on the keys brought a thrilling, mellow, clear sound up from under the battered lid. My double take at the nameboard found there "J. Blüthner, Leipzig," a name I had never before heard. Since that afternoon, I have played a good number of Blüthners, many made in the late nineteenth or early twentieth century. Not one has been poor, and two have been, for sound quality and responsiveness of touch, among the best pianos I have ever played. (Subjectivity informs any such judgment, of course, and I do not wish to impose my personal affection for Blüthners on anyone else.)

Julius Blüthner may have embraced much of Steinway's technology, but he was independent for all that. In 1856 he patented his own repetition action. It was a modification of a type designed in 1844 by Jean George Kriegelstein of Paris, and though not as rapid in repetition as the actions developed from Erard's model, it was simpler in construction and entirely adequate for anyone short of Liszt or von Bülow.[6] Blüthner also offered the standard repetition action in his pianos. One-piece cast-iron frames were

By courtesy of Händel-Haus, Halle, GDR

FIG. 8.3. *Grand piano, Julius Blüthner, Leipzig, c. 1878.* Serial no. 15332. *Action:* Blüthner repetition action; felt-covered hammers. *Stops:* 2 pedals: una corda, dampers to c♯³. *Range:* AAA–a⁴. *Stringing:* AAA–DD single-strung wound, DD♯–G♯ double-strung wound, A–a⁴ triple-strung plain; cross-strung; AAA 157.1 cm, c² 39 cm, a⁴ 6.3 cm; "Aliquot" stringing. *Framing:* One-piece cast-iron frame with 6 tension bars cast in. *Case:* Oak veneered, French-polished black; 220 cm long, 143.2 cm wide. *Location:* Händel-Haus, Halle, GDR. Catalog no. MS-49.

standard on Blüthners, but the firm continued to make straight-strung grands long after most German makers had abandoned them. The Blüthner generally had a lighter sound than the Steinway, partly because Blüthner used lighter hammers and felts as well as his own, lighter action.

Blüthner's best-known development was his pattern of stringing, patented in 1873 and pictured in Figure 8.4. Called the Aliquot system, it consists of a fourth string for each note in the upper three octaves, strung above the other three and not struck by the hammer. The fourth, or aliquot, string has its own damper, attached to and working with the damper of the other three strings, and when the note is struck, the fourth string vibrates sympathetically with it. When the damper pedal raises all of the dampers, the aliquot strings vibrate in sympathy with partials of the lower notes. The result is a strengthening of the enriching partials and an evenness of quality throughout the range of the piano, a smoothing of hard qualities in the topmost notes, and a mellow clarity of tone, enhanced by the presence of upper partials but not hardened by them. Reactions to the Aliquot stringing have varied

FIG. 8.4. *Aliquot stringing on a Blüthner grand.*   The fourth string is above and to the right of each set of three struck strings, passing through a projection in the agraffe and through its own bridge (the row of vertical brass pieces beyond the dampers). Photograph by Gretchen Steffy-Bond.

from scorn to enthusiasm, but the company still uses the design in its grands today. It makes life slightly difficult for the technician if a string has to be replaced.

Blüthner grew up in a small village, had little formal education, and started, like so many of his colleagues in the piano trade, as an apprentice cabinetmaker. But he trained himself extremely well and even, together with Heinrich Gretschel, wrote a textbook on piano making that is technically sound and historically useful.[7] He knew what he was doing, did Julius Blüthner, as his instruments show.

Cyril Ehrlich rightly called 1853 the *annus mirabilis* of piano making.[8] In that year, Julius Blüthner in Leipzig, Steinway & Sons in New York, and Carl Bechstein in Berlin all began manufacturing pianos. Bechstein's rise to prominence in Germany pretty well coincided with the rise of Prussia to dominance and of Berlin to the status of the German capital and a full-fledged cultural center.

The Bechstein grand pictured in Figure 8.5 has a plaque at the left of the keyboard that says: "This pianoforte was manufactured expressly for the Abbé Franz Liszt, and was placed in his study at Westwood House, Sydenham, where it was used by the great master during his last visit to England, April 3–19, 1886." That was just under four months before his death at the age of seventy-four on Aug. 1, 1886. The old man played a surprising number of times during those two weeks in England, and on this piano we know he played Chopin's Nocturne in A-flat, op. 32, no. 2, two Chopin études, parts of his own E-flat Major Concerto, the Crusaders' March from his oratorio *The Legend of St. Elizabeth* as well as improvisations on some of its themes, and his Fantasia on the Tarantella de Bravura from Daniel François Esprit Auber's opera *Masaniello*—enough to impress his powers, probably not greatly diminished, on the Bechstein.[9] Liszt, of course, owned a Bechstein on which his students played in his classes in Weimar after 1880; that instrument is now in the Liszt Museum in Weimar.

The pianist most closely associated with Bechstein was not Liszt, though, but Hans von Bülow, his former pupil and sometime son-in-law. Von Bülow gave the very first Bechstein grand its

FIG. 8.5. *Grand piano, Carl Bechstein, Berlin, 1886.* Serial no. 19002. *Inscription:* "C. Bechstein, Hof-Lieferant Sr. Maj. des Kaisers u. Königs, Berlin." *Action:* Repetition action; felt-covered hammers. *Stops:* 2 pedals: una corda, dampers to c^3. *Range:* AAA–c^5. *Stringing:* AAA–FF single-strung copper-wound, FF♯–BB double-strung copper-wound, C–C♯ triple-strung copper-wound, D–c^5 triple-strung plain; cross-strung; AAA 196 cm, c^2 34 cm, c^5 4.4 cm. *Framing:* One-piece cast-iron frame. *Case:* Oak veneered, lacquered black; 260.4 cm long, 153 cm wide. *Location:* Helen Foresman Spencer Museum of Art, University of Kansas, Lawrence. Accession no. 77.105.

baptism of fire in 1856, playing Liszt's Sonata in B minor. From then on, von Bülow played Bechsteins whenever he could, though he made an American tour in the 1870's for Chickering. He was well known as an acid-tongued critic of everything and everyone,* but the sharp criticism he directed to Bechstein was applied in a constructive cause. Von Bülow promoted the Bechstein piano, suggested places where it could be sold, and expressed his satisfac-

---

*"Hans von Bülow's praise," Brahms once observed, "smarts like salt in the eyes so that tears run" (Harold C. Schonberg, *The Great Pianists*, p. 234). Brahms himself was not noted for his tact.

tion at the way his name and Bechstein's were linked in the public mind. This did not keep him from making the most minute criticisms of the pianos themselves, showing Bechstein what needed to be improved in a manner that the builder found helpful.

Thanks to Bechstein's talent and von Bülow's criticism, the Bechstein piano had the reputation of being matched only by the Steinway in quality of construction and tone. Indeed, to the dismay of the British piano-trade press, German manufacturers made a considerable dent in the British market between 1880 and 1914.[10] Both Bechstein and Blüthner had permanent branches and showrooms in London, and in 1901, the Bechstein company built a fine concert hall there, which bore its name.* Bechstein was felt to be in the front rank of German pianos, noted for its strength and what was frequently called a "velvety" tone. Instruments from that period are still found on the floors of dealers in used pianos, and they command high prices even at this advanced age. Bechsteins are still made in Berlin, though the company is now a wholly owned subsidiary of the D. H. Baldwin company.

As for this Bechstein, what sets it off from a contemporary Steinway is mainly the styling of the case. The action is the standard Herrburger-Schwander repetition action on the Herz-Erard model, which Bechstein imported from Paris. The frame is crossstrung on the Steinway pattern. Of course, by the time this Bechstein was made, Steinway had introduced the third, sostenuto, pedal, which Bechstein, like most European makers, never really accepted. I do not mean to make the Bechstein sound like an unexceptional, run-of-the-mill instrument. When one finds oneself in a range of mountain peaks, descriptive superlatives about each one become boring. No one would deliberately provide Franz Liszt with a mediocre piano. Instruments like this were as a group considered among the best available and, if second to any other, then by no large interval.

————————◄◆►————————

More disagreement might be found about the grand pictured in Figure 8.6. Taken as an exemplar of technology alone, Erard's no. 71390, dating from about 1894, is a nice instance of the fact that

*In 1917, with the wave of anti-German feeling during the First World War, Bechstein Hall became Wigmore Hall.

known innovations are not necessarily adopted on introduction. We have here a seven-octave piano, not terribly uncommon at the time it was built, but not encountered as frequently as the AAA–c⁵ of the modern standard. The seven octaves are straight-strung, and that was uncommon as late as 1894 (though in 1895

FIG. 8.6. *Grand piano, Erard, Paris, c. 1894.* Serial no. 71390. *Action:* Erard double-escapement repetition action, under-dampers; felt-covered hammers. *Stops:* 2 pedals: una corda, dampers to b². *Range:* AAA–a⁴. *Stringing:* AAA–GG single-strung wound, GG♯–C♯ double-strung wound, D–F♯ triple-strung wound, G–a⁴ triple-strung plain; straight-strung; AAA 159.9 cm, c² 32.7 cm, a⁴ 5.9 cm. *Framing:* Composite iron frame with 6 tension bars bolted to string plate; gap-stretcher under strings between pin block and belly rail. *Case:* Quarter-sawn rosewood veneered with rosewood cross-banding; 212.5 cm long, 141 cm wide. *Location:* Collection of William E. Garlick, Boston, Mass.

Alfred J. Hipkins used a photograph of a straight-strung Broad-wood for the frontispiece of his book, *Description and History of the Pianoforte*). Not until 1901 did Erard issue a cross-strung grand. The frame of no. 71390 is composite, the tension bars being bolted into the string-plate and into the pin block, with a gap-stretcher beneath the strings. Except for some aspects of design, it is not substantially changed from the composite frames that Erard was using in the late 1820's, when they were the great new thing. The action is a slight development on the repetition action that Pierre Erard had designed about 1840, including the use of under-dampers, which were needed mainly because the tension bars ran so close to the strings that they would interfere with over-dampers. The hammers were certainly covered by hand. In 1894, the very year this instrument was built, the editor of the *Musical Courier* of New York visited the Erard factory in Paris and re-ported that each hammer received four successive covering oper-ations by hand.[11]

Taking the Steinway as the norm, the Erard looks obsolete. I have already warned that such a conclusion is too simple. Erard was conservative, as no one would deny. But it is not clear that the conservatism was based merely on a French chauvinism that would not admit that anyone but French makers could produce the finest instruments, though the sentiment was sometimes heard.[12] Albert-Louis Blondel, who took over the direction of Erard in 1873, insisted that the opinion against cross-stringing and one-piece iron frames was solidly based on tone quality.[13]

There is that matter of preference, about which argument is difficult if not impossible. The Polish pianist Ignace Jan Pade-rewski managed to sit on both sides of the fence. He played Steinways exclusively in America, and Erards exclusively in Europe. And he stoutly maintained, even to William Steinway, who was invited to leave the Paderewski house one day for arguing too long, that whatever the faults of other pianists, when he played the Erard it sounded just fine.[14] Perhaps. But George Ber-nard Shaw thought otherwise. In his days as a music critic, he wrote that "in most of the big climaxes [Paderewski] is making such a thundering noise that he cannot hear the orchestra, whilst the orchestra is making such a thundering noise that the audience cannot hear him, and can only gaze raptly at the inspiring specta-cle of his fists flying in the air as he trounces the keyboard."[15] The

American composer and pianist Edward MacDowell took the opposite tack, objecting that an Erard on which he was to play his Second Concerto in Paris in 1889 could not be heard over the orchestra. Casting about, he found a small American grand (probably not a "baby" grand) made by Albert Weber of New York, which he proceeded to use in preference to the Erard.[16] It is always possible, of course, that MacDowell had some nationalistic agenda of his own, and wanted to insult the Erard company. Unquestionably, some Erards were the equal in volume and richness of Steinways and Bechsteins. Nevertheless, the "typical" Erard sound was lighter than that of its competitors, and French musical preferences may have had something to do with the fact.

Though Claude Debussy preferred the Bechstein, Maurice Ravel liked the glassy sound of the Erard.[17] When one listens to the piano music of the leading French composers of the late nineteenth century, such as Camille Saint-Saëns, Gabriel Fauré, and Emmanuel Chabrier, one hears musical textures for which a relatively thin sound and clarity at the expense of richness is appropriate. It is a sound rather the opposite of that implied by the orchestra used by Richard Wagner, whose cult swept Europe. There were Wagnerians in France, but it can be argued that more French composers rejected the "music of the future" in favor of their own styles than accepted it. Perhaps the Wagner sound and its popularity had something to do with the German and American adoption of the Steinway technology, which could approximate that sound. And perhaps the preference for a smaller texture with elegance still remembered from the great eighteenth-century French composers for the harpsichord had something to do with the French preference for the straight-strung, composite-framed Erards and Pleyels. That is speculation.

What is not, as I showed in Chapter Seven, is that the French makers took a severe beating in the international market in the years up to the First World War. Reconstruction after the war was difficult enough, but the economic and political troubles from 1930 to 1945 piled Pelion on Ossa, and the piano manufacture of France never really recovered. In 1971, the Schimmel company of Braunschweig, Germany, took over the production of pianos under the three leading French names, Erard, Pleyel, and Gaveau. Erards are still made, but they are no longer made in France.

Some chauvinism certainly informed French persistence in the older technology, as conservatism informed Austrian persistence. Some Europeans viewed the American successes of 1867 as a European defeat, unexpected from America—"nothing but a land of steam engines," as old Pierre Zimmermann had said cuttingly to the thirteen-year-old Louis Moreau Gottschalk in refusing him admission to piano classes at the Paris Conservatory in 1842.[18] American had "outdone" the Old World not in some engine or railroad, but in a tool of the highest art.

Some took the "defeat" as a signal to stand fast, and some did not. The official jury report of the 1878 Paris Exposition explicitly condemned the Steinway system, and the French makers swept the medal lists. Pleyel had by then begun cross-stringing, but it stood by the composite frame (and made it of wrought iron, not cast iron). In 1888, Broadwood took out a patent for a one-piece cast-steel frame that dispensed with the tension bars crossing over the strings. But the "barless" Broadwood was still straight-strung; the company did not make a cross-strung piano until 1897.[19] By that time, the Germans and Americans had captured the export territory, and the catching-up was all but impossible. As sailors say, "A stern chase is a long chase."

In one respect the Germans led the way. The firm of Moritz Pöhlmann of Nuremberg began to make steel piano wire about 1850. For a long time, German piano wire had had a high reputation for quality. Pöhlmann not only made good wire, but worked very hard to improve it. His success can be seen in the tabulation below, which shows the results of breaking tests of his no. 13-gauge wire at a series of international expositions. This wire, about .08 cm or .03 inch in diameter, is used in the relatively high treble. The figures are in pounds of tension at breaking:[20]

Paris Exposition, 1867	226 lbs.
Vienna Exposition, 1873	232 lbs.
Centennial Exhibition, Philadelphia, 1876	265 lbs.
Chicago World's Fair, 1893	325 lbs.

Even in 1867, Pöhlmann's wire was greatly superior to that of his competitors. The constant improvement in the material, amounting to close to a 50 percent increase in tensile strength over 26 years, testifies to high craftsmanship and care for engineering. Such improvements in material explain why, though Beethoven and Liszt were notorious for breaking strings by the fistful, modern concert audiences very seldom hear a piano string break. A fair amount of the credit can be laid at Pöhlmann's door.

Today we can see that the modern piano was the one that the Steinways devised in the late 1850's and the two following decades. This chapter should make it clear that this development was not a foregone conclusion. Indeed, I know of no way to account for the fact that one inventor's innovation rather than another's ultimately becomes the norm for its kind. One can conceive of various different outcomes. Exactly why, for example, Erard's action came to be the standard grand action cannot now be explained. The assertion that it was objectively better than the competition is undemonstrable. Conceivably Kriegelstein's action could have been developed; in fact, Blüthner did adapt that form. But Erard's action was the one finally adopted, and Kriegelstein's was not. Steinway's cross-stringing did not win the day by some mystical predestination. I find no explanation for the fact that it did win the day except that Steinway and its imitators persuaded the piano-buying public throughout the world that the Steinway system was the norm. Once the public had been persuaded that it was the norm, it had become the norm.

9

Some Odds and Dead Ends

This chapter digresses to some extent from the line of the story. The foregoing chapters have mapped the main path of development with occasional side trips into interesting byways. But even those lesser paths have had certain connections with the main one, whereas the experiments described in this chapter are only distantly related.

I will discuss, first, one radical and two mild experiments in redesigning the piano keyboard, and, second, experiments in automating the piano (the player-piano phenomenon). The first discussion shows some seeming dead ends, but in the second, one cannot speak certainly of a dead end, for the automatic piano has recently made a comeback, after falling distinctly out of favor more than 40 years ago.

Of unsuccessful experiments the history of the piano has many. Some were simply poor ideas, or ideas that resulted in poor instruments, such as the "sewing-table" pianos of the first half of the nineteenth century. Some were perfectly good ideas that were never widely adopted, such as repetition actions other than Erard's in the 1820–1840's. In many of these cases, no clear explanation of the lack of success can be made. A third group of experiments entailed good or decent ideas whose success was temporary or whose lack of success can be explained in terms of what was happening in the mainstreams of the industry. The experiments described below belong to the third category, unless the current resurgence of the player piano turns out to be longer-lived than one might expect. In that case, I will have been wrong to discuss it in this chapter.

Paul von Jankó, who in 1882 invented the keyboard shown on the Decker Brothers upright in Figure 9.1, studied under Hermann Helmholtz. Whether his teacher approved Jankó's musical invention, as he approved the work of Theodore Steinway, we do not know. Helmholtz certainly knew of Jankó's keyboard; an example of it came from his collection of instruments to the Neupert

By permission of the Smithsonian Institution, Washington, D.C.

FIG. 9.1. *Upright piano, Decker Brothers, New York, c. 1890. Action:* Tape-check upright action, with Jankó keyboard; felt-covered hammers. *Stops:* 2 pedals: "soft" (moves hammers forward), dampers. *Range:* AAA–c⁵. *Stringing:* AAA–GG♯ single-strung brass-wound, AA– E double-strung wound, F–c triple-strung wound, c♯–c⁵ triple-strung plain; cross-strung; AAA 140.4 cm, c²?, c⁵ 4.4 cm. *Framing:* One-piece cast-iron frame. *Case:* French-polished black; 134.3 cm high, 152.4 cm wide. *Location:* Smithsonian Institution, Washington, D.C. Catalog no. 299,840.

collection. For the present discussion, the Decker Brothers piano, which is very like the Chr. Schmidt upright discussed in Chapter Eight, is of less interest than the keyboard fitted to it.

Jankó's redesigned keyboard was an ingenious attempt to overcome some of the physiological problems posed by the standard piano keyboard. One of these problems is its width, slightly over four feet, which some people find difficult to span. The Jankó keyboard is relatively compact, and its extremities are easily reached. Another problem is that the keys on the standard keyboard are far enough apart that reaching certain chords and intervals is hard for people with small hands. Perhaps the worst problem is the plain inconvenience of the standard keys. The black keys, raised above the level of the white ones and coming in irregular intervals in groups of two and three, uneasily fit the contours of the hand. Learning to play fluently on both white and black keys has been the bane of many a young pianist.

The picture of the Jankó keyboard, Figure 9.2, may aid in seeing its virtues and vices. The photo shows only two octaves, but

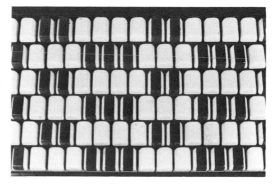

FIG. 9.2. *Jankó keyboard.* The photo shows just over two octaves of the keyboard. The first, third, and fifth rows have the notes C, D, E, F♯, G♯, A♯ in the octave, and the second, fourth, and sixth rows have C♯, D♯, F, G, A, and B. The sharps are the black keys, and the keys are about the same width as on a standard keyboard. The keyboard pictured is on a Decker Brothers, New York, upright, serial number 27218 (to be dated c. 1898–1900), owned by the College of Notre Dame, Belmont, California. Photograph by Gretchen Steffy-Bond.

the keyboard itself covers the entire seven octaves and a third of the modern piano. The keys are approximately the same width as those of a conventional keyboard but are not nearly so deep, being almost square in shape. The six rows of keys are banked up behind each other, like rows of seats in a theater balcony, as the photograph of the Decker piano shows. All the keys in each row are on the same level and are equidistant. The rows are arranged in pairs: rows 1, 3, and 5 are identical, as are rows 2, 4, and 6. The rows are offset from each other, so that the centers of the keys in one row are between the keys of the rows above and below it. Each row is arranged in whole tones: rows 1, 3, and 5 have C, D, E, F♯, G♯, A♯ and C; rows 2, 4, and 6, C♯, D♯, F, G, A, B, and C♯.

The pairing of the rows greatly reduces the distance that the player must reach for an interval. Moreover, it is always the same distance for any specified interval, no matter which two notes form the interval, and it is always in the same pattern. That is not the case with the standard keyboard, on which there is no consistency in finding the same interval starting from different keys. The reach of a major sixth, for example, may be from a white key to the fifth white key above (C to A), from a black key to the fourth black key above (C♯ to A♯), from a white key to the fourth black key above (E to C♯), from a black key to the sixth white key above E♭ to C), and so on. To play a major sixth on the Jankó keyboard, you need go only from any key to the fourth key to the right in the next row, either up or down, and to play a minor sixth, you reach from any key to the fourth key to the right in the same row.

Scales, too, cease to be difficult to remember. How forbidding is the prospect before the young pianist to learn that the fingering for the major scale, say, of E-flat is different from that of C. You must start with the second finger of the right hand, the third of the left, remember which of those wretched black keys you must stretch for, and when you turn your thumb under. On the Jankó keyboard, all of the major scales are played in the same pattern and with the same fingering. Whichever note you start with on whichever row, you play the first three notes on that row, the next four on the adjacent row, and the last on the row with which you started. C♯ major is exactly like C major. The minor scales are a bit more complicated, but no more so than on the standard keyboard, and, like the major ones, their fingerings are all the same.

The reduced width of the keyboard means that the player can reach stretches hitherto undreamed of. On a standard keyboard, I myself can play rather easily an octave and a third (say, C to E an octave above), and a hard stretch will cover an octave and a fourth—but not going from F♯ to B. On the Jankó keyboard, the reach of an octave is about as far as that of a sixth on the conventional keyboard, an octave and a fifth (C to G an octave above) is not at all difficult, and my hard stretch covers an octave and a seventh. Someone with a big hand could doubtless reach beyond two octaves. The multiple rows, moreover, allow the fingers to reach intermediate notes for easily played, widely spaced chords.

Each row is coupled to its two mates. When you play a note on row 1, the same keys go down on rows 3 and 5, or if you play it on row 3 or 5, the keys go down on the other two rows, and likewise for rows 2, 4, and 6. The player can freely move up and down from one row to another, however the hand feels most comfortable in the passage being played. If, playing on row 3, you must reach for a note on the adjacent row, you can reach up to row 4 or down to row 2, whichever is more convenient, without worrying about hitting the wrong note.

It sounds like a piano player's dream: easy, consistent fingering of scales, wide reaches, comfortable options for fingering. Why did it not take hold? Why was Alfred Dolge, an enthusiastic proponent of the Jankó keyboard, mistaken when he said that it was "destined to inaugurate a new era for the piano industry"?[1] Well, it is not quite the dream it sounds. The Jankó keyboard clearly does make better sense for the human hand than the standard keyboard in several ways. But it posed three problems, one mechanical, one psychological, and one musical.

The mechanical problem was that the touch of the keyboard was extraordinarily stiff. Putting down one key, you are actually putting down three, and the farther up you move on the six rows, the less advantageous becomes the leverage, because the finger comes ever closer to the key's fulcrum. It was a very hard touch, especially difficult to control in soft passages. In about 1910, Paul Perzina of Schwerin, Germany, attempted a modification of the action to remove the stiffness, but it was too little and too late. By then the nonacceptance of the Jankó keyboard was evident.

The psychological problem was with pianists, piano teachers, and music publishers. The pianists would have had to relearn their entire repertoires, for all of their habitual muscular movements were completely wrong on the Jankó. Imagine sitting down to play a piece you have performed correctly and eloquently hundreds of times, only to find that nothing you do on the keyboard is right. Piano teachers too would have had to learn a completely new technique in order to teach it. Easier the technique might be, but unlearning an old one for a new one is not at all easy. The publishers would have had to throw away all of their fingered editions, thus wasting millions of pounds, francs, marks, or whatever, and put out new ones with fingerings adapted to the new keyboard. None of these problems was in theory insoluble, but they *looked* insoluble to those who would have faced them. It was psychologically enough to spoil any success the Jankó keyboard might have had.

The musical problem was more subtle. The Jankó keyboard makes a number of pianistic gestures easier to execute. Skips, arpeggios, scales, wide chords, all are rendered less difficult with this system. But composers, in writing for the standard keyboard, had written the music not merely as a series of notes to be played mechanically in certain rhythms at certain speeds. The fast scales, the brilliant arpeggios, the wide, breathtaking leaps, are part of the musical texture, the very difficulties themselves aspects of the work's musical communication. Remove the struggle through which the performer must pass in order to master and execute those difficulties, and you have removed a considerable part of the character and quality of the piece. Arthur Loesser has beautifully chronicled the wishes of young pianists and their parents, as the piano took central place in European and American homes, for "brilliant but not difficult" music, music that sounded hard to play but was not hard to play.[2] Most of the music produced to meet such demands was trash. Perhaps Liszt's "La Campanella" étude would be more easily mastered on the Jankó. But only through the labor of surmounting the difficulties in that work on the standard keyboard does it possess the musical tension and hair-raising risks that Liszt wrote into it. Walk around the risks and tensions, and "La Campanella" will be tame—will, indeed, be a different work.

Jankó's own motivations are not at issue, nor do I claim to know exactly what they were. But music is a demanding art, calling for relentless discipline and years of hard work to approach its vision of perfection. The easy availability of pianos and other instruments after the 1850's or so made for a tremendous surge in the numbers and activities of amateur musicians and increased their quite natural desire to sound better than they actually were. It is a delusion. The Jankó keyboard, whatever its inventor's intentions, actually put forth a hollow promise. Difficult music, rendered easier, no longer sounds difficult, for it does not contain the subtle, necessary intensities and hazards that underlie all genuine difficulty. Jankó apparently wanted his keyboard to attract the highest levels of the performing art, and he failed. Science does not always answer the problems of art.

Jankó was not the only person or even the first to address the problems of the keyboard. In 1907, Ferdinand Clutsam, an Australian, devised a concave keyboard in order to exploit the natural tendency of the arms to move around the body in an arc. (Other concave keyboards had been attempted in Vienna around 1824 by Johann Georg Staufer and Max Haidinger.) The Clutsam keyboard found even less favor than the Jankó, though the Kunsthistorisches Museum in Vienna has a Bösendorfer grand that was modified in 1910 to receive a Clutsam keyboard.[3]

Over the decade from 1922 to 1932, Emanuel Moór, a Hungarian-born composer and pianist, was granted a series of patents for a double-keyboard piano in which the upper manual played an octave higher than the corresponding notes on the lower. Moór's invention required only one standard action and one set of strings, though transmitting energy from key to hammer required some relatively intricate engineering. Since the upper keyboard activated the strings an octave above where its keys were, a kind of "tracker" device provided the sideways motion. About 64 pianos were made with Moór's keyboard, and after his death, his widow, the pianist Winifred Christie-Moór, and others interested in the instrument attempted to persuade contemporary makers to take it up anew, an effort that continues today. In 1978, the Emanuel Moór Double Keyboard Piano Trust in England published a detailed history of the invention and its career.[4]

Some of the same kinds of problems that prevented acceptance of the Jankó keyboard have hindered the Moór double keyboard. There are some mechanical difficulties involved with it. The two manuals can be coupled together, thus producing an octave by the playing of only one note, but the coupling seriously increases the weight of touch. Certain combinations of notes prevent the coupling from working properly. Perhaps the major shortcoming of the Moór double keyboard, though, is not the idea itself but, as with the Jankó, the fact that new playing techniques must be learned for it. And, unlike the Jankó, the Moór keyboard requires the player to start with a first-class technique on the conventional keyboard.[5]

———◆———

With the automatic piano, I shall depart from my pattern of focusing on a specific instrument in order to discuss the entire phenomenon more generally. It seems fair to me to put this in the same musical category with the Jankó keyboard, namely the search for that which is "brilliant but not difficult."

The automatic piano uses a "programmed" device to play either an ordinary instrument or one especially constructed. Automatic musical instruments have a long history, into which we need not enter here.[6] Composers as important as Mozart and Beethoven produced works for some of them. The application of automatic programming to the piano seems to have begun as far back as the 1820's, when no less a musician and manufacturer than Muzio Clementi devised a model.

There came to be four types of automatic piano. The *barrel-organ* had no keyboard.* Inside the case was a cylinder studded with pins, and as the cylinder was rotated these pins tripped the hammer mechanisms to strike the strings. The *piano player* was a machine that was set in front of an ordinary piano, with mechanical "fingers" programmed to strike the keys. When the piano player box was wheeled away, the piano was played like any other. The *player piano*, by contrast, had the automatic mechanism contained within the piano, which was otherwise an ordinary instrument, and the player mechanism bypassed the keys to activate the action from the inside. When the mechanism was turned off, the piano could be played manually. Both the piano player and the player piano (it is unfortunate that these conventional terms can so easily be confused) had controls so that a "performer" could govern dynamics, tempo, accents, and other such niceties of interpretation. Finally, the *reproducing piano*, usually a player piano in the above definition, simply played back a recorded performance by a professional pianist. In the reproducing piano, the expressive di-

---

*"Organ" is a misnomer, since this is a stringed instrument activated by hammers, though its operators were often called organ grinders. It should perhaps be called a barrel-piano, but I know of no one who has done so.

rections were contained in the perforated paper roll, or "program."

Two kinds of mechanisms worked these instruments: mechanical and pneumatic. The barrel-organ was entirely mechanical. Without a keyboard, it had only a rudimentary upright piano action operated by the revolving barrel, a cylinder from which the pins stuck out like so many porcupine quills. As the cylinder revolved by hand crank or motor, the pins activated the hammers by striking tails attached to the action. Along the length of the barrel the pins were spaced to correspond to the notes, and their placement around the circumference represented the time sequence. The larger the barrel's circumference, the longer the works that could be played. Some barrels were pinned with as many as 10 different tunes, the barrel being moved a tiny distance sideways to bring the pins for each successive tune into play.

The barrel-organ was not exactly a subtle instrument, being incapable of musical expression. It frequently had drum, triangle, and bell stops, reminiscent of those Janissary music stops that we saw in the early nineteenth century, and was generally to be found in the street or in noisy eating and drinking establishments, where it served as the jukebox of its day. Many have been the expressions of disgust at these machines by people with sensitive ears. The editor of the *Franklin Journal*, commenting on an Irish barrel-organ of the 1820's, wrote: "Such instruments, although they may serve to show the consummate skill of the workman, ought never to be admitted as improvements, so far as the science of music is concerned, and will never be highly valued, excepting by those who cannot play."[7]

Some of the piano players were also mechanical in operation. They used a device, found earliest in automatic organs and reed organs, that shows the influence of an entirely different technology. The Jacquard loom, invented in 1801 by Joseph Marie Jacquard in France, was a successful introduction of automatic machinery to the weaving industry. By means of perforated cards, whose holes mechanically worked levers govering the woof, the loom could automatically weave very complex designs. The idea of doing other kinds of work by Jacquard-type perforated cards was taken up by the English mathematician Charles Babbage in his experiments with a calculating machine in the second quarter of the nineteenth century. It was apparently after Babbage that people began to attempt to use Jacquard cards to work automatic musical instruments.* From 1847 or so, a number of experiments, especially with wind instruments and organs, used perforated cards to open wind passages mechanically. But cardboard never proved satisfactory for the mechanical operation of piano actions, because the actions had become heavy enough that they too easily damaged the cardboard.

Pneumatic devices using perforated paper rolls worked better than mechanical ones for automatic pianos. They too were derived from small organs. In certain forms of the reed organ, or harmonium, the bellows, operated by pedals, blew air across the reeds to make them vibrate. As the harmonium became more sophisticated, it was found that moving air in the other direction, by sucking it into a partial vacuum created by the pumping of the bellows, produced a more controlled and better tone. The same method was soon adapted to work the action in the automatic piano. The principle is that lessening air pressure inside a collapsible chamber causes the chamber to collapse because of the excess of atmospheric pressure outside it. The collapsing chamber closes in such a way as to move the hammer action.[8]

The diagram in Figure 9.3 may aid understanding. This kind of mechanism was applied to both piano players and player pianos. In the piano player, the action pneumatic (*C* in the diagram) pushed a mechanical finger downward on the piano's key; in the player piano, the push rod, *F*, moved up against the wippen of the action.

The player pumps pedals that operate suction bellows below, establishing a partial vacuum throughout the system. The suction moves the take-up spool and draws the paper roll across the tracker bar. The pneumatic tube, *D*, is partially vacated of air through the bleed hole, *G*. The pouch, *E*, pulled down by that partial vacuum, draws down the valve, *B*, so that it covers the opening between the vacuum chamber and the atmospheric chamber.

When a perforation in the paper roll crosses the hole in the tracker bar, air rushes down the tube, *D*, and into the chamber

---

*It is worth noting that the Jacquard perforated card also developed into the punch cards of earlier generations of digital computers.

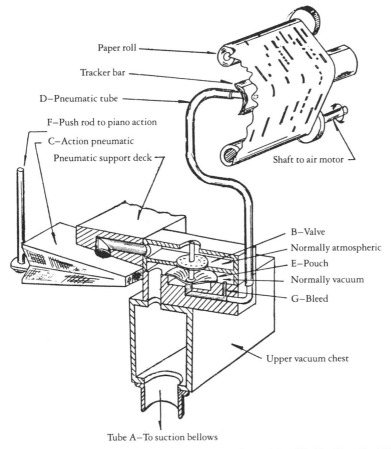

Paper roll

Tracker bar

D—Pneumatic tube

F—Push rod to piano action

C—Action pneumatic

Pneumatic support deck

Shaft to air motor

B—Valve

Normally atmospheric

E—Pouch

Normally vacuum

G—Bleed

Upper vacuum chest

Tube A—To suction bellows

FIG. 9.3. *Single-valve pneumatic player-piano mechanism.* Diagram from Larry Givens, *Rebuilding the Player Piano* (Vestal, N.Y., 1963).

beneath the pouch, *E*, pushing it and the valve, *B*, upward. The valve, seated now against the upper opening, closes off air from entering the atmospheric chamber and opens the passage from it to the vacuum chamber and tube *A*, leading down to the bellows. Air in the atmospheric chamber and in the action pneumatic, *C*, rushes out through those passages, and the collapsible action pneumatic closes quickly from the bottom, raising the push rod, *F*, to work the hammer and sound the note. When the perforation in the music roll moves on, the hole in the tracker bar is closed, the air pressure in the pneumatic tube is lessened, and the pouch relaxes, letting the valve fall back down. The valve closes the passage to the vacuum chamber and the suction bellows, and opens the atmospheric chamber and the action pneumatic to air, which fills the action pneumatic and brings down the push rod.

This operation takes much less time to happen than to explain. It is, indeed, nearly instantaneous. In some forms of action, a system of double valves gives backup power to the drive. These machines must be operated by a performer, who pumps the pedals to keep up the suction and moves control levers for volume changes, tempo changes, emphasis for a melody line in treble or bass, and occasional strong accents (sometimes calling into play what was vividly termed a "crash valve"). The controls have valve systems that open and close to admit much air or little to the various chambers or to close them to the air. The less air admitted, the stronger the suction, the faster the closure of the pneumatic chamber, and the louder the tone. Varying the amount of pressure makes the crankshaft running the take-up spool run faster or more slowly.

The machine needs to generate a great deal of suction in order to run the take-up spool smoothly, handle dynamic and tempo controls, and play all the notes. It is not surprising that inventors looked for ways to reduce the muscle power needed to work it. Hot-air motors were tried in Germany but were not efficient enough to do the job properly. Better was the electric motor, used with a belt drive to work the bellows and to relieve the pianist of the need to thrust with the feet the entire time. A few designers even used electrical contacts through the perforations in the music roll to work levers mechanically and move the piano action. They were dangerous, since electricity was still imperfectly understood in the late nineteenth century. The machines gave off spectacular blue sparks as they played, and if the designer was not careful about grounding the mechanism, the player was in danger of serious shock. Though an electric player would seem, from our vantage point, to be potentially the most efficient, it was not widely taken up.

There were even instruction books for performers on the player piano. One of them, Sidney Grew's *The Art of the Player-Piano* (1922), starts from the assumption that the student does not read music and has access only to the directions for loudness, accent,

By permission of the Smithsonian Institution, Washington, D.C.

FIG. 9.4. *E. S. Votey's "Pianola" piano player, Aeolian Company, New York, 1896.* Pneumatic, pedal-operated cabinet. *Range:* C–a³ (58-note model). *Location:* Smithsonian Institution, Washington, D.C. Catalog no. 324,741. The instrument is the patent model made by the inventor, E. S. Votey.

and tempo that were printed on the roll itself. "I find," Grew says, "it takes about three years to make a good player-pianist of a man or woman of average musical intelligence."⁹ There follow chapters on how to use the pedals and manipulate the control levers. Such handling of the controls was, of course, the means by which a rather flat "performance" of a work on a roll was given shape and musical sense.

The earliest pneumatic piano players, around 1880, had few notes, some as few as 39. The range moved sequentially up to 58, then to 65, and finally to the entire 88. The famous Pianola, pictured in Figure 9.4, was made at first with either 58 or 65 notes, but very soon achieved the entire range of the piano. E. S. Votey, the inventor, was an organ maker, doubtless getting his experience with pneumatic drive from that background and from his work with reed organs. He devised the Pianola (by no means the last automatic piano to be named with the suffix "-ola") in 1897, when he joined the Aeolian Company, and the patent was granted in 1900. The name was one of those successes of which marketing people dream: it came to be used as a generic term for piano players, in the way that Frigidaire and Kleenex have become generic names for refrigerators and facial tissues. Indeed, outside of North America one hears of pianolas rather than of player pianos.

Votey's Pianola was a bulky affair. As designers learned to pack more machinery into less space, and experience taught that some of the large-capacity mechanisms of earlier days carried more reserve power than they needed,[10] the instruments became smaller. With the development in the 1890's of the player piano, which fit inside the case of a piano that had been enlarged to receive it, the day of the player cabinet separate from the piano it played was shortened. An advanced form of the Pianola was used in 1912 for performances of Edvard Grieg's Piano Concerto and Liszt's Hungarian Fantasy with the London Symphony; the conductor on that occasion, Arthur Nikisch, gave the instrument a qualified advertising endorsement: "Save for the fact that the instrument supplies the performer with absolutely perfect technique, the Pianola should never again be referred to as a mechanical instrument."[11] But by this time the piano player was obsolete, rendered so both by the self-contained player piano and by the reproducing piano.

The important difference between the piano player and the player piano on the one hand and the reproducing piano on the other was that in the first two, a performer could operate controls while the music roll was playing, whereas in the reproducing piano, a human operator was needed only to turn on the machine. The mechanisms themselves did not differ in their essentials except as different companies made different designs. The tracker bar in the reproducing piano had more holes in it than did that of a player piano, the tubes from the additional holes leading to devices to modify the touch and dynamics and the speed of the take-up spool for ritards and accelerations, to work the pedals, and to provide accents. All of these aspects of the performance were programmed to the paper roll by the recording processes used.

Four reproducing mechanisms took most of the market. The Aeolian Company in New York put out the Duo-Art Reproducing Piano in 1913. (Indeed, by rights I should have put the term reproducing in quotation marks throughout the discussion above, since Aeolian copyrighted that term for the Duo-Art machine. Like Pianola, however, the copyright name came to be used generically.) The American Piano Company, also of New York, produced the Ampico "re-enacting" action in 1913, though it was not made public until 1916 (see Fig. 9.5).[12] The Welte-Mignon mechanism, first brought out in Germany in 1901, was made by Welte und Sohn in Freiburg, in southwestern Germany. An American man-

By courtesy of Q. David Bowers

FIG. 9.5. *Ampico player-piano mechanism in a Mason & Hamlin grand, c. 1931.* From the collection of Terry Hathaway. This photo originally appeared in Q. David Bowers, *The Encyclopedia of Automatic Musical Instruments* (Vestal, N.Y., 1972).

ufacturer made the Welte-Mignon after the First World War under license, and altered it to a small degree. These three, the Duo-Art, the Ampico, and the Welte-Mignon, took the greatest share of the "reproducing" market. A fourth successful one was the Phonola mechanism of the Ludwig Hupfeld company of Böhlitz-Ehrenburg, near Leipzig. Hupfeld had the biggest factory for automatic musical instruments in Europe, occupying a six-story building. A ready arrangement with a neighbor brought the Hupfeld mechanism wide use in Blüthners, also made in Leipzig.*

The sophistication of these machines was such that performances by famous pianists were not only rendered accurately, but could be edited and improved (as can modern recording tape). Percy Grainger, the popular British pianist, remarked of his Duo-Art rolls that they represented him not as he actually played, but as he "would *like* to play."[13] And Sergei Rachmaninoff, hearing one of his performances for the first time, told the assembled Ampico dignitaries, "Gentlemen, I have just heard myself play."[14] On the whole, these rolls reflect the playing styles of pianists in the early decades of the twentieth century better than their phonograph recordings do. Not until after the Second World War did electronic recording give sufficient fidelity to capture piano sound. And in the early days, the pianists suffered loudly under the hardships of playing 10-minute pieces within the four-minute limit of an ordinary record, in wretchedly hot studios to utterly inadequate recording equipment. No such problems were presented for the reproducers. In recent years, some Duo-Art and Ampico rolls have been played on original machines, recorded to tape, and released on commercial discs. The result is perhaps not as impressive to ears accustomed to high-fidelity reproduction as it was to the original listeners, but it is quite faithful.

Alfred Dolge, as we saw, was mistaken in his estimation in 1911 of the future of the Jankó keyboard. He was not so mistaken in evaluating the player piano. "The player piano," he said, "is the musical instrument for the home of the future, barring all others. . . . Eventually a player piano will be evolved with an action which will be capable of producing the long-sought-for effects of tone sustaining, losing its mechanical character entirely, and thus

---

*As I write this, an old Blüthner grand with a Hupfeld Phonola player mechanism sits on the show-room floor of a local piano dealer, a rare sight in America.

becoming the superior of the present-day piano, as that instrument has superseded the clavichord."[15] If one takes Dolge's remarks for the future up to our own present, he overstated the case. But Dolge himself might have been surprised at his own accuracy for the 20 years after he wrote those words. At that time, neither the Duo-Art nor the Ampico action had been produced, and a number of small improvements to the instrument had yet to be made.

Some figures from the American trade are eye-openers.[16] In 1909, 330,000 conventional pianos were manufactured in the United States, compared with only 34,000 automatic pianos. Five years later, in 1914, the figures were 238,000 conventional pianos, 98,000 automatics. In 1919, the tide came to its highest point, with 180,000 automatic pianos manufactured to only 156,000 conventional ones. In 1925, the year William Braid White's book *Piano-Playing Mechanisms* was published, the automatics were still ahead in a somewhat reduced output, 169,000 to 136,000 conventional instruments. With the stock-market crash in 1929 and the ensuing depression, piano manufacture went into a tailspin, and the 1930's saw the disappearance of the player piano.

But the depression explains no more than the decline of piano production in general. The automatic piano succumbed, most scholars agree, to the competition of the radio and the phonograph, technologies of which Dolge could have had little inkling in 1911. For all their early faults, they did for the household listening public more than the player piano did, were packaged in much smaller spaces, and as the technologies developed, did all this at lower prices. The radio and the phonograph provided entertainment of an extremely varied sort. The player piano, for all its virtues, has the limitation that it can produce only the sound of a piano.

In the 1970's the traditional player piano began to return to favor, even to the point of being the subject of a front-page story in the *Wall Street Journal* in 1978.[17] Most commentators on the player-piano craze ascribe it to nostalgia, though one wonders if nostalgia alone can account for the 7,000 new instruments produced in 1978.[18] Yet the technology of most of these new instruments is no different from that of the 1920's. The resurgence of an old instrument with its old technology is not unheard of. It has happened in our own century with the harpsichord, to a lesser extent with the clavichord, and even with the fortepiano, which can be found in modern copies, often made deliberately with the old craft technologies. The player piano's comeback reminds one of those resurrections, and all bespeak an antiquarian motivation.

One modern player-piano design is distinctly not antiquarian. The Piano-corder, made by the Superscope Corporation, encodes the musical program digitally on an ordinary magnetic tape cassette. A digital-to-analog converter changes the digital commands on the tape to electric commands to solenoid switches, which move levers to operate the piano's action. The home pianist, in fact, can record to the Piano-corder's cassette and play it back immediately. The Piano-corder also comes in the form of a piano player, a box wheeled up to the keyboard, where the solenoids work mechanical fingers on the keys. This design certainly exemplifies the application of new electronic technology to the old problem of an automated piano. One wonders only whether the Piano-corder is really superior to a tape recorder.

In the circumstances, it appears we cannot yet call the automatic piano a dead end. But it cannot conceivably compete on even terms with a recording industry as zealous, effective, and innovative as the one European and American nations know. The automatic piano will likely remain a curiosity, for the old pneumatic technology will hardly capture millions of imaginations that look forward to storing recorded music in home computers.

That a radically reformed keyboard might make a comeback seems an even more dubious proposition. Perhaps something like the Jankó keyboard could be adapted for electronic synthesizers; those that use keyboards are at present only hampered by the standard keyboard's limitations. But if the piano continues its long career in homes and auditoriums, it seems likely that it has reached its definitive forms. The violin, after all, has been unchanged for about 180 years now and shows little sign of declining, and the acoustic guitar has been improved very little since the middle of the eighteenth century. No preordained necessity decrees that an instrument undergo constant innovation.

10

The Modern Piano

At every time in its history, except the first few years, the piano has taken a number of forms. In the early nineteenth century there were squares, large and small grands, large cabinet uprights, giraffes, pyramid pianos, and small uprights. Similar diversity characterizes the modern piano: grands of many sizes, ranging from about four and a half to nine and a half feet, and uprights of three basic sizes. And though the square piano became obsolete in the last years of the nineteenth century, it has, wonder of wonders, returned as one of the typical forms of the electronic piano.

But for all the diversity, the forms of the piano as we know them today have been more or less standardized since about the turn of the century. Modifications since then have been nothing more than variations, none extensive enough even to be called mutants. The one exception is the electric and electronic forms.

This chapter has two purposes: to present the basic forms of the modern piano, first, in terms of its variety and, second, in terms of its leading makers. Brands not mentioned here are by no means meant to be relegated to insignificance. But, as most would agree, I am sure, for the quality of their products and their contributions to the tradition of the piano, Steinway, Baldwin, and Bösendorfer are properly included. Nor can anyone object to calling Yamaha of Hamamatsu, as the world's largest producer, a "leading" maker.

For our first form and maker, we have the piano shown in Figure 10.1—a small grand made by the Yamaha company. Small grands were made long before the modern piano came into being;

By courtesy of Nippon Gakki Co., Ltd., Hamamatsu, Japan

FIG. 10.1. *Grand piano, Yamaha (Nippon Gakki Co., Ltd.), Hamamatsu, Japan.* Model G-3. *Action:* Yamaha repetition action; felt-covered hammers. *Stops:* 3 pedals: una corda, sostenuto, dampers to f³. *Range:* AAA–c⁵. *Stringing:* AAA–FF♯ single-strung copper-wound, GG–B♭ double-strung copper wound, B–c⁵ triple-strung plain steel; cross-strung; AAA 135 cm, c² 35.6 cm, c⁵ 5.2 cm. *Framing:* One-piece cast-iron frame. *Case:* Black lacquer over sheet resin veneer; 182.9 cm long, 148 cm wide.

Broadwood made what it called a semi-grand as early as 1831. As the nineteenth century wore on, the standard instrument for concert use came to be about nine feet long, and so it has remained to this day. But a grand of that length would not do for home consumption, and most makers began in the last half of the century to produce various sizes of smaller grands. (Charles Gounod, the French composer, disapproved; he called one of them a *crapaud*, "toad," and the term has stuck as French slang for a small grand.)[1] Steinway exhibited a "parlor" grand at the 1876 Centennial Exhibition in Philadelphia that was six feet, eight inches long. Sizes of less than six feet were tried. In about 1900, the Albert Weber company in New York began to make a five-foot grand, which they were the first to call a "baby grand." The term is sometimes misapplied to any grand smaller than the concert instrument. "Baby grand" is probably best used for a piano five feet long or smaller—and some have been smaller.

Yamaha's G-3 model is not, by that definition, a baby grand. This instrument has few features not common to all modern grands. Yamaha follows Theodore Steinway in making the hammer rail, to which the hammers are hinged, of metal. Theodore Steinway patented a tubular metal action frame in 1875.[2] Yamaha's is of aluminum alloys, a metallurgical technology not available to Steinway in the nineteenth century. Yamaha has adopted another famous Steinway success in using a modification of the Steinway duplex scale, which proportioned the lengths of the strings between the agraffes and the tuning pins to the speaking lengths of the strings so that those parts of the string would vibrate as enhancing partials. Yamaha has gone further. The section of strings between bridge and hitch-pins passes over a second, metal bridge, which exactly sets the proper length of that portion of the string so that it also vibrates sympathetically as a partial of the main note. Though Yamaha still calls this a duplex scale, it is actually "triplex."

Yamaha is perhaps the best example of a manufacturing technology utilizing machine accuracy and efficiency and automation. I can describe only parts of the process. For example, the Sitka spruce planks for the soundboard are first sawn, naturally dried for six months or more, kiln-dried in automated chambers to about a 10 percent moisture content,* and planed; they are then put through a patching machine in which a special urea glue is applied, and the planks are automatically glued side by side to form the basic soundboard. Keys are simultaneously and automatically sawed from a single block of wood (silver fir in one Yamaha account, spruce in another). Keys have been made from a single block for several centuries, but only in modern days have

---

*The 10 percent figure applies only to the soundboard and may be a simplification. Yamaha cures the wood to be used in its pianos to three different specifications, depending on the countries to which the instruments are to be sent: "standard" for Japan and most other Asian countries; "dry" for Europe; and "super dry" for North America. (I am indebted to LaRoy Edwards of Yamaha International Corporation for this information.)

automatic multiple saws cut them all at once. Figure 10.2 is a photograph of the interior of the Yamaha factory in Hamamatsu, Japan, showing some of the machinery in use.

Not every stage of the assembly of a Yamaha is automated. Action parts are assembled by hand, though many of them are automatically milled, and strings are put on tuning pins and hitch-pins by hand. But the string is wound on the tuning pin by a machine, and another machine drives the tuning pins into the pin block. Hammer felts are attached by machine, as they have been in the United States since the 1850's, but the finishing of the bridges is handwork, as is the attachment of the ribs to the machine-glued soundboard.

The technology of a distinctively modern machine has had its impact on one of Yamaha's processes. The iron frames are cast by what is called the vacuum-shield mold process, which Yamaha first used in casting engine parts for motorcycles.[3] Iron has long been cast in "green sand," a mixture of sand, clay, and water that is made into a mold by being applied under pressure to the pattern. Yamaha's process uses dry sand that is hardened by air pressure when suction tubes pull the air out of the sand in the mold box. A thin film of plastic between the sand and the pattern adheres exactly to the pattern and ensures the finest detail in the casting. Yamaha claims more faithful casting for this process and a more uniform structure of the metal because of balanced cooling times between the thick and thin parts.

As far as I have been able to discover, Yamaha alone among contemporary piano makers is responsible for manufacturing everything that goes into the instrument. Years ago that was a relatively common claim, but no longer. The economies of independent, specializing companies, as I have said elsewhere, have led almost all makers to subcontract frames, keys, and sometimes actions. Doubtless Yamaha's volume of production has some effect on the economy of maintaining the entire manufacturing process under its own control.

For all its leadership in manufacturing technology (something not unexpected in a Japanese firm), Yamaha may best represent a success story of a different kind. After the Meiji restoration in 1868 made Westernization a Japanese policy, pianos, along with many other artifacts of Western culture, soon appeared in Japan.

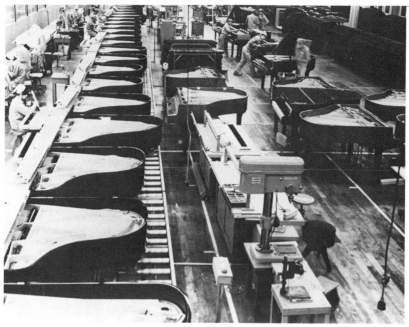

By courtesy of Nippon Gakki Co., Ltd., Hamamatsu, Japan

FIG. 10.2. *Interior of Yamaha factory, Hamamatsu.* The grands, of various sizes, are moving away from the camera for the final stages of assembly. The woman on the line at left is completing assembly of a keyboard, and men toward the back seem to be putting actions and keyboards into the instruments.

There is some question about just when this happened. Sumi Gunji, sketching the history of the piano trade in Japan, says that European pianos, from Blüthner and Carl Otto, both German makers, first came to Japan in 1882.[4] But Cyril Ehrlich notes that a Japanese square piano (I have been unable to discover the maker's name) was exhibited, and ignored, at the Paris Exposition of 1878, and Daniel Spillane asserts that the Japanese government contracted in 1879 with Knabe of Baltimore to provide pianos for public schools.[5] Since a government program for teacher training, inaugurated in 1880, included lessons in piano, organ, and violin, as well as in traditional Japanese instruments, pianos were almost certainly imported into Japan earlier than Gunji thinks.* At any rate, Nishikawa & Son of Tokyo began to make pianos in 1885.[6]

*See Cyril Ehrlich, *The Piano*, p. 195. *Frank Leslie's Illustrated Newspaper*, a New York weekly, reported on June 23, 1860, that a square made by John B. Dunham of New York had been sent to Japan in 1859.

Torakusu Yamaha, who was making reed organs in Hamamatsu in 1887, formed his company, Nippon Gakki, in 1897 and entered the piano trade in 1899. Other makers would appear in time.

By 1911, Yamaha was outpacing Nishikawa in production, with a yearly output of 600, compared with Nishikawa's 200.[7] By 1930, total Japanese production had risen to more than 2,000 yearly, and in 1935 it was double that amount. However, the real success, not only of Yamaha, but of Japanese piano manufacture generally, came in a torrent after the Second World War, when Nippon Gakki's new president decided to go in heavily for automation. By 1960, Japan had taken third place to the United States and the USSR, making 48,000 pianos that year as against 160,000 for the United States and 88,000 for the USSR; by the end of the decade, Japan had leaped past both countries, to move into first place. U.N. data for 1970 show 273,000 pianos for Japan, 220,000 for the United States, and 200,000 for the USSR. Next to these figures, the 1970 totals for France (1,000), England (17,000), and Germany (45,000, East and West together) are more than a little anemic. In the next eight years Japanese output increased more than 25 percent, to stand at 374,000 units in 1979.[8]

Yamaha is by far the largest Japanese maker—followed by Kawai—with an annual production (238,000 units in 1979) higher than the total U.S. production.[9] The company is engaged in much more than piano production; it manufactures electronic organs and pianos, guitars, accordions, harmonicas, band instruments, stereo systems, tape recorders, motorcycles, boats, skis, and bathtubs. A widespread system of Yamaha instruction on keyboard instruments, not only in Japan but also in the United States, is doing for children's instruction on the piano what Suzuki has done for it on the violin.

In commercial terms, then, Yamaha's is a success story even more than Steinway's. Yamaha would like to match Steinway in all respects, but even one of its own officials was quoted recently as saying that to compare the two is "like comparing Rolls-Royces with Toyotas."[10] The pianos themselves are tough, well made, and attractively styled. The conservatory models stand up well to the acid test of conservatory and college practice-room use, and a number of concert pianists have recently given high praise to Yamaha's concert grand. The G-3 is a worthy exemplar of the modern small grand.

———————◆———————

The upright piano has been the instrument of the masses—except where the guitar has displaced it—since long before the square became obsolete. In Europe especially, the square was replaced in modest homes around the middle of the nineteenth century by the upright. Some of these instruments, like the Schmidt and Decker Brothers uprights in Chapters Eight and Nine, were quite large. Others, like Pape's consoles, were small, comparable in size to the Baldwin pictured in Figure 10.3. The modern upright has settled down to three basic sizes. The largest, usually called a studio piano, stands about 3 feet, 9 inches; next comes the console, at 3 feet, 4½ inches (the size of the Baldwin); and finally there is the spinet, at just over 3 feet.

"Studio" is a purely modern appellation and was probably coined to avoid the word upright, but the other two names have a long history. A spinet was first a type of harpsichord, possibly named either for Giovanni Spinetti, alleged to have been the first to make them, or from the Italian *spinetta* ("little thorn"), descriptive of the instrument's plectra.[11] But since the earliest references to spinets are French, it is also possible that the term originated in France.[12] However that may be, the word later denoted small harpsichords shaped either trapezoidally or in a modified wing form, in which the spine or long side of the case ran at an acute angle from the keyboard.[13] I have been unable to discover who among modern makers first used the term spinet for a very small upright piano, but it seems to have happened in the mid-1930's. "Console" we have met before as the term Henri Pape used for his tiny uprights in the 1830's and 1840's. Indeed, Pape's console piano of about 1840 was only about one inch smaller than Baldwin's console of 1980.*

The small case puts some cramping constraints on designers. Pape, back in the 1820's, devised cross-stringing to meet the problem of his low uprights. Without it, these small instruments would be very poor in tone quality, requiring excessively short strings to fit inside the cabinet. Cross-stringing allows the maxi-

---

*A beautiful Pape console of 1840 in the Colt Clavier Collection is 39½ inches high (a color photograph appears in C. F. Colt, *The Early Piano*, p. 123). Our Baldwin measures 40½ inches.

mum length consistent with the size of the case. It is still not long, as the figures for the Baldwin show, and the possibilities of rich tone quality in small uprights are distinctly limited because of it. Were it not that the upright design affords space for the largest soundboard area proportional to the case, the prospects for uprights would be even less promising. Here Steinway's advance in combining cross-stringing with a single soundboard gives modern consoles and spinets a great advantage compared with Pape's little instruments.

The upright's other principal constraint has to do with the action. The diagram in Figure 10.4 shows the "drop" action of the

FIG. 10.3. *Console piano, Baldwin Piano and Organ Company, Cincinnati, Ohio.* Model 914. *Action:* Baldwin drop action; felt-covered hammers. *Stops:* 3 pedals: "soft" (shortens hammer blow), bass dampers, dampers to e♭³. *Range:* AAA–c⁵. *Stringing:* AAA–BB single-strung wound, C–e double-strung wound, f–c⁵ triple-strung plain; cross-strung; AAA 112.1 cm, c² 37.8 cm, c⁵ 5.1 cm. *Framing:* One-piece cast-iron frame. *Case:* Cherry veneered over hardwood panels, lacquered over filler and stain; 102.9 cm high, 149.8 cm wide.

FIG. 10.4. *Baldwin drop action*. The wire abstract joins the end of the key to the wippen below. When the key is depressed, the abstract pulls the wippen up, and the jack pushes the hammer to the string. Shaded areas are rails that run horizontally all through the action. Drawing by Bayard H. Colyear, III.

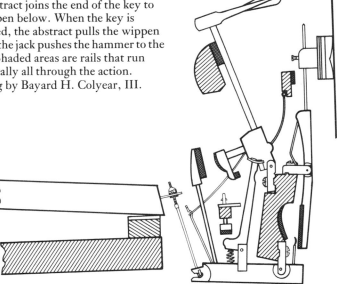

Baldwin. The height from the end of the key to the wippen is dictated by the height of the case. The keyboard must be at a standard height from the floor, about 28⅝ inches, in order to be played comfortably by a seated pianist. On the console model, the keys are just under 12 inches below the top of the case. To leave space in the case for the pin block with the tuning pins, the length of string above the capo tasto and the agraffes, and some string length for the proper striking point, the hammers actually strike the strings at about keyboard level. Thus the action must be arranged as the diagram shows it, so that the leverage on the hammer butt comes from considerably below the level of the key. In a spinet, the drop must be even lower, since the keyboard level is only about 8 inches below the top of the case.

Baldwin's is an interesting action, operating on a slightly different principle from other vertical actions we have seen. Ordinarily the wippen is pushed up by the key to raise the jack against the hammer butt. Baldwin's is of a type that has been called the "pulling action."[14] The wire connector between the end of the key and the wippen pulls the wippen upward when the key goes down, raising the jack to propel the hammer. If the key were angled down, as we saw, for example, with the Stein giraffe in Chapter Four, the dropped part of the key would undergo some wasted forward motion on the wippen, since the wippen operates only on vertical motion. The pulling arrangement is more efficient, because the vertical motion of the key is entirely translated into the vertical motion of the wippen and the jack.

D. H. Baldwin was a music teacher in Cincinnati, Ohio, who, among other things, sold Decker Brothers pianos. The piano business so flourished that Baldwin was able to establish branches. From there he went on in 1889 to found an organ manufacturing subsidiary, the Hamilton Organ Company, in Chicago. By 1891 Baldwin was manufacturing pianos, and several subsidiaries (one picturesquely named Valley Gem Piano Company) were bought. When Baldwin died in 1899, the company was bought by Lucien Wulsin and George W. Armstrong, who had been with the company for some time. The Baldwin company won a grand prize at the Paris Exposition of 1900, only nine years after it began to build pianos. Baldwin was never a high-volume manufacturer but made a solid reputation for solid instruments. Not until the 1930's or so was its name counted among the top few pianos made in the United States. Since then, it is fair to say that by virtue of its attention to concert grands, Baldwin has moved above names like Knabe, Chickering, Mason and Hamlin, and Kimball to become second in reputation only to Steinway among U.S. makers. Baldwin took controlling interest of the Bechstein company in Berlin in 1963, and in 1974 made it a wholly owned subsidiary.

Baldwin's experiments with electronic pianos issued in 1968 in a system to use such instruments in class instruction.[15] In the Baldwin system, each student has an electronic piano and a headset. The teacher operates a console that can tune in to each student in turn, and the teacher can give instructions through the headphones. It is a much less noisy method of class piano teaching than others.

———————— ◆▶ ————————

With the mention of electronic pianos we come to another modern modification of the piano, perhaps the only serious one since

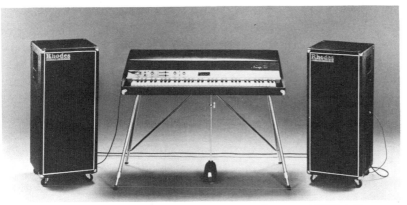

FIG. 10.5. *Electric piano, Rhodes (CBS Music), Fullerton, Calif.* Model 73. *Action:* Anglo-German action, hammers molded plastic with neoprene tips; felt under-dampers. *Stops:* 1 pedal: dampers. *Range:* EE–e⁴. *Vibrators:* Metal rods of varying lengths; larger metal resonator rods attached to vibrators by metal bridges, magnetic coil pickups for each note. *Controls:* Volume, tone (treble, bass equalizers), vibrato (intensity, speed). *Case:* Plastic; 115.3 cm wide, 55.6 cm deep.

the Jankó keyboard: the use of electrical and electronic means to amplify or generate sound in keyboard instruments.

The instrument you see in Figure 10.5 is not a piano. The piano, as I explained in Chapter One, is a struck chordophone. Having no strings, our example is not a chordophone and is therefore not a piano. It is probably best classed as a struck idiophone. Invented in 1969 by Harold Rhodes, the instrument is manufactured by the Rhodes Division of CBS Musical Instruments in Fullerton, California. Looking at it, you might think that you were seeing the resurrection of one of Zumpe's little squares, were it not for the plastic case, the metal legs, and the loudspeaker housings. Shaped like a square, not as wide as the 1767 Zumpe discussed in Chapter Two, and, in truth, sounding less like a modern piano than the Zumpe does, it is almost wholly a product of twentieth-century technology. It has hammers, to be sure, and they are activated by keys. However, the hammers strike not strings, but metal rods that are free at one end, in effect very small tuning forks.

In that respect, we have nothing new. Tuning-fork pianos, bearing names such as Adiaphone, Dulcitone, Euphotine, and

Melodikon, were invented from 1788 to about 1885. (Charles Clagett of London was the first to introduce them.)[16] The Rhodes differs from them in its resonation. The vibrating rods are attached to larger resonating metal bars, and the vibrations of resonators and vibrators affect the magnetic fields of coils for each note. The resulting electric current runs through a pre-amplifier with volume and tone controls and then into an amplifier and a transducer, which produces the mechanical vibrations for the cone of the loudspeaker or the similar membrane of a set of headphones. This means of amplifying sound could not have been conceived before the twentieth century and the exploitation of electricity.

Perhaps the most surprising feature of this instrument, one that also brings to mind the pianos of a much earlier day, is that its action is of the Anglo-German type: the hammers, pivoted on a rail at the back of the keys, point forward toward the player. A jack mounted on the key propels the hammer to the vibrating rod. The hammer and shank are one piece of molded plastic, and the striking tip is neoprene. The action in the Rhodes is ordinarily a good deal stiffer than a piano action.

The sound, I said, is little like that of the piano, rather resembling a vibraphone. The reason lies in the vibrators. A struck metal rod does not produce the same pattern of fundamental and partials as a struck string. The tone is entirely different, from attack and partials to decay characteristics. Tone electronically amplified can, of course, be electronically modified, but to make the Rhodes sound like a piano would require a kind of modification that cannot be accomplished with this particular instrument.

Since the Rhodes is not a piano, I do not wish to spend much space on it. But since it is *called* a piano, it is worth at least a little space. Such instruments are to be heard mostly in popular music groups, where they are compatible with other electronically amplified instruments, can be run through a mixer with them, and are extremely light and easy to transport. An instrument like this has one other very convenient aspect: since the tone is amplified entirely through a loudspeaker or headphones, no one but the player can hear the sound if headphones are chosen. For those who need to practice at 3:00 A.M. in a thin-walled apartment, this is the perfect answer.

The instrument shown in Figure 10.6 is another Yamaha—the CP-80 grand. It has a standard grand action with a damper system somewhat modified from the usual, in the interest, the promotional literature says, of rapid response. The hammers set strings to vibrating. At that point, however, the familiarity begins to recede. Unlike any other instruments we have discussed, except the Rhodes, this one has no soundboard. The amplification of the strings' vibrations is electronic. Instead of a wooden bridge that conveys the vibrations to a sympathetically vibrating soundboard, the bridge for each string is a piezoelectric element, like a small microphone installed under each note's strings. At the other end of the wire, a transducer converts the electrical impulses to the mechanical vibrations of a loudspeaker. Between the pickups and the loudspeaker are all the paraphernalia of circuit boards, resistors, capacitors, pre-amplifiers, and the like, which both boost the impulses received through the pickups and modify them through manipulation of the control knobs and switches on the fall-board.

But this is a piano. With the loudspeaker off, the instrument produces a small, unresonated sound, recognizable as a piano sound because the strings vibrate as they do on an acoustic piano. Thus the tone coming out of the loudspeaker is much like the tone of a conventional piano. It is still not quite the same thing, partly because electronic modifications can be introduced into the tone, partly because the pickups are not the last word in fidelity of reproduction. The player who wants grand piano tone will not get it out of this instrument, no matter how fine the speakers.

Another thing that detracts from the tone is that the volume level does not depend on the player's touch. To be sure, hitting the keys harder produces more volume. But the general volume level can be raised by the volume control, and the pickups are responsive enough to allow high volume without the necessity of long, tightly stretched strings. Thus the CP-80 has short strings and is only double-strung in the treble. The very short strings require considerably less tension than in a conventional piano, and the relative shortness, hence stiffness, and low tension mean that the strings do not produce the partials that a standard piano does.

By courtesy of Yamaha International, Buena Park, Calif.

FIG. 10.6. *Electronic grand, Yamaha (Nippon Gakki Co., Ltd.), Hamamatsu, Japan.* Model CP-80. *Action:* Repetition action, modified damper assembly; synthetic leather hammer covering. *Stops:* 1 pedal: dampers to b♭³. *Range:* AAA–c⁵. *Stringing:* AAA–F♯ single-strung wound, G–d¹ double-strung wound; e♭¹–c⁵ double-strung plain; cross-strung; AAA 75.6 cm, c² 34.1 cm, c⁵ 5.1 cm. *Controls:* Volume (resistor), tone (bass, middle, treble; tremolo speed, depth). *Framing:* One-piece cast-iron frame. *Case:* Plastic; 115 cm long, 146 cm wide. The instrument has no soundboard. Piezoelectric pickups form bridges for the strings of each note.

Notice that the bottom AAA has a string merely 75.6 cm long, only about two-thirds the length of the same string in the Baldwin console and just over half the length of the same string on the six-foot Yamaha grand discussed above. The hammers, moreover, may remind us a bit of the eighteenth century. Into the end of the quite small wooden hammer is set a urethane rubber crown, which is covered with a thin layer of synthetic, buckskin-like material. This artificial leather is glued to the hammer and can easily be replaced when grooves cut by the strings become too pronounced.

The tremolo and tone controls are completely different from

anything on a standard piano. What is called tremolo is actually a vibrato, worked by an oscillator that rapidly modifies the volume level up and down. The rapidity is controlled by a "speed" knob and the amplitude by a "depth" knob. The vibrato gives a certain "live" quality to the sound, much as the right amount of it in the human voice or on a violin does, but it is a quality of sound that no standard piano can give. The tone controls provide selective enhancement and filtering of certain frequency levels within the tone. Such electronic modifications allow a range of timbre changes far beyond anything of which a conventional piano is capable. To be sure, the more modification is used, the less the tone resembles ordinary piano tone.

This is an acoustic instrument, a piano where the Rhodes is not. It is also electronic, capable of sounds that fit better into certain kinds of popular music and of a volume level that only extraordinary muscle-power could produce on a standard piano. But it is a compromise, as every effort to eat your cake and have it too necessarily is. The satisfaction that one may derive from such an instrument depends, I suppose, on one's expectations. For some purposes it is an entirely adequate solution. Those purposes do not, in my judgment, include performances of art music.

There is another type of electronic piano that is completely electronic. In this type (Yamaha's CP-30 is an example), the keys, weighted to give the feeling of a standard piano action, activate pressure-sensitive switches. The player can control the volume with finger pressure on the key, and the switches bring into play premixed, electronically generated vibrations that are electronically amplified.

This instrument is in no sense at all a piano, and its tone is no nearer that of the piano than is the tone of the Rhodes. Some instruments of this kind have harpsichord stops that simulate the plucking attack, and some have clavichord stops. There may be several different tonal varieties of what the switches that activate particular mixtures call "piano." These "piano" tones are synthesized so as to approximate—but not really closely—the mix of fundamental and partials of the piano, the attack and decay characteristics, and even on some an initial attack component remarkably similar to the "hammer slap" of a conventional piano, that slight thud made by the felt on the string. The programmers of the sound deserve credit for trying. But I wonder how long makers will go on pretending that these instruments are pianos. Surely the time will, and should, come when buyers will want them for their own sound quality and not for their dubious approximation to piano sound. Imitation may be flattery, but to leave off imitating in this instance would seem a greater freedom for an electronic keyboard instrument to produce unabashedly electronic sounds, something approaching the versatility of a synthesizer that a musician could play and not pretend to be playing something else.

--------◆▶--------

Pianos are the subject of this book, and I return to them. The Bösendorfer in Figure 10.7 is the largest piano made today. Its nine-and-a-half-foot length makes it 6¼ inches longer than the standard concert grand, and it is also 6⅝ inches wider. It has, moreover, a wider range than any successful piano in the history of the instrument: eight full octaves, nine keys more than the regular seven octaves and a third of the modern piano. On the Bösendorfer Imperial one fingers not "the 88" but "the 97." Though larger pianos have been made, this is more piano than most of us ever need.*

The standard range encompasses nearly all the music ever written for the piano. A few composers have used notes lower than the AAA that is the usual bottom note. The Hungarian composer Zoltán Kodály called for pitches down to CCC♯ in his early set of pieces, op. 3 (1909–10), and other occasional forays below AAA turn up in modern piano scores. The CCC on the Bösendorfer, if it is in tune, has a frequency of 16.5 Hz. The lowest vibration frequency that the normal human ear can detect as sound is 15 Hz.[17] When that CCC is played, many listeners will *feel* it as vibration but will not *hear* it as a pitch. The tuner must use an electronic device to be sure that the string is in tune; the ear may not tell.

This is not the only Bösendorfer model that exceeds the standard range. The firm's Concert Grand, just over nine feet in length, and its seven-foot, four-inch Half-Concert Grand (yes, the company calls it that: *Halbkonzertflügel*) both extend to FFF, four keys below the standard range. The amateur who wants a very fine

---

*In 1935, Challen of London celebrated the silver jubilee of King George V with a grand 11 feet, 8 inches long. Pictures of the instrument exist, but I do not know whether the company made more than one such behemoth, nor have I discovered any public testimony to its musical qualities.

By courtesy of Kimball Piano and Organ Company, Jasper, Ind.

FIG. 10.7. *Grand piano, Bösendorfer, Vienna.* Model 290 "Imperial." *Action:* Renner repetition action; felt-covered hammers. *Stops:* 3 pedals: una corda, sostenuto, dampers. *Range:* CCC–c⁵. *Stringing:* CCC–DD♯ single-strung copper-wound, EE–C♯ double-strung copper-wound, D–c⁵ triple-strung plain steel; cross-strung; CCC 221.8 cm, c² 34.9 cm, c⁵ 5.1 cm. *Case:* Mahogany veneered with two surface veneers, black lacquer finish; 290 cm long, 168 cm wide.

piano—at a rather fine price—may be encouraged to know that Bösendorfer also makes two smaller grands with the standard AAA–c⁵ range. In fact, the company makes nothing but grands.

Bösendorfer has never gone in for large production. Before 1975, when 515 pianos were produced, the greatest output in a single year was 434 in 1913. It is not surprising that this should be so. The market for grands has always been far below that for the smaller pianos. Bösendorfer's concentration on grands to the exclusion of other shapes means that no matter how fine a machine it makes, sales will be limited. And since the Imperial goes in the United States for about the price of a small house, it has restricted appeal to the mass market.

Bösendorfer is a relatively old company in Vienna, though

since 1973 the factory has been in Wiener Neustadt, 54 kilometers south of Vienna. It started in 1828 when Ignaz Bösendorfer took over the shop of the deceased Josef Brodmann, to whom he had been apprenticed. Brodmann was one of Vienna's leading makers in the early nineteenth century, and no less a pianist than Carl Maria von Weber purchased a Brodmann grand in 1813.* Shortly after Bösendorfer entered the trade for himself, he was given the opportunity to see one of his grands reduced to rubble by the ministrations of Franz Liszt. To everyone's surprise, even Liszt's and Bösendorfer's, the piano withstood the beating that other Viennese pianos had not survived, and Bösendorfer had a new friend. At Ignaz's death in 1859, his son Ludwig took direction of the firm; he sold it in 1909 to Carl Hutterstrasser.

In 1966, Bösendorfer was purchased by Kimball International, Inc., an American conglomerate based in Jasper, Indiana, that grew out of the W. W. Kimball Company (more recently Kimball Piano and Organ Company), a builder of pianos in Chicago since 1857. The Kimball name had never been associated with the highest quality instruments in the United States, and its acquisition of the highly respected Bösendorfer firm had mixed reviews. It appears that Kimball has made no moves that have compromised Bösendorfer's reputation. For a company with testimonials in its files from satisfied users like Franz Liszt, Johannes Brahms, Anton Rubinstein, Alfred Cortot, Béla Bartók, Artur Rubinstein and Sviatoslav Richter, to say nothing of Victor Borge and Oscar Peterson, the reputation carries no little weight.

Bösendorfer does not make any pretense of total manufacture. The frames of its grands are cast in Czechoslovakia, and the actions are made by Renner in Stuttgart, the leading European action specialists. It is not clear whether the company has followed other makers in using the urea resin glues that became available after the Second World War. Unlike most contemporary makers, Bösendorfer has not adopted plastics for key coverings; the white keys are still ivory. The relatively small production bespeaks the company's continuance of the craft tradition. Some companies went

---

*The piano is part of the Musikinstrumentensammlung in Berlin. It may be the instrument that Alfons Kontarsky plays in a recording of Schubert's Sonata for Arpeggione and Piano, D. 821, Archiv-Produktion no. 2533 175. The record's liner notes do not refer to Weber's ownership, but the piano that was used dates from the same year, 1810, and has the same pedal configuration and range (FF–f⁴).

down the drain in the early twentieth century because they failed to keep up with the technology that could make them participants in the world markets. Bösendorfer remained alive and solvent through those times with small production, while larger firms like Streicher died, and others like Erard lost their place in the market. Perhaps success is to be marked up to a tradition of high craft and effective quality control.

There is no question that playing an Imperial is something like sitting down to a feast of haute cuisine. The piano has long had the reputation of a smooth clarity of tone across the entire range. With a well-regulated Bösendorfer, one feels that the sound may never die completely away but will vibrate on and on. Perhaps that smoothness is not the best quality for some twentieth-century music that calls for the sharpest contrasts of loudness and an occasional strident crash. But in music of melodic warmth and harmonic color, one has the feeling that the instrument nearly plays itself.

———————◄◆►———————

With the instrument in Figure 10.8, we bring the Steinway story to the present. This sort of piano is played, according to one estimate, in 90 percent of the American concerts using pianos,[18] though in some of those concerts, models other than the nearly nine-foot concert grand are certainly used. In design technology the modern Steinway has few improvements over earlier models. The action is now the "accelerated" action, not merely a "repetition" action. The changes are not great, consisting first of careful adjustments of the lead weights in the keys in order to ensure an even balance across the entire range (something any pianist wants and a superior pianist recognizes) and second, of a change in the design of the fulcrum on which the key pivots. Merely rounding the edges of the fulcrum produced a greater ease of swing for the key, making it more responsive to the touch. These design changes were the work of Frederick A. Vietor, an employee of the company, in the early 1930's.[19]

More significant changes have been made in materials. One does not, on a Steinway or on any piano made in the United States, "tickle the ivories" any longer. For one thing, an act of Congress in 1973 forbade the importation of ivory or objects made

By courtesy of Steinway & Sons, New York

FIG. 10.8. *Grand piano, Steinway & Sons, New York.*   Model D. *Action:* Steinway accelerated action; felt-covered hammers. *Stops:* 3 pedals: una corda, sostenuto, dampers to g³. *Range:* AAA–c⁵. *Stringing:* AAA–EE single-strung wound, FF–AA double-strung wound, BB♭–E triple-strung wound, F–c⁵ triple-strung plain; cross-strung; AAA 201.5 cm, c² 34.5 cm, c⁵ 5 cm. *Framing:* One-piece cast-iron frame. *Case:* Laminated maple, lacquered with black nitro-cellulose; 273.7 cm long, 151.3 cm wide.

of it. For another, ivory has always tended to crack and become yellow with age. Improperly glued, ivory curls up and falls off the keys. In the early 1960's, Steinway began to use a plastic key covering that neither cracks nor yellows. At the start, some pianists complained that the plastic felt wrong under the fingers, but even they have perforce become used to it. Ivory was always expensive, and various other materials have been tried over the years, all the way from strips of cattle bone to celluloid. The cattle bone did not polish to a smooth enough surface, and celluloid was strictly for cheap pianos made before the Second World War.[20] The plastic now used is probably a better key covering than ivory, however one might yearn sentimentally for the old "natural" material. But to get that particular natural material, you must kill an elephant. Fortunately, the perception of the elephant's ecological value has coincided with the availability of an entirely adequate alternative technology.

Along with others, Steinway now uses the urea resin glues that were one of the technological outcomes of the Second World War. Things glued to hold in temperate climates come distinctly unglued in tropical ones. Because much of the war was prosecuted in the tropics, the search for ways to hold military equipment together took on great importance, and piano technology was one of the beneficiaries. These glues have been improved to the point that 20 minutes in the vicinity of a high-frequency generator sets them forever. Unlike the old animal glues, they are water-proof, humidity-proof, rot-proof, and for all practical purposes, vermin-proof, being utterly unattractive to rats, mice, and the like.

Still another difference in materials, one in which Steinway has pioneered, is the use of Teflon (polytetrafluoroethylene) in the action. One of the requirements of an action is that it be absolutely noiseless. In fact, all actions make small sounds apart from what they produce on the strings, and acousticians have suggested that one of the subliminally recognized aspects of piano sound is the tiny clicks and thumps in the action—a difficult thing to calculate and one of the reasons it is so hard to synthesize piano sound, even with a computer. No company will publicly admit, of course, that its actions make any noise. To avoid it, any point at which part touches part is lined with a noise-reducing material, and any place where a part pivots on a pin or flange is bushed. Traditionally bushings have been cloth, leather, or felt, materials that wear thin with use, altering the tolerances of the moving parts, until they finally wear out, permitting the clicks and bumps they were designed to suppress. In the 1970's, Steinway began to use Teflon in certain parts of the action, especially around the pins on which the keys pivot. Teflon never wears thin under the kind of use a piano action gives. It also reduces friction, which cloth, leather, and felt do not, and thus it is supposed to increase responsiveness. It has been alleged that the innovation has not been a total success, indeed, by some pianists, that it is disastrous. The argument is that Teflon does not expand and contract with the wood in changes of humidity, thus altering the tolerances of parts either to bind the keys so that they stick or to allow them to thump.[21] Steinway has stoutly defended the product, and some of the problems are said to be reduced by the use of a ribbed Teflon in the bushings.

As for the technology of manufacture at Steinway, it has not changed as much as one might suppose. The high-frequency generator sets resin glues in a very short time. Some testing machines have been introduced, including one jocularly called a "piano banger," which plays all of the keys 10,000 times in an hour with cam-operated plungers, both testing their resilience and doing a very quick aging job on the hammers. (Yamaha has machines like this too.) Critical operations like stringing, the assembly of actions, the voicing of hammers, and action regulation—the operations that determine the musical quality of a particular instrument—are still done by hand. But actions are assembled from parts milled by machine, and the strings are machine drawn and machine wound.

In one respect, though, Steinway has indeed changed its manufacturing technology. When the plant was moved from the old Fifty-third Street factory in Manhattan to Long Island City in 1910, Steinway claimed to do everything in manufacture and assembly itself (though the firm probably did not draw its own wire). That is no longer the case. Frames are bought from an independent foundry; the keys are made by Pratt, Read & Company, the foremost American firm specializing in action manufacture; and such hardware as hinges and casters is purchased. For its Hamburg manufacturing plant, Steinway has its actions manufactured by the Renner company of Stuttgart. Renner is the major action maker in Western Europe, and its own actions, which are used in Bösendorfers among many other European makers, are slightly different in design from Steinway's.

There is one other respect in which Steinway & Sons is not what it once was (a descriptive, not critical, statement). In 1972, the company was purchased by CBS, Inc., and made a part of the Musical Instruments division of that corporation. People with the name of Steinway continue to occupy high offices in the company, but in 1977, for the first time in its history, Steinway & Sons found itself with a president whose name was not Steinway. (Still, Robert P. Bull, though he came from the electronic instruments group of the CBS division, had a link with the piano trade: his great grandfather was one of the founders of the Story & Clark Piano Company in Chicago. At this writing, Peter M. Perez is the president of the firm, and John H. Steinway the chairman.)[22] The sentimental may mourn that the great families of the piano-making past choose our time to relinquish the reins of direction—yet there are still Broadwoods in the saddle at John Broadwood & Sons in London and Blüthners in charge in Leipzig. Even the sentimental may take comfort from the remark of a younger Steinway, newly come into the employ of the company: "The continuity of the piano is the most important thing. Not the family—the piano."[23]

———————◆◆———————

It is time to conclude the story. It might seem to have been concluded at about the end of Chapter Eight. Of technological changes in design, materials, and manufacturing there have been precious few since the early years of the twentieth century: some efforts to improve the responsiveness of an already standard action, the development of relatively standardized sizes, and the use of some new materials such as resin glues and plastics. The introduction of electronic sound generation and amplification is a novelty, but it has issued rather in other instruments than in important effects on the piano.

Yet even avant-garde composers continue to write for the instrument. To be sure, they sometimes call for untraditional uses of it, such as hand-plucking the strings or drumming on the case to produce musical sounds (some will dispute the adjective) that are different from those employed by Haydn, Liszt, and Debussy. Of course, composers also continue to write for violins, in which no substantial design or material changes have been made since early in the nineteenth century, and for other instruments with long periods of static design behind them.

The question that arises, however, is, does the piano have a future? To that kind of question, only the prophet and seer can confidently give an answer, and perhaps even they ought not do so. "I am no prophet nor the son of a prophet" (Amos 7:14), and speculation must be cautious if not downright timid. More telling yet, anyone who knows the past knows that all along there have been those who falsely predicted the future (Alfred Dolge on the Jankó keyboard, for example), those who luckily landed on a correct perception of the future even when it turned out to be more temporary than the predictor thought (Dolge, again, on the player piano), and those who could not imagine that the future might produce anything superior to what the present had. Surely at every stage in the piano's evolution, those engaged in designing and making quality pianos thought they were putting out an instrument that was as good as it could possibly be. Then someone came along with something more useful for some musical purpose.

Perhaps the piano has no future, will simply go on being made in the ways it is now made, to the designs now employed, in order to play the music it has always been there to play. Perhaps it will fade away as an obsolete instrument that was once useful for playing outdated tunes that no one wants to hear any more. That happened to the harpsichord and the clavichord, and just as they have been to some extent revived in our own times (not merely for the music current when they were dominant, but also for modern works written for them), perhaps the piano would at some time be rescued from museums and oblivion to render its sounds again for the edification and delight of antiquarians. The harpsichord and clavichord, however, receded because the piano increasingly supplanted them. I do not see at present another instrument usurping the piano's place.

Some now unconceived change in design or materials could turn it in a new direction. Might electronics provide the new impulse? If electronic pianos catch on with the masses of amateur pianists (and they have not done so yet), their difference in tone quality from the acoustic piano may cease to be a problem simply by its becoming more and more familiar, until ultimately it becomes the norm for the perception of keyboard instruments' tone. This has happened in the case of the electric guitar, which has gained ascendancy over all other instruments in popular music.

Or the music synthesizer might succeed the piano as the home instrument, perhaps driven by a home computer. The advantage of the synthesizer (to which I have not felt required to pay attention in this book) is that it can be programmed either for the diatonic and chromatic scales of traditional Western music or for the more subtle, microtonal gradations of pitch and timbre that twentieth-century electronic and computer-generated music has been exploring and exploiting. Just as players today feel free to play Bach's harpsichord music on the piano, those of the future might play Brahms's piano music on synthesizers. Indeed, a record like Walter Carlos's "Switched-On Bach" (1968) may represent the future already in our midst.

On the other hand, the appearance of a number of people making exact or general copies of fortepianos (in the United States such names as Frank Hubbard, Philip Belt, Robert Smith, and Philip Wolf are becoming better known, and one can purchase at least two different kits for the home construction of eighteenth-century-style Viennese fortepianos) might point toward the revitalization of early forms of the piano. So far, they have been almost exclusively late-eighteenth-century forms, but a few copies of the Grafs of the early nineteenth century have been made. The continuing production of accurate and well-made copies of these types of pianos would greatly enhance the variety of instruments available and the enjoyment of the music written for them. Such a prospect is pleasant to those of us who enjoy playing and hearing fortepianos. And it is highly unlikely that the growth of available fortepianos would put any dent in the production of modern pianos.

My discomfort about guessing the future of the piano stems from my certainty that, had I been asked in 1819 what would happen next to the piano, I could not in the wildest fantasies about my own prescience have predicted the technological explosion in piano design in the 1820's. If, then, prediction is to be approached only fearfully, is any conclusion to be drawn from the history sketched in these pages? Any storyteller hopes that the story is self-explanatory, that commentary is unnecessary and morals redundant. The drawing of "lessons" from history is a hazardous if not a silly undertaking. But the storyteller must be aware of aspects of the story that still want investigation, and of those I am sensible.

To look back over the long years in which the piano dominated the musical world and to see in some detail the kinds of pianos used proposes some implications about the changing musical scene. We now learn to play on modern pianos the range of works for the piano from, say, Carl Philipp Emanuel Bach to Pierre Boulez. Therefore we tend too easily to overlook the long distances we leap in textural and tonal expectations. The differences among a Stein grand of the 1780's, a Graf of 1839, and a Bechstein of 1910, in the ranges of their dynamics, the kinds of textures they are capable of, and the styles of playing that they demand and imply, reflect differences of musical conceptions from Mozart to Schumann to Debussy. Looked at only on the page, music resolves itself into factors of melody, rhythm, and harmony, and studied in those terms, Mozart, Schumann, and Debussy have certain affinities with one another. But music as played adds the factor of tone, sound heard not only as pitch and duration, but also as timbre—in short, of sound as texture. There the understanding of the history of instruments makes its musical impact and ought to be a factor in the education of performers, no matter what their instruments. Viewed from the perspective of the history of the piano, the Classical music of Mozart differs far more from the Romantic music of Chopin than many a music historian will admit.[24] Since the difference shows up crucially in performance, pianists at least need to take it into consideration and ponder the instrument in its many stages of development. It is tempting to play early Beethoven on a modern piano as if it were Liszt. Acquaintance with the instruments both composers knew is the best safeguard against the anachronism.

Another kind of distance is present in the differing forms of the piano. That we find both concert instruments and instruments for the home is not surprising. What must be realized, however, is how very different they were and are. Whereas the guitar that John Williams plays on the concert stage is different from the one you buy in the local shop only in the care the maker took in its building and in the choice of its materials, the piano that Misha Dichter plays in the concert hall is very different in its capabilities from the little spinet on the showroom floor. The two are similar only in the sense that their principle of tone production is the same and their keyboards are identical.

I suspect that the deep gulf between the concert piano and the home piano is related to the increasing difference in European and American culture between art music and popular music. The melodies that composers like Mendelssohn or Liszt wrote were not very different from, though they were more subtle than, those of their contemporary popular composers, such as Stephen Foster. Brahms was a great admirer of Johann Strauss, the Waltz King. Aaron Copland freely adopted jazz idioms. But the cleavage between the two realms began to take place long ago.* As the technology of the piano proceeded, more was demanded of its musical practitioners, and the amateur was less and less capable of playing the great works. Mozart's and Haydn's sonatas were written as teaching pieces for their dilettante pupils; Liszt's and Brahms's were not. The technique requisite for them was too difficult for the ordinary pianist to acquire. Viennese lovers of Johann Strauss's waltzes would have had an awful time bending their fingers around Brahms's waltzes, until he published a simplified version. Copland's Piano Sonata is beyond the reach of most jazz pianists, just as the jazz improvisations of Thelonious Monk are outside the capacities of most classical pianists.

I would not claim to explain fully the distance between popular music and art music in the Western world merely by the history of the shapes of pianos. But I believe that that history may form some part of an explanation. Such cultural criticism is far beyond any of the modest aims of this book. If an explanation is found, someone besides me will certainly be the finder.

I said at the outset that I would not enter on the connections between the piano in its various stages and the music that was written for it. That I enter on it here is only in order to suggest some topics for others to pursue, some lines of perspective on a subject that a single book could not conceivably exhaust. Perhaps no book short of an encyclopedia of the piano could encompass the whole of the instrument's history—its technologies, its social contexts, its economic conditions, the techniques of its performance and its pedagogy, its implications for musical style. Perhaps that whole history can be written only at a time when the piano itself is retiring into the past. And then surely someone will make a sarcastic reference to its successor in people's musical affections as a tinker's kettle.

---

*The distance between the two seems to me to have increased in my own lifetime, though the techniques of the higher realms of popular music (e.g., in our period, of jazz) always verge on those of art music. Popular music has, of course, been much readier than art music to adopt the new technologies of electronic amplification and tone production. Where art music has gone in for the new technology, as in computer-generated music, it has not so far carried very many ordinary art-music lovers with it.

Notes

Notes

————◄◆►————

Citations in the notes are to short titles (e.g., Hollis, *The Piano*) when more than one work of an author is listed in the Bibliography. Otherwise citations are to author (and page, where appropriate). I have used the following abbreviations in the Notes: *DJM*, *Dwight's Journal of Music*; *FJ*, *Franklin Journal*. Complete authors' names, titles, and publication data are in the Bibliography, pp. 277–86.

CHAPTER ONE

   1. See Loesser on social history; Ehrlich on economic history; Bie, Gillespie, and Matthews, among others, on piano music; and Schonberg on pianists and piano-playing.

   2. More extensive discussions of the physics of music are in such works as Roederer, Backus, Levarie and Levy, and Benade, *Fundamentals*.

   3. The most influential book is Sachs.

   4. Helmholtz, pp. 52–4.

   5. See Kock.

   6. Wolfenden, p. 91. Compare Grover, p. 56.

   7. See Wolfenden, p. 94.

   8. See White, *Theory and Practice*, pp. 63–64.

   9. Pfeiffer, *Piano Hammer*, pp. 85–88.

  10. Norton, pp. 107–8.

CHAPTER TWO

   1. Much of the information in the next paragraphs comes from Fabbri.

   2. Quoted by Fabbri, p. 165.

   3. Fabbri, p. 167.

   4. Marcuse, *Musical Instruments* and *A Survey*.

   5. Hubbard, p. 28.

   6. Maffei, "Nuova invenzione." Rimbault gives the Italian text (with one or two errors) and an English translation (pp. 95–102). I am grateful to my colleague Eric Hutchinson for lending me his copy of the 1711 volume of the journal in which this article appeared.

   7. On 1732 rather than 1731, the usual date given for Cristofori's death, see Fabbri, p. 172.

8. Harding, pp. 28–29.

9. The Bach anecdote was related by Johann Friedrich Agricola; see translation in David and Mendel, p. 259. The account of Frederick's pianos (by Johann Nikolaus Forkel) and the following story are on pp. 305–6 of the same work.

10. A report of this visit in the *Spenersche Zeitung*, Berlin, is translated in *ibid.*, p. 176.

11. Wolff, p. 403.

12. I am indebted to my colleague Albert Cohen for the citation that provided Jean Marius's death date: Institut de France, *Index biographique des membres et correspondantes de l'Académie des Sciences* (Paris, 1968), pp. 369–70.

13. Edwin Ripin, "Pianoforte, I," in Sadie, 14: 683.

14. De Pontécoulant, 1: 227, says that he did not. All four drawings are reproduced in Harding, pp. 12–15, and Rimbault, pp. 104–7; those of the first two models in Marcuse, *A Survey*, pp. 322–23.

15. Closson, p. 91.

16. Badura-Skoda, p. 83.

17. Schröter, "Herrn Christoph Gottlieb Schröters . . . Beschreibung," pp. 87–88.

18. Schröter, "Sendschreiben." The letter is dated 1738 but was published by Mizler only in 1747.

19. Schröter, "Herrn Christoph Gottlieb Schröters . . . Beschreibung."

20. Harding, Appendix G, pp. 385–409.

21. Buntebart appears in a London directory of 1794 cited in Rimbault, p. 147, with the English-sounding name of Buntlebart; only Dale, p. 50, names Garcka among the apostles, and he also includes a Froeschley, probably the George Froeschle, active from 1788 to 1800, listed in Harding, p. 393.

22. Dolge, p. 48.

23. Rupprecht, pp. 54–55, quoting an article of 1782.

24. Pfeiffer, *Piano Hammer*, p. 30.

25. Hollis, in conversation. See also Harding, pp. 23–24.

26. Harding, pp. 38–42.

27. Mozart was referring to Franz Jakob Späth of Regensburg.

28. Anderson, *Letters of Mozart*, 2: 478–81.

29. A photograph of Mozart's Walter is in Paul Henry Lang, ed., *The Creative World of Mozart* (New York, 1963), between pp. 64 and 65.

30. Badura-Skoda, p. 80.   31. Von Schönfeld, p. 88.

32. *Ibid.*, p. 90.   33. *Ibid.*, p. 91.

34. Loesser, p. 133; Folker Göthel, "Stein, Familie," in Blume, 12: col. 1231.

35. Sasse, p. 139.

36. Newman and Williams, pp. 52–53.

37. Hipkins, p. 32.

38. Marcuse, *A Survey*, p. 279.

CHAPTER THREE

1. So Czerny remembered. See Sonneck, *Beethoven*, p. 26.

2. Thayer, p. 335.

3. Anderson, *Letters of Beethoven*, 1: 292.

4. Luithlen, p. 36.

5. De Pontécoulant, 1: 230.

6. Reichardt, *Vertraute Briefe aus Paris*, pp. 151–52.

7. Quoted by Newman, "Beethoven's Piano," p. 498.

8. Reichardt, *Vertraute Briefe aus Paris*, p. 154.

9. Walter, p. 269.

10. Invoice cited in Wainwright, pp. 36–37. See also Loesser, p. 246. Sheraton's design was not entirely successful. Disliking the looks of pedals, he omitted them.

11. Luithlen, p. 39, quoting a manuscript biography of Johann Georg Roser by his son, Franz de Paula Roser, in the Gesellschaft der Musikfreunde in Vienna.

12. Hoover and Odell, p. 14.

13. Loesser, p. 241; Schonberg, p. 58.

14. Loesser (p. 133) disagrees, holding that the Streicher workshop was a factory, or close to it.

15. Anderson, *Letters of Beethoven*, 1: 271, 292.

16. Newman, "Beethoven's Piano," p. 488.

17. Anderson, *Letters of Beethoven*, 2: 505, 507, 523.

18. Loesser, p. 139; Harding, Plate I, facing p. 98; Newman, "Beethoven's Piano," p. 492.

19. Colt, pp. 48–49.

20. Anderson, *Letters of Beethoven*, 2: 755n; Thayer, pp. 694–95.

21. Loesser, pp. 147–48.

22. See Gábry, p. 382n; Ernst, p. 120.

23. The letter, in French, is quoted in Thayer, p. 694.

24. Colt, pp. 73, 138.

25. Letter to Nannette Streicher, July 7, 1817, in Anderson, *Letters of Beethoven*, 2: 686.

26. See Newman, "Beethoven's Piano," p. 490; Edward Larkin, "Beethoven's Medical History," Appendix A of Cooper, pp. 440–41.

27. Sonneck, *Beethoven*, pp. 188–89, translating Rellstab, *Aus meinem Leben* (Berlin, 1861), 2: 224ff.

28. Melville, p. 47.

29. Grover, p. 88; Van Barthold and Buckton, p. 42.

30. Newman, "Beethoven's Piano," p. 493.

31. Schindler, p. 372.   32. Quoted by Grover, p. 103.

33. Hipkins, p. 15.   34. Clemen, p. 112.

35. Van der Meer, p. 262; Michel, p. 118.

36. Letter to Nannette Streicher, Aug. 26, 1817, in Anderson, *Letters of Beethoven*, 2: 702.

37. Closson, p. 93n; Dolge, p. 219.

38. See *Bericht über die . . . Gewerbsprodukten-Ausstellung*, p. 319.

39. *Ibid.*, pp. 319–21.

40. Grover, p. 150; Van Barthold and Buckton, p. 70.

41. Newman, "Beethoven's Piano."

42. Thayer, p. 984.

CHAPTER FOUR

1. Harding, p. 56.
2. *Ibid.*, p. 64.
3. Hubbard, p. 161.
4. See Loesser, pp. 167–72.
5. Hollis, *The Piano*, p. 75, citing F. C. Morse, *Furniture of Olden Times* (New York, 1902), p. 262.
6. English patent no. 2028.
7. Gerber, pp. 494–95; Marcuse, *A Survey*, p. 257.
8. Gallini and Gallini, p. 251. Del Mela's 1739 upright is pictured in both Hirt, p. 383, and Gai, 181–82.
9. Marcuse, *A Survey*, pp. 281–82.
10. An illustration of this interior arrangement in an 1816 Clementi upright is in Colt, p. 62.
11. See the illustration in eye-popping color in Clemencic, Plate 113, p. 103.
12. See Harding, Chap. 6, pp. 124–50.
13. A small 1812 Wilkinson and Wornum upright with diagonal stringing is pictured and discussed in Colt, pp. 58–59.
14. English patent no. 2591, quoted in Harding, p. 225. Italics in the patent.
15. A photograph is in *ibid.*, Plate IIb, facing p. 30.
16. Cripe, pp. 55–57.
17. An example made in 1812 by Clementi, with whom Collard worked, is in Colt, pp. 54–56.

CHAPTER FIVE

1. Clemen, p. 112.
2. Schonberg, p. 119.
3. *FJ*, o.s. 3 (1827): 140.
4. *FJ*, n.s. 2 (1828): 310–12.
5. See Bridenbaugh, pp. 141–43.
6. Sonneck, *Early Concert-Life*, p. 265.
7. Grafing, "Alpheus Babcock: Pianoforte Maker," p. 11. Spillane, p. 56, gives the mistaken date of 1817.
8. Babcock's patent, Dec. 17, 1825, quoted by Grafing, "Alpheus Babcock: Pianoforte Maker," p. 71. I was unable to obtain a copy of the patent specifications from the U.S. Patent Office.
9. *FJ*, o.s. 4 (1827): 406.
10. Spillane, p. 122.
11. See Grafing, "Alpheus Babcock: Pianoforte Maker," pp. 38–42; and Grafing, "Alpheus Babcock's Frames," *passim*.
12. Hipkins, "Pianoforte," in *Encyclopaedia Britannica*, 9th ed. (1895), 19: 77.
13. Spillane, p. 122.
14. Patent quoted by Grafing, "Alpheus Babcock: Pianoforte Maker," p. 72. I have corrected the spelling of the words "affected," which Babcock consistently spelled with an "e," and "tension" ("tention").
15. *Ibid.*, p. 38.
16. Information on this episode comes from Grafing, "Alpheus Babcock's Frames."
17. Spillane, p. 27.
18. Grafing, "Alpheus Babcock: Pianoforte Maker," p. 60; see also p. 77.
19. *Ibid.*, p. 1.

CHAPTER SIX

1. *Revue et Gazette Musicale*, 6 (1839): 73.

2. For a diagram and explanation, see Harding, pp. 171–72, and Fig. 11.

3. Hirt, p. xxii.

4. Quoted by Friedheim, pp. 148–49.

5. Hirt, p. 106.

6. In the Kunsthistorisches Museum, Vienna (Gesellschaft der Musikfreunde no. 383); description in Luithlen, pp. 74–76.

7. In the Kunsthistorisches Museum, Vienna (inventory no. 612); description in *ibid.*, pp. 78–79.

8. Catalog no. MS-42. Description and photograph in Sasse, pp. 94–95.

9. Loesser, pp. 407–9.   10. Harding, pp. 179–82.

11. De Pontécoulant, 1: 231; 2: 359.   12. Harding, p. 368.

13. Loesser, p. 409, favors 1826; both Dolge, p. 123, and Marcuse, *A Survey*, p. 346, 1838; and Hirt, p. 95, 1850.

14. Harding, Appendix D, p. 372. She refers to Sanguinède as Sanguinède et Capt, perhaps a typographical error for Sanguinède et Comp. See De Pontécoulant, 2: 451–52, on Sanguinède's patent.

15. Wolfenden, p. 6. See also Holland, p. 339, who thought the idea "fanciful."

16. C. S. Smith, "Discovery of Carbon."

17. Marcuse, *A Survey*, p. 343, makes a good deal of this influence.

18. Schumann, 2: 484–85.   19. Harding, pp. 229–30.

20. Grover, p. 139.   21. Loesser, pp. 267–83.

22. Orga, p. 113.   23. Liszt, p. 90.

24. Grover, p. 120.

25. Quoted from an unidentified source, surely *Das Wissenschaftliche der Fortepiano-Baukunst* (Bern, 1844), by Pfeiffer, *Piano Hammer*, p. 86.

CHAPTER SEVEN

1. Ehrlich, p. 221; Van Barthold and Buckton, p. 26.

2. De Pontécoulant, 2: 552, 553.   3. Ehrlich, p. 35.

4. Rosenberg, pp. 286–87.   5. See Ehrlich *passim*.

6. *DJM*, 4 (1853–54): 133.   7. Spillane, p. 153.

8. Personal letter, dated Sept. 27, 1978, from John H. Steinway.

9. Hoover, p. 53.   10. MacArdle and Misch, p. 18.

11. Rosenberg, Table 1, p. 54.   12. This is the thesis of Habakkuk.

13. Rosenberg, p. 42, quoting the Whitworth Committee's Report, *The American System of Manufactures* (1855).

14. See Loesser, p. 552.   15. Harding, p. 305.

16. Loesser, p. 235.   17. Steinway, p. 93.

18. Ehrlich, pp. 57–58.   19. Quoted in *ibid.*, p. 61.

20. Derived from *ibid.*, Appendix 2, p. 221.

21. *Ibid.*, p. 108.   22. *Ibid.*, p. 110.

23. Quoted in *ibid.*, p. 63.   24. *DJM*, 9 (1856): 133.

25. Gottschalk, p. 134.   26. Dolge, p. 397.

27. *Ibid.*, p. 398.

28. Hollis, "Jonas Chickering," p. 228.
29. Dolge, pp. 99–100.
30. Steinway, p. 31.
31. *Ibid.*, p. 32.
32. Ehrlich, p. 54. The patents were in the name of Albert Steinway, the youngest son.
33. *Ibid.*, p. 51.
34. Junghanns, p. 49.
35. New York *Tribune*, Nov. 11, 1856, quoted in *DJM*, 10 (1856–57): 52.

CHAPTER EIGHT

1. See Ehrlich, pp. 65–67.   2. Luithlen, p. 55.
3. Sasse, p. 211.   4. Harding, p. 148.
5. *Ibid.*
6. See *ibid.*, p. 175, for a discussion of Kriegelstein's action, together with its patent description in French.
7. J. Blüthner and H. Gretschel, *Der Pianofortebau* (Berlin, 1909).
8. Ehrlich, p. 27.   9. Sitwell, pp. 321–23.
10. Ehrlich, pp. 88–107.   11. Quoted in *ibid.*, p. 113.
12. Constant Pierre is a notable example.
13. Blondel, p. 2069.   14. Ehrlich, p. 144.
15. Shaw, p. 300.   16. Ehrlich, p. 114.
17. Orenstein, p. 126.   18. Gottschalk, p. 52.
19. Ehrlich, p. 146.   20. Data from Dolge, pp. 125–26.

CHAPTER NINE

1. Dolge, p. 80.
2. Loesser, pp. 291–92.
3. Inventory no. 434 (9194). The material in this paragraph is from Luithlen, p. 62.
4. Shead.
5. *Ibid.*, pp. 226–27.
6. Ord-Hume, *Player Piano*, Chap. 1, gives an excellent presentation.
7. *FJ*, o.s. 2 (1826): 188.
8. White, *Piano Playing Mechanisms*, pp. 1–37, is a clear discussion of the principles and general mechanisms.
9. Grew, p. 1.
10. See White, *Piano Playing Mechanisms*, pp. 52–54.
11. Advertisement in *The Connoisseur* (London), April 1912, reproduced in Ord-Hume, *Clockwork Music*, p. 277.
12. See Givens for the complete history of the Ampico mechanism.
13. Ord-Hume, *Player Piano*, p. 39.   14. *Ibid.*, p. 97.
15. Dolge, p. 160.   16. Ehrlich, Table 7, p. 134.
17. "Where Does a Roll Play a Very Key Role?," *Wall Street Journal*, Sept. 15, 1978, p. 1.
18. Figures from *ibid*.

CHAPTER TEN

1. Marcuse, *Musical Instruments*, p. 132, *s.v.* "Crapaud."

2. Diagram in Spillane facing p. 224.

3. Stokes.

4. Gunji, p. 213.

5. Ehrlich, p. 67 (see also Dolge, p. 265); Spillane, p. 298.

6. Loesser, p. 598.

7. Ehrlich, p. 197, quoting the *Music Trade Review*. Dolge, p. 266, gives the same figures, as does Loesser, p. 598.

8. Stokes.   9. *Ibid.*

10. *Ibid.*   11. Marcuse, *A Survey*, pp. 291–92.

12. Marcuse, *Musical Instruments*, pp. 489–90.

13. A plan view of a Hitchcock spinet in a modified wing form, c. 1770, is in Marcuse, *A Survey*, p. 294.

14. Pfeiffer, *Piano Hammer*, pp. 32–35.

15. Grover, p. 203.

16. Marcuse, *Musical Instruments*, pp. 4, 7, 160, 176, 337, 550, 553.

17. Backus, p. 110. Roederer, p. 19, says 20 Hz.

18. Segal.

19. Steinway, p. 85.

20. Grover, pp. 183–84.

21. See Reblitz, pp. 112–13, on the problems and their solutions from a piano technician's point of view.

22. Segal; Rothstein.

23. Segal.

24. See, for example, Friedrich Blume, *Classic and Romantic Music: A Comprehensive Survey* (New York, 1970), tr. M. D. Herter Norton, p. vii.

Bibliography

Bibliography

Anderson, Emily, ed. and trans. *The Letters of Beethoven: Collected, Translated and Edited with an Introduction, Appendixes, Notes and Indexes.* 3 vols. New York, 1961.

————. *The Letters of Mozart and His Family.* 3 vols. London, 1938.

Arnold, Denis, and Nigel Fortune, eds. *The Beethoven Companion.* London, 1971.

Art du faiseur d'instruments de musique et lutherie: Extrait de l'Encyclopédie Méthodique: Arts et métiers méchaniques. Vol. 4, part 1. Geneva, 1972. Reprint of 1785 Paris ed.

Bach, Carl Philipp Emanuel. *Essay on the True Art of Playing Keyboard Instruments.* Tr. and ed. William J. Mitchell. New York, 1949.

Backus, John. *The Acoustical Foundations of Music.* New York, 1969.

Badura-Skoda, Eva. "Prolegomena to a History of the Viennese Fortepiano," *Israel Studies in Musicology*, 2 (1980), pp. 77–99.

Baines, Anthony, ed., for the Galpin Society. *Musical Instruments Through the Ages.* Rev. ed. Harmondsworth, Eng., 1969.

Barbour, J. Murray. *Tuning and Temperament: A Historical Survey.* 2d ed. East Lansing, Mich., 1953.

Benade, Arthur H. *Fundamentals of Musical Acoustics.* New York, 1976.

————. *Horns, Strings, and Harmony.* Science Study Series. Garden City, N.Y., 1960.

Bericht über die erste allgemeine österreichische Gewerbsprodukten-Ausstellung im Jahre 1835. Vienna, n.d.

Bernal, J. D. *Science and Industry in the Nineteenth Century.* London, 1953.

Berner, A., J. H. van der Meer, and G. Thibault, with the collaboration of Norman Brommele. *Preservation and Restoration of Musical Instruments: Provisional Recommendations.* London, 1967. Published by the International Council of Museums.

Bie, Oscar. *A History of the Pianoforte and Pianoforte Players.* Translated and revised by E. E. Kellett and E. W. Naylor. Foreword by Aube Tzerko. New York, 1966. Reprint of 1899 London ed.

Bilhuber, Paul H., and C. A. Johnson. "The Influence of the Soundboard on Piano Tone Quality," in Kent, ed., *Musical Acoustics*, listed below, pp. 99–108. Reprint from *Journal of the Acoustical Society of America*, 11 (1940), pp. 311–20.

Blackham, E. Donnell. "The Physics of the Piano," in *The Physics of Music: Readings from Scientific American*. Introduction by Carleen Maley Hutchins. San Francisco, 1978, pp. 24–33. Reprint from *Scientific American*, 92 (Dec. 1965), pp. 88–99.

Blanchet, Armand François N. *Méthode abrégée pour accorder le clavecin et le fortepiano*. Geneva, 1976. Reprint of 1801 Paris ed. Combined in one volume with Loüet, listed below.

Blom, Eric. *The Romance of the Piano*. New York, 1969. Reprint of 1928 London ed.

————, ed. *Grove's Dictionary of Music and Musicians*. 5th ed. 9 vols. with supplementary vol. New York, 1954–61.

Blondel, Albert-Louis. "Le Piano et sa facture," in Albert Lavignac and Lionel de la Laurencie, eds., *Encyclopédie de la musique et dictionnaire du Conservatoire* (Paris, 1927), vol. 3, part 2, pp. 2061–72.

Blume, Friedrich, ed. *Die Musik in Geschichte und Gegenwart: Allgemeine Enzyklopädie der Musik*. 15 vols. Kassel and Basel, 1949–73.

Boalch, Donald H. *Makers of the Harpsichord and Clavichord, 1440–1840*. 2d ed. Oxford, Eng., 1974.

Boomkamp, C. van Leeuwen, and J. H. van der Meer. *The Carel van Leeuwen Boomkamp Collection of Musical Instruments: Descriptive Catalogue*. Amsterdam, 1971.

Bridenbaugh, Carl. *The Colonial Craftsman*. Chicago, 1950.

Brinsmead, Edgar. *The History of the Pianoforte: With an Account of the Theory of Sound and also of the Music and Musical Instruments of the Ancients*. The Music Story Series. Detroit, 1969. Reprint of 1879 London ed.

Broder, Nathan. "Mozart and the 'Clavier,'" in Paul Henry Lang, ed., *The Creative World of Mozart* (New York, 1963), pp. 76–85.

Cardwell, D. S. L. *Technology, Science and History: A Short Story of the Major Developments in the History of Western Mechanical Technology and Their Relationships with Science and Other Forms of Knowledge*. London, 1972.

Casella, Alfredo. *Il Pianoforte*. 2d ed. Milan, 1954.

Clemen, Otto. "Andreas Streicher in Wien," *Neues Beethoven-Jahrbuch*, 4 (1930), pp. 107–17.

Clemencic, Réné. *Old Musical Instruments*. Tr. David Hermges. New York, 1968.

Closson, Ernest. *History of the Piano*. Tr. Delano Ames. Edited and revised by Robin Golding. 2d ed. London, 1974.

Clutton, Cecil. "The Pianoforte," in Baines, ed., *Musical Instruments*, listed above, pp. 88–102.

Colt, C. F., with Anthony Miall. *The Early Piano*. London, 1981.

Cooper, Martin. *Beethoven: The Last Decade, 1817–1827*. With a medical appendix by Edward Larkin. London, 1970.

Cripe, Helen. *Thomas Jefferson and Music*. Charlottesville, Va., 1974.

Czerny, Carl. *On the Proper Performance of All Beethoven's Works for Piano: Czerny's "Reminiscences of Beethoven" and Chapters II and III from Volume IV of the "Complete Theoretical and Practical Piano Forte School, op. 500."* Edited with commentary by Paul Badura-Skoda. Vienna, 1970.

Dale, William. *Tschudi the Harpsichord Maker*. Boston, 1973. Reprint of 1913 London ed.

David, Hans T., and Arthur Mendel, eds. *The Bach Reader: A Life of Johann Sebastian Bach in Letters and Documents*. Rev. ed., with a Supplement. New York, 1966.

De Pontécoulant, Louis Adolphe. *Organographie*. 2 vols. Amsterdam, 1971. Reprint of 1861 Paris ed.

Doerschuk, Bob. "Bösendorfer: Celebrating 150 Years of Piano-Building Excellence," *Contemporary Keyboard*, 5.6 (1979), pp. 8–14.

Dolge, Alfred. *Pianos and Their Makers: A Comprehensive History of the Development of the Piano from the Monochord to the Concert Grand Player Piano*. New York, 1972. Reprint of 1911 Covina, Calif., ed.

Ehrlich, Cyril. *The Piano: A History*. London, 1976.

Einstein, Alfred. *Mozart: His Character, His Work*. Tr. Arthur Mendel and Nathan Broder. Corr. ed. New York, 1962.

Ernst, Friedrich. "Der Instrumentenbauer Johann Andreas Stumpff: Ein Freund Beethovens," in *Jahrbuch des Staatlichen Instituts für Musikforschung Preussischer Kulturbesitz*, 1968, pp. 119–27.

Fabbri, Mario. "Il primo 'pianoforte' di Bartolomeo Cristofori," *Chigiana Rassegna Annuale di Studi Musicologici*, n.s. 1. 21 (1964), pp. 162–72.

Fay, Amy. *Music-Study in Germany: From the Home Correspondence of Amy Fay*. Ed. Fay Pierce. 18th ed. New York, 1903.

Fellerer, K. G. "Musikforschung und Klavierinstrumente," in Herzog et al., eds., *Europiano Kongress*, listed below, pp. 27–32.

Ferguson, Howard. *Keyboard Interpretation from the 14th to the 19th Century: An Introduction*. New York, 1975.

Fisher, Douglas Alan. *The Epic of Steel*. New York, 1963.

The Franklin Journal and American Mechanics' Magazine, vols. 1–4 (1826–27); n.s. vols. 1–2 (1828).

Friedheim, Arthur. *Life and Liszt: The Recollections of a Concert Pianist*. Ed. Theodore L. Bullock. New York, 1961.

Gábry, György. "Das Klavier Beethovens und Liszts," *Studia Musicologica*, 8 (1966), pp. 379–90.

Gai, Vicinio. *Gli Strumenti Musicali della Corte Medicea e il Museo del Conservatorio "Luigi Cherubini" di Firenze: Cenni Storici e Catalogo Descrittivo*. Florence, 1969.

Gale, W. K. V. *Iron and Steel*. Industrial Archaeology Series no. 2. London, 1969.

Gallini, Natale, and Franco Gallini, eds. *Commune di Milano: Museo degli Strumenti Musicali: Catalogo*. Milan, 1963.

Geiringer, Karl. *Instruments in the History of Western Music*. 3d (revised and enlarged) ed. New York, 1978.

Geiringer, Karl, with the collaboration of Irene Geiringer. *The Bach Family: Seven Generations of Creative Genius*. New York, 1954.

Gerber, Ernst Ludwig. *Historisch-Biographisches Lexicon der Tonkünstler*. Ed. Othmar Wessely. Graz, 1977. Reprint of 1790–92 Leipzig ed.

Gillespie, John. *Five Centuries of Keyboard Music: An Historical Survey of Music for Harpsichord and Piano*. New York, 1972.

Givens, Larry. *Re-enacting the Artist . . . A Story of the Ampico Reproducing Piano*. Vestal, N.Y., 1970.

Gottschalk, Louis Moreau. *Notes of a Pianist*. Edited, with a Prelude, a Postlude, and Explanatory Notes, by Jeanne Behrend. New York, 1964.

Grafing, Keith Gerhart. "Alpheus Babcock: American Pianoforte Maker (1785–1842): His Life, Instruments, and Patents," D.M.A. thesis, University of Missouri–Kansas City, 1972.

————. "Alpheus Babcock's Cast-Iron Piano Frames," *The Galpin Society Journal*, 27 (1974), pp. 118–24.

Grew, Sidney. *The Art of the Player-Piano: A Text-Book for Student and Teacher*. London, 1922.

Grover, David S. *The Piano: Its Story from Zither to Grand*. London, 1976.

Grundmann, Herbert. "Per il clavicembalo o piano forte," in Siegfried Kross and Hans Schmidt, eds., *Colloquium Amicorum: Joseph Schmidt-Görg zum 70. Geburtstag* (Bonn, 1967), pp. 100–117.

Gunji, Sumi. "Japan und sein Klavierbau," in Herzog et al., eds., *Europiano Kongress*, listed below, pp. 213–16.

Habakkuk, H. J. *American and British Technology in the Nineteenth Century: The Search for Labour-Saving Inventions*. Cambridge, Eng., 1962.

Hahn, Kurt. "Schumanns Klavierstil und die Klaviere seiner Zeit," in Hans Joachim Moser and Eberhard Rebling, eds., for the Deutsche Schumann-Komite, *Robert Schumann: Aus Anlass seines 100. Todestages* (Leipzig, 1956), pp. 120–28.

Hammerich, Aagul. *Musikhistorisk Museum: Beskrivende illustreret Katalog*. Copenhagen, 1909.

Harding, Rosamond E. M. *The Piano-Forte: Its History Traced to the Great Exhibition of 1851*. Cambridge, Eng., 1933. 2d ed., Old Woking, Eng., 1978. All citations are to the first edition unless otherwise noted.

Helmholtz, Hermann L. F. *On the Sensations of Tone as a Physiological Basis for the Theory of Music*. 2d ed. Tr. Alexander Ellis. With a new Introduction (1954) by Henry Margenau. New York, 1954. Reprint of 1885 London ed.

Herrmann, Heinrich. "Die Regensburger Klavierbauer Späth und Schmahl und ihr Tangentenflügel," dissertation, Erlangen, 1928.

Herzog, H. K., ed. *Europe Piano Atlas: Piano-Nummern*. 4th (expanded) ed. Frankfurt am Main, 1978.

Herzog, H. K., Eckart Rohlfs, and Georg Preiss, eds. *Europiano Kongress Berlin. 1965: Dokumentation: Kongressbericht, Referate, Podiumgespräche, Arbeitsgemeinschaften, Schlussberichte*. Frankfurt am Main, 1966.

Hill, Jackson. *The Harold E. Cook Collection of Musical Instruments*. Lewisburg, Pa., 1975.

Hindle, Brook. *Technology in Early America: Needs and Opportunities for Study*. With a directory of artifact collections by Lucius F. Ellsworth. Needs and Opportunities for Study Series. Chapel Hill, N.C., 1966.

Hipkins, Alfred J. *A Description and History of the Pianoforte and of the Older Keyboard Stringed Instruments*. 3d ed. Introduction by Edwin M. Ripin. Detroit Reprints in Music Series. Detroit, 1975. Reprint of 1929 London ed.

Hirt, Franz Josef. *Stringed Keyboard Instruments, 1440–1880*. Tr. M. Boehme-Brown. Boston, 1968.

Holland, John. *A Treatise on the Progressive Improvements & Present State of the Manufactures in Metal*. Vol. 2: *Iron and Steel*. London, 1833.

Hollis, Helen Rice. "Jonas Chickering: 'The Father of American Pianoforte-Making,'" *The Magazine Antiques*, Aug. 1973, pp. 227–30.

———. *The Musical Instruments of Joseph Haydn: An Introduction*. Smithsonian Studies in History and Technology no. 38. Washington, D.C., 1977.

———. *The Piano: A Pictorial Account of Its Ancestry and Development*. New York, 1975.

———. *Pianos in the Smithsonian Institution*. Smithsonian Studies in History and Technology no. 27. Washington, D.C., 1973.

Hoover, Cynthia Adams. "The Steinways and Their Pianos in the Nineteenth Century," *Journal of the American Musical Instrument Society*, 7 (1981), pp. 47–89.

Hoover, Cynthia Adams, and Scott Odell, eds. *A Checklist of Keyboard Instruments at the Smithsonian Institution*. 2d ed. Washington, D.C., 1975.

Hubbard, Frank. *Three Centuries of Harpsichord Making*. Cambridge, Mass., 1965.

Jeans, Sir James. *Science & Music*. New York, 1968. Reprint of 1937 Cambridge, Eng., ed.

Junghanns, Herbert. *Der Piano- und Flügelbau*. 5th ed. Ed. H. K. Herzog. Frankfurt am Main, 1979.

Kent, Earle L. "Influence of Irregular Patterns in the Inharmonicity of Piano Tone Partials upon Tuning Practice," in Kent, ed., *Musical Acoustics*, listed below, pp. 58–68. Corrected translation of article with same title in Herzog et al., eds., *Europiano Kongress*, listed above, pp. 133–54.

———. ed. *Musical Acoustics: Piano and Wind Instruments*. Benchmark Papers in Acoustics no. 9. Stroudsburg, Pa., 1977.

Kinsky, Georg. *Musikhistorisches Museum von Wilhelm Heyer in Cöln: Katalog*. Vol. I: *Besaitete Tasteninstrumente, Orgeln und orgelartige Instrumente, Friktionsinstrumente*. Cologne, 1910.

Klemm, Friedrich. *A History of Western Technology*. Tr. Dorothea Waley Singer. Cambridge, Mass., 1964.

Kock, Winston E. "The Vibrating String Considered as an Electrical Transmission Line," in Kent, ed., *Musical Acoustics*, listed above, pp. 27–33. Reprint from *Journal of the Acoustical Society of America*, 8 (1937), pp. 227–33.

Landon, H. C. Robbins. *Haydn: Chronicle and Works*. Vol. 3: *Haydn in England, 1791–1795*. Bloomington, Ind., 1976.

Laslett, Peter. *The World We Have Lost*. New York, 1965.

Levarie, Siegmund, and Ernst Levy. *Tone: A Study in Musical Acoustics*. Kent, Ohio, 1968.

Levine, Jo Ann. "Battle of the Concert Grands," *Christian Science Monitor*, Dec. 13, 1977, pp. 18–19.

Libin, Laurence. *Musical Instruments in the Metropolitan Museum*. New York, 1978.

Liszt, Franz. *Frederic Chopin*. Translated, with an Introduction, by Edward N. Waters. New York, 1973.

Loesser, Arthur. *Men, Women and Pianos: A Social History*. Preface by Jacques Barzun. New York, 1954.

Loüet, Alexandre. *Instructions théoriques et pratiques sur l'accord du pianoforte: Ouvrage qui apprend en très-peu de temps aux personnes les moins exercées, à accorder parfaitement cet instrument*. Geneva, 1976. Reprint of 1797 Paris ed. Combined in one volume with Blanchet, listed above.

Luithlen, Victor, ed. *Katalog der Sammlung alter Musikinstrumente*. Part 1: *Saitenklaviere*. Vienna, 1966.

MacArdle, Donald W., and Ludwig Misch, trans. *New Beethoven Letters*. Norman, Okla., 1957.

McFerrin, W. V. *The Piano—Its Acoustics*. Boston, 1972.

Maffei, Scipione. "Musicalischer Merckwürdigkeiten. Des Marchese, Scipio Maffei, Beschreibung eines neuerfundenen *Claviceins*, auf welchem das *piano* und *forte* zu haben, nebst einigen Betrachtungen über die Musicalische Instruments. Aus dem Welschen ins Teutsche übersetzt von König," *Criticae Musicae*, 2 (1725), pp. 335–42.

————. "Nuova invenzione d'un Gravecembalo col piano e forte; aggiunta alcune considerazioni sopra gli strumenti musicali," *Giornale de' Letterati d'Italia*, 5 (1711), pp. 144–59.

Marcuse, Sibyl. *Musical Instruments: A Comprehensive Dictionary*. Corrected ed. New York, 1975.

————. *A Survey of Musical Instruments*. New York, 1975.

Marpurg, Friedrich Wilhelm, ed. *Kritische Briefe über die Tonkunst*. 3 vols. Berlin, 1759–64.

Matthews, Denis, ed. *Keyboard Music*. Harmondsworth, Eng., 1972.

Melville, Derek. "Beethoven's Pianos," in Arnold and Fortune, eds., *The Beethoven Companion*, listed above, pp. 41–67.

Mendel, Hermann. *Musikalisches Conversations-Lexicon: Eine Encyklopädie der gesammten musikalischen Wissenschaften*. 11 vols. Berlin, 1870–79.

Meyer, Jürgen. "Die Richtcharacteristik des Flügels," in Herzog et al., eds., *Europiano Kongress*, listed above, pp. 155–66.

Michel, N. E. *Historical Pianos, Harpsichords and Clavichords*. Pico Rivera, Calif., 1970.

Mizler (von Kolof), Lorenz Christoph. *Neu eröffnete Musikalische Bibliothek*. 4 vols. Hilversum, Netherlands, 1966. Reprint of 1739–54 Leipzig ed.

Montal, Claude. *L'Art d'accorder soi-même son piano d'après une méthode sure, simple et facile, déduite des principes exactes de l'acoustique et de l'harmonie*. Geneva, 1976. Reprint of 1836 Paris ed.

Moscheles, Charlotte. *Life of Moscheles, with Selections from His Diaries and Correspondence, by His Wife*. Adapted from the original German by A. D. Coleridge. 2 vols. London, 1873.

Moscheles, Ignatz. *Recent Music and Musicians: As Described in the Diaries and Correspondence of Ignatz Moscheles*. Edited by Charlotte Moscheles and adapted from the original German by A. D. Coleridge. New York, 1879.

Müller, Werner. *Auf den Spuren von Gottfried Silbermann: Ein Lebensbild des berühmten Orgelbauers nach urkundlichen Quellen gezeichnet*. Kassel, Germany, 1968.

Newman, Sidney, and Peter Williams, eds. *The Russell Collection and Other Early Keyboard Instruments in Saint Cecilia's Hall, Edinburgh*. Edinburgh, 1968.

Newman, William S. "Beethoven's Piano Versus His Piano Ideals," *Journal of the American Musicological Society*, 23 (1970), pp. 484–504.

———. *A History of the Sonata Idea*. 3 vols. 2d ed. New York, 1972.

———. *Performance Practices in Beethoven's Piano Sonatas: An Introduction*. New York, 1971.

Norton, Edward Quincy. *The Construction, Tuning and Care of the Pianoforte*. Boston, 1887.

Ord-Hume, Arthur W. J. G. *Clockwork Music: An Illustrated History of Mechanical Musical Instruments from the Musical Box to the Pianola, from Automaton Lady Virginal Players to Orchestrion*. Illustrated with contemporary material. New York, 1973.

———. *Player Piano: The History of the Mechanical Piano and How to Repair It*. Illustrated by the author. South Brunswick, N.J., 1970.

Orenstein, Arbie. *Ravel: Man and Musician*. New York, 1975.

Orga, Ateş. *Chopin: His Life and Times*. Rev. 2d ed. Tunbridge Wells, Eng., 1978.

Pacey, Arnold. *The Maze of Ingenuity: Ideas and Idealism in the Development of Technology*. Cambridge, Mass., 1976.

Pearse, John B. *A Concise History of the Iron Manufacture of the American Colonies up to the Revolution, and of Pennsylvania until the Present Time*. New York, 1970. Reprint of 1876 ed.

Pfeiffer, Walter. *The Piano Hammer: A Detailed Investigation into an Important Facet of Piano Manufacturing*. Tr. J. Engelhardt. Frankfurt am Main, 1978.

———. *The Piano Key and Whippen: An Analysis of Their Relationships in Direct Blow Actions*. Tr. J. Englehardt. Frankfurt am Main, 1967.

Pierce, Bob. *Pierce Piano Atlas*. 7th ed. Long Beach, Calif., 1977.

Pierre, Constant. *Les Facteurs d'instruments de musique, les luthiers, et la facture instrumentale: Précis historique*. Paris, 1893.

Pistone, Daniele. *Le Piano dans la littérature française: Des origines jusqu'en 1900*. Paris, 1975.

Rapin, Eugène. *Histoire du piano et des pianistes*. Bologna, 1969. Reprint of 1904 Lausanne-Paris ed.

Reblitz, Arthur A. *Piano Servicing, Tuning, and Rebuilding for the Professional, the Student, the Hobbyist*. Vestal, N.Y., 1976.

Reichardt, Johann Friedrich. *Vertraute Briefe aus Paris geschrieben in den Jahren 1802 und 1803*. Part I. Hamburg, 1804.

———. *Vertraute Briefe geschrieben auf einer Reise nach Wien und den Österreichischen Staaten zu Ende des Jahres 1808 und zu Anfang 1809*. Introduced and annotated by Gustav Guglitz. 2 vols. Munich, 1915.

Rephann, Richard. *Checklist: Yale Collection of Musical Instruments*. New Haven, Conn., 1968.

Rimbault, Edward F. *The Pianoforte, Its Origin, Progress, and Construction*. London, 1860.

Roederer, Juan G. *Introduction to the Physics and Psychophysics of Music*. 2d ed. New York, 1975.

Rosenberg, Nathan. *Perspectives on Technology*. Cambridge, Eng., 1976.

Rothstein, Edward. "At Steinway, It's All Craft," *New York Times*, Feb. 22, 1981, p. 8E.

Rupprecht, Margarete. "Die Klavierbaufamilie Schiedmayer: ein Beitrag zur Geschichte des Klavierbaues," dissertation, Erlangen, 1954. Photocopy of typescript, Nuremberg, 1954.

Russell, Raymond. *Victoria and Albert Museum: Catalogue of Musical Instruments*. Vol. 1: *Keyboard Instruments*. With an Appendix, "Catalogue of Pianos and Organs," by Austin Niland, and an Appendix, "The Decoration of Keyboard Instruments," by Peter Thornton. London, 1968.

Sachs, Curt. *Handbuch der Musikinstrumentenkunde*. Leipzig, 1920.

Sadie, Stanley, ed. *The New Grove Dictionary of Music and Musicians*. 20 vols. London, 1980.

Sakka Keisei. "Beethovens Klaviere: Der Klavierbau und Beethovens künstlerische Reaktion," in Siegfried Kross and Hans Schmidt, eds., *Coloquium Amicorum: Joseph Schmidt-Görg zum 70. Geburtstag* (Bonn, 1967), pp. 327–37.

Sasse, Konrad. *Katalog zu den Sammlungen des Händel-Hauses in Halle*. Part 5: *Musikinstrumentensammlung: Besaitete Tasteninstrumente*. Halle an der Saale, 1966.

Schindler, Anton Felix. *Beethoven as I Knew Him: A Biography*. Ed. Donald W. MacArdle, tr. Constance S. Jolly. New York, 1972.

Schonberg, Harold C. *The Great Pianists*. New York, 1963.

Schröter, Christoph Gottlieb. "Christoph Gottlieb Schröter (ex autogr.)," in Marpurg, ed., *Kritische Briefe*, listed above, vol. 2, part 4, pp. 456–60.

———. "Herrn Christoph Gottlieb Schröters, Organistens an der Hauptkirche in Nordhausen, umständliche Beschreibung seines 1717. erfundenen Clavier-Instruments," in Marpurg, ed., *Kritische Briefe*, listed above, vol. 3, part 1, pp. 81–104.

———. "Sendschreiben an ***Lorenz Mizler," in Mizler (von Kolof), ed., *Neu eröffnete Musikalische Bibliothek*, listed above, vol. 3, pp. 464–77.

Schubert, H. R. "Extraction and Production of Metals: Iron and Steel," in Singer et al., eds., *History of Technology*, listed below, vol. 4, pp. 99–117.

Schuck, O. H., and R. W. Young. "Observations on the Vibrations of Piano Strings," in Kent, ed., *Musical Acoustics*, listed above, pp. 40–50. Reprint from *Journal of the Acoustical Society of America*, 15 (1943), pp. 1–11.

Schumann, Robert. *Gesammelte Schriften über Musik und Musiker*. 4th ed., ed. F. Gustav Jansen. 2 vols. Leipzig, 1891.

Scott, Marion M. "Haydn in England," *Musical Quarterly*, 18 (1932), pp. 260–73.

Segal, Stuart. "Pianomaker Henry Steinway and Family," *Town & Country*, Dec. 1977, no pagination.

Shaw, Bernard. *Shaw on Music: A Selection from the Music Criticism of Bernard Shaw*. Selected by Eric Bentley. New York, 1955.

Shead, Herbert A. *The History of the Emanuel Moór Double Keyboard Piano*. Old Woking, Surrey, 1978.

Singer, Charles, E. J. Holmyard, A. R. Hall, and Trevor I. Williams, eds. *A History of Technology*. Vol. 4: *The Industrial Revolution, c. 1750 to c. 1850*. Oxford, Eng., 1958.

Sitwell, Sacheverell. *Liszt*. New York, 1967.

Skinner, William, comp. *The Belle Skinner Collection of Old Musical Instruments, Holyoke, Massachusetts: A Descriptive Catalogue*. Philadelphia, 1933.

Slonimsky, Nicolas. *Baker's Biographical Dictionary of Musicians*. 6th (rev.) ed. New York, 1978.

Smith, Cyril Stanley. "Art, Technology, and Science: Notes on Their Historical Interaction," *Technology and Culture*, 11 (1970), pp. 493–549.

––––––. "The Discovery of Carbon in Steel," *Technology and Culture*, 5 (1964), pp. 149–75.

––––––. ed. *Sources for the History of the Science of Steel, 1532–1786*. Cambridge, Mass., 1968.

Smith, Eric. *Pianos in Practice*. London, 1978.

Smith, Fanny Morris. *A Noble Art: Three Lectures on the Evolution and Construction of the Piano*. New York, 1892.

Sonneck, Oscar. *Early Concert-Life in America (1731–1800)*. Leipzig, 1907.

––––––. ed. *Beethoven: Impressions by His Contemporaries*. New York, 1967. Reprint of 1926 ed.

Spillane, Daniel. *History of the American Pianoforte: Its Technical Development, and the Trade*. New Introduction by Rita Benton. New York, 1969. Reprint of 1890 ed.

Stanley, Albert A. *Catalogue of the Stearns Collection of Musical Instruments*. 2d ed. Ann Arbor, Mich., 1921.

Steinway, Theodore E. *People and Pianos: A Century of Service to Music*. New York, 1953.

Stokes, Henry Scott. "On Yamaha's Assembly Line," *New York Times*, Feb. 22, 1981, p. 8E.

Strong, Charles Wm. "Brass Strings on Italian Harpsichords," *The Galpin Society Journal*, 23 (1970), pp. 167–68.

Sumner, William Leslie, *The Pianoforte*. 3d ed. London, 1971.

Thayer, Alexander Wheelock. *Thayer's Life of Beethoven*. Revised and edited by Elliot Forbes. Princeton, N.J., 1967.

Thibault, G. (Mme. de Chambure), Jean Jenkins, and Josiane Bran-Ricci. *Victoria and Albert Museum: Eighteenth Century Musical Instruments: France and Britain. Les Instruments de musique au XVIIIe siècle: France et Grand-Bretagne*. Exhibition catalogue. London, 1973.

Thomas, Michael. "Brass Strings on Italian Harpsichords," *The Galpin Society Journal*, 23 (1970), pp. 166–67.

Thomas, W. B., and J. J. K. Rhodes. "Brass Strings on Italian Harpsichords," *The Galpin Society Journal*, 23 (1970), pp. 168–70.

Tomek-Schumann, Sabine. "Akustische Untersuchungen an Hammerflügeln," *Jahrbuch des Staatlichen Instituts für Musikforschung Preussischen Kulturbesitz*, 1974, pp. 127–72.

Ure, Andrew. *A Dictionary of Arts, Manufactures, and Mines: Containing a Clear Exposition of Their Principles and Practice*. London, 1839.

Van Barthold, Kenneth, and David Buckton. *The Story of the Piano*. London, 1975.

Van Beijnum-von Essen, Bertha. *Bouwe en Geschiedenis van het Klavier*. Rotterdam, 1932.

Van der Meer, John Henry. "Die klavierhistorische Sammlung Neupert," *Anzeiger des Germanisches Nationalmuseum*, 1969, pp. 255–66.

Von Frimmel, Theodor. "Von Beethovens Klaviere," *Die Musik*, 2. 14 (1903), pp. 83–91.

Von Lenz, Wilhelm. *The Great Piano Virtuosos of Our Time from Personal Acquaintance: Liszt, Chopin, Tausig, Henselt*. Tr. Madeleine R. Baker. New York, 1973. Reprint of 1899 ed.

Von Schönfeld, Johann Ferdinand. *Jahrbuch der Tonkunst von Wien und Prag*. Ed. Otto Biba. Munich, 1976. Facsimile reprint of 1796 Vienna ed.

Wainwright, David. *The Piano Makers*. London, 1975.

Walter, Horst. "Haydns Klaviere," *Haydn-Studien*, 2 (1969–70), pp. 256–88.

Weinreich, Gabriel. "The Coupled Motions of Piano Strings," *Scientific American*, 240. 1 (Jan. 1979), pp. 118–27.

Wertime, Theodore A. *The Coming of the Age of Steel*. Chicago, 1962.

White, William Braid. *Piano Playing Mechanisms: Being a Treatise on the Design and Construction of the Pneumatic Action of the Player-Piano and of the Reproducing Piano*. New York, 1925.

———. *Theory and Practice of Piano Construction: With a Detailed, Practical Method for Tuning*. New York, 1975. Reprint of *Theory and Practice of Pianoforte Building*, New York, 1906.

Wilson, Charles West. "Instructions for Adjusting the English Piano Action," *The Galpin Society Journal*, 24 (1971), pp. 105–6.

Winter, Robert. "Performing Nineteenth-Century Music on Nineteenth-Century Instruments," *19th Century Music*, 1 (1977–78), pp. 163–75.

Wolfenden, Samuel. *A Treatise on the Art of Pianoforte Construction*. Introduction by David S. Grover. Preface by Frank W. Holland. Rev. ed. Old Woking, Eng., 1977. Reprint of the 1916 London and Woking ed., together with the Supplement of 1927.

Wolff, Christoph. "New Research on Bach's Musical Offering," *Musical Quarterly*, 57 (1971), pp. 379–408.

Index

Index